PARTICIPATORY RESEARCH METHODOLOGIES

Participatory Research Methodologies

Development and Post-Disaster/Conflict Reconstruction

Edited by

ALPASLAN ÖZERDEM
University of York, UK

RICHARD BOWD
University of York, UK

ASHGATE

Published by
Ashgate Publishing Limited
Wey Court East
Union Road
Farnham
Surrey, GU9 7PT
England

Ashgate Publishing Company
Suite 420
101 Cherry Street
Burlington
VT 05401-4405
USA

www.ashgate.com

British Library Cataloguing in Publication Data
 Participatory research methodologies : development and post-
   disaster/conflict reconstruction.
   1. Participant observation. 2. Disaster relief--Research--
   Methodology. 3. Postwar reconstruction--Research--
   Methodology.
   I. Özerdem, Alpaslan. II. Bowd, Richard.
   363.3'48'0723-dc22

Library of Congress Cataloging-in-Publication Data
Participatory research methodologies : development and post-disaster/conflict
reconstruction / [edited by] Alpaslan Özerdem and Richard Bowd.
       p. cm.
   Includes bibliographical references and index.
   ISBN 978-0-7546-7735-2 (hbk) -- ISBN 978-0-7546-9454-0 (e-book)
1. Economic development projects--Planning. 2. Participant observation. 3. Postwar
reconstruction--Planning. 4. Emergency management. 5. Economic assistance. 6.
International relief. I. Özerdem, Alpaslan. II. Bowd, Richard.

   HD75.8.P377 2009
   363.34'8--dc22

ISBN 9780754677352 (hbk)
ISBN 9780754694540 (ebk)

Mixed Sources
Product group from well-managed
forests and other controlled sources
www.fsc.org Cert no. SGS-COC-2482
© 1996 Forest Stewardship Council
FSC

Printed and bound in Great Britain by
TJ International Ltd, Padstow, Cornwall

Contents

List of Tables

List of Figures

List of Contributors

Editors

Alpaslan Özerdem teaches in the areas of post-conflict recovery and politics of humanitarianism, and he is Convenor of the MA in Post-war Recovery Studies Course at the Post-war Reconstruction and Development Unit (PRDU). With field research experience in Afghanistan, Bosnia-Herzegovina, El Salvador, Kosovo, Liberia, The Philippines, Sierra Leone, Sri Lanka and Turkey, Dr Özerdem's research interests centre around post-conflict reconstruction, reintegration of former combatants and disaster management. He is the author of *Post-war Recovery: Disarmament, Demobilization and Reintegration* (I.B. Tauris, 2008), and co-author of *Disaster Management and Civil Society: Earthquake Relief in Japan, Turkey and India* (I.B. Tauris, 2006). He has also taken an active role in the initiation and management of several consultancy and commissioned research projects at the PRDU.

Richard Bowd has completed his PhD research at the Post-war Reconstruction and Development Unit (PRDU) at the University of York, which examined the social reintegration of ex-combatants in Rwanda and its implications on social capital restoration and reconciliation. Richard has also conducted extensive research in Kosovo, Rwanda, The Democratic Republic of Congo, Kenya and Ethiopia and has written and presented research papers based on this research. He has held a research position at the University of Salford and has taught on a number of politics modules at the University of York, including convening the Graduate Research Methods module. His research interests include: post-conflict reconstruction, reintegration of ex-combatants, reconciliation, security sector reform, African conflicts and social capital and social development.

Authors

Victor Asiedu is a doctoral student in Post-war Recovery and Development Unit (PRDU) at the University of York. His research explores how community-based disarmament, demobilization and reintegration (DDR) can facilitate a more sustainable peace-building. Victor is an ex-artillery officer in the Ghanaian Army and has a wide peacekeeping experience in Liberia, Sierra Leone, and Lebanon.

John Burns is a senior researcher based at the Feinstein International Centre office in Addis Ababa. Since early 2006, John has worked in partnership with seven organizations in Africa, looking at the development and application of an approach and tools to measure the impact of humanitarian assistance programs. Prior to joining the Centre, John worked as a consultant for the European Commission and was responsible for their food security initiatives in southern Sudan. He has also worked in various capacities for the United Nations Food and Agriculture Organization and the World Food Programme in Africa and Central Asia.

Andrew Catley is the Research Director at the Tufts University, Feinstein International Centre office in Addis Ababa. Andrew has been adapting participatory approaches to impact assessment in the horn of Africa since the mid-nineties. An early pioneer of privatized, community-based approaches to primary veterinary care in pastoral areas, he co-developed the participatory epidemiological methods now recognized as standard approaches for epizootic disease investigation and surveillance in marginalized areas.

David Connolly is a Research Fellow at the Post-war Reconstruction and Development Unit, University of York. He specializes in the theory and practice of post-war recovery and conflict resolution. Practical insight is fundamental to David's research, teaching and writing. Since 2000, he has conducted and led numerous participatory research projects and capacity support initiatives for communities in Afghanistan, Indonesia, Northern Ireland and Sierra Leone.

Sohini Dutt is a doctoral student in geography at Kansas State University, USA. Her research interests include environmental hazards and health/medical geography. She is also interested on gender issues and her areal speciality is in South Asia.

Maria Holt is a Lecturer at the Centre for the Study of Democracy (University of Westminster, London). She has carried out considerable research on Muslim women and violent conflict in Lebanon and the Palestinian territories, and has published a book and several chapters and articles on this subject.

Rohit Jigyasu is a conservation architect and risk management consultant from India, currently working as invited professor at Ritsumeikan University in Kyoto, Japan. After undertaking his postgraduate degree in Architectural Conservation from School of Planning and Architecture in Delhi, he obtained a PhD in Engineering from the Norwegian University of Science and Technology, Trondheim, Norway. He has contributed to several national and international conferences and meetings in India and abroad. He has several publications to his credit.

Richard Jones is currently a Stabilization Advisor in Helmand, Southern Afghanistan for the UK Government's tri-departmental Stabilization Unit made up of the Department for International Development, the Foreign and Commonwealth Office and the Ministry of Defence. Prior to his appointment in Afghanistan,

Richard worked extensively in the Great Lakes Region for National Governments, UN Agencies and NGOs where he has undertaken situation assessments, strategy formulation, programme planning and monitoring and participatory evaluation focused mainly on livelihoods and economic development. His chapter is written in a personal capacity and does not reflect UK Government policy.

Bimal Kanti Paul is a Professor of Geography at Kansas State University, USA. He is a hazard geographer with additional interests on health and population geography, and quantitative analysis. Although his areal speciality is in South Asia, he has conducted research on tornadoes, flash floods, blizzards, and hurricanes in the United States. Dr Paul received fellowships and grants from many external sources including the National Science Foundation (NSF) and the Natural Hazards Center, University of Colorado at Boulder, USA. He has published more than 120 papers including 60 in refereed journals. He is currently editor of the Special Publications of the National Council for Geographic Education (NCGE).

Derese Getachew Kassa is currently a PhD candidate at the School of Urban and Public Affairs in the University of Louisville (KY), USA. He earned his BA in Sociology and Social Administration from the Addis Ababa University (2000) before attending the University of Bath (UK) in 2004/5 where he completed his Master of Research (MRes) in International Development Studies. Over the last three years, Derese was a full time lecturer at the Department of Sociology in Addis Ababa University. He was also involved in various research projects around issues of wellbeing and quality of life, rural development, and urban social transformations in Ethiopia. He also served as an Executive Committee member of the Ethiopian Society of Sociologists, Social Workers and Anthropologists (ESSSWA) and is a member of the Organizations of Social Science Research in Southern and Eastern Africa (OSSSREA).

Anna Mdee (neé Toner) is Senior Lecturer in Development Studies at the University of Bradford. Her research focuses on livelihoods, community-driven development and social enterprise in Africa and the UK.

Sukanya Podder is a PhD candidate in Post-war Recovery at the Post-war Reconstruction and Development Unit (PRDU) at the University of York working under the supervision of Alpaslan Özerdem. Her research focuses on child soldier reintegration outcomes, particularly the problem of re-recruitment in Disarmament, Demobilization and Reintegration (DDR) processes. She was until recently a researcher with the Institute for Defence Studies and Analyses (IDSA) (New Delhi), a premier think tank affiliated to the Ministry of Defence in India.

Simon Robins is a humanitarian professional and researcher with an interest in transitional justice, humanitarian protection and human rights. He has worked as a delegate of the International Committee of the Red Cross (ICRC) in conflict and post-conflict contexts in Africa and Asia with a mandate to protect and assist victims of conflict. Since late 2007 he has been a PhD candidate at the Post-war Reconstruction and Development Unit (PRDU) at York University, doing research into the issue of disappearances and persons missing in conflict and victim-centred approaches to transitional justice, with an interest in Nepal and Timor-Leste.

Acknowledgements

We would first like to thank all the contributors to this volume for participating in a truly fascinating effort to share their research experiences from many different parts of the world. Without their spirit of collaboration and good will, this complex undertaking would not have been realized.

On behalf of all contributors in this project, we also wish wholeheartedly to thank all those research participants, local researchers, translators, respondents, and interviewees, who took part in the research processes incorporated in this book. This book is about the relationship between the researcher and the researched, and we hope that the voice of the researched in all case studies is heard loud and clear.

We would also like to express our gratitude to Kirstin Howgate and her editorial team at Ashgate for their tireless and great support throughout this project, and Gavin Ward Design Associates for their excellent proofreading.

Preface

Participatory research methodologies have, since the 1970s, been used as a tool to garner accurate information about communities in which development practitioners operate. In particular the key tenets of Participatory Rural Appraisal (PRA), those of participation, teamwork, flexibility and triangulation, make it a valuable set of approaches through which we can better understand communities and therefore design and implement programmes that not only have a more significant impact on those intended, but that also are locally owned thereby enjoying stronger commitment from these communities.

Whilst participatory research techniques have, in the past, been predominately utilized by development practitioners their usefulness as a collection of research techniques has been evident in academic disciplines such as politics, sociology, anthropology and economics, among others. Over recent years participatory methods have proven to be advantageous to the researcher and their use for this purpose has increased. However, with its wide range of challenges from accessing populations to the low levels of security and ethical concerns, conducting research in development, post-disaster and post-conflict contexts present a set of challenges to the beneficial use of participatory research methodologies. More importantly, there lacks any comprehensive study comparing its application in such environments.

This gap in the literature represents a particular problem as the lessons to be learnt for the various applications of participatory research methodologies may be lost. With the increasing use of participatory methodologies as a research toolset it is evident that a publication addressing the lessons learned and the experiences of researchers using participatory research techniques in different contexts would be highly valuable to methodological literature.

The key objective of this proposed text is, therefore, to assess the use of participatory methods as a research tool in the contexts of development and reconstruction after conflict and disasters through identifying the cross-cutting themes and establishing a comparative lessons learned framework that can help inform future uses of them, both for practitioners and researchers. More importantly, rather than adopting a prescriptive perspective, the volume aims to provide a critical analysis of such methodologies. Specifically, this text brings together a wide range of experiences on the utilization of participatory research methods from both academic and practitioner perspectives in different operational contexts and countries.

The book is structured around two main sections in order to explore the participatory research method experiences of development and post-disaster in the first part and those in the context of post-conflict reconstruction in the second one. In addition to overall introduction and conclusion chapters, each section has its own separate introduction and conclusion chapters, which helps establish a coherent argument from chapter to chapter and section to section, and allows the book to focus on a comparative analysis in the final chapter. In Chapter 1, 'A Theoretical and Practical Exposition of "Participatory" Research Methods', Richard Bowd, Alpaslan Özerdem and Derese Getachew Kassa introduce theoretical understandings of participatory methodologies before progressing to examine the evolution of their use. The primary purpose of this chapter is to provide a theoretical exposition of participatory research methodologies that underpin the practical focus of the remainder of this publication, and also avoid the repetition of a generic literature review on research methods in each case study chapter. The only literature review in each case study chapter will be specifically related to those particular research methods used or conceptual issues in focus.

In Chapter 3, 'Who Speaks for the Community? Negotiating Agency and Voice in Community-based Research in Tanzania', Anna Mdee from the University of Bradford explores an attempt to work in partnership with active local community researchers in Uchira, Tanzania. The basis for doing this was to go beyond the application of PRA tools to have community involvement in the research from inception to final analysis. The project set out to analyse collective village life and in particular the operation and impacts of a community-managed water project and investigates those tensions relating to power, resources and capacity in the interaction and the evolving relationship of the research team. In Chapter 4, 'Poverty Assessment in Rwanda through Participatory Rural Appraisal', Richard Jones from the Department for International Development demonstrates the use of PRA techniques in an economic assessment context in Rwanda as part of the methodology used to research poverty baselines in preparation for the Rwandan Poverty Reduction Strategy Paper (PRSP). Chapter 5, 'Participatory Approaches to Impact Assessment: Experiences from Humanitarian Interventions in Zimbabwe', by John Burns and Andrew Catley from the Feinstein International Center at Tufts University, reviews the use of participatory methods in measuring the impact of a drought response livelihoods project implemented by Africare. Describing the systematic use of participatory tools to generate a set of representative qualitative and quantitative data demonstrating project impact, based on the perceptions of project participants, the chapter investigates the strengths and weaknesses of the methodology, as well as some of the methodological and organizational challenges involved in measuring impact within the humanitarian sector.

In Chapter 6, 'Applications of Participatory Research Methods in a Post-disaster Environment: The case of Cyclone Sidr, Bangladesh', Bimal Kanti Paul and Sohini Dutt from Kansas State University examine the prevalent conditions under which participatory methods have been used in natural disasters, as well as the suitability of these techniques. Based on existing literature and personal field research experience, PRA methods along with their scope in future disaster research in Bangladesh, are evaluated. In Chapter 7, entitled 'Rediscovering

Traditional Knowledge for Post-disaster Reconstruction through "Participatory" Research Methods in India and Nepal', Rohit Jigyasu from Ritsumeikan University in Kyoto, Japan explores the participatory research challenges and opportunities in the context of the research aimed at rediscovering traditional knowledge systems for post-earthquake reconstruction in Marathwada and Gujarat in India and Kathmandu valley in Nepal.

The first case study chapter on post-conflict reconstruction, Chapter 10, 'Understanding Social Capital and Reconciliation in Rwanda through Participatory Methods', by Richard Bowd from CARE International, draws on PRA research conducted in Rwanda to provide an appreciation as to how participatory research methods contribute to our understanding of social capital and reconciliation in war-torn communities. Based on an empirical appraisal of the author's field work in Sierra Leone on the study of how community-based disarmament, demobilization and reintegration (DDR) can facilitate a more sustainable peace-building, in Chapter 11, 'Door Knocking in Sierra Leone: A Necessity in Post-conflict Research', Victor Asiedu from the University of York argues that door knocking facilitates the building of trust and addresses some methodological and ethical challenges in post-conflict environment. Given that the dynamics of child soldiers' reintegration continues to be understudied, together with evidence that young child soldiers might not respond best to survey questionnaire and semi-structured interview techniques, Chapter 12, 'Mapping Child Soldiers' Reintegration Outcomes in Liberia: A Participatory Approach' by Sukanya Podder from the University of York, explores the role of PRA techniques in mapping child soldier reintegration outcomes in the context of Liberia.

In Chapter 13, 'A Participatory Approach to Ethnographic Research with Victims of Gross Human Rights Violations: Studying Families of the Disappeared in Post-conflict Nepal', Simon Robins from the University of York describes research into the needs of families of persons disappeared during the decade long Maoist People's War in Nepal. The chapter shows that through the use of a participatory approach to ethnographic methods an understanding can be developed that allows efforts to address violent pasts to be made that go beyond the currently favoured prescriptive approaches. This methodology also represents an effort to go beyond the purely consultative to a research concept in which conflict victims participate in research planning and implementation in a way that both uses and strengthens their own organizations, providing a platform for the mobilization of victims to advance their own agendas.

In Chapter 14, 'Unexamined Lives: a Methodology of Women, Violence and War in Lebanon', Maria Holt from the University of Westminster develops an appropriate participatory methodology for carrying out research into the experiences of Arab–Muslim women who find themselves caught up in violent conflict. By adopting feminist research methods and placing the voices of women at the centre of the research, the chapter explores the possibility of a more egalitarian relationship between the researcher and the researched. In Chapter 15 entitled 'Participatory Research in Programme Evaluation: The Mid-term

Evaluation of the National Solidarity Programme in Afghanistan', David Connolly from the University of York examines the use of participatory research methods in the mid-term evaluation of post-war recovery programmes. The analysis concentrates on the effectiveness of such methods in terms of three overlapping domains: gathering valid evidence; meeting the aims and objectives of a mid-term evaluation; and managing the expectations of both research participants and programme stakeholders. The chapter argues that participatory research methods are effective with particular focus on their ability to manage the inevitable tensions between the three mid-term evaluation domains. Nevertheless, it identifies reasons why such methods can fail to develop the capacities of research participants and programme stakeholders and explore ways to overcome specific challenges in the post-war context.

Differently from the preceding case studies, in Chapter 17, 'Participatory Research Methods in Post-conflict Reconstruction Study Visits', Alpaslan Özerdem from the University of York explores the ways of teaching participatory research techniques as part of conventional postgraduate research method courses and the way such techniques can be used in study visits individually or as a group by MA and PhD students. Starting its investigation from a set of ethical concerns in using such techniques by students under or without supervision in disaster and conflict-affected areas, the chapter questions how such methodologies can be taught, tested and practised in an ethical, effective and efficient way in the preparation of future researchers.

The final chapter of this book presents the overall conclusions by undertaking a comparative analysis of the use of participatory research methods in the three contexts of development, post-disaster and post-conflict, and, in order to achieve this, the chapter uses the taxonomy of participation, power and empowerment to analyse the similarities and contrasts between them. Having focused on the benefits of participatory research methods for triangulation, the chapter presents a set of recommendations for an improved practice in the use of such methods by focusing on the issues of flexibility and multi-disciplinarity, diversity and interpretation, trust and confidence building, and finally the ethics of participatory research methods, which all can serve as the main principles for an improved practice.

Chapter 1

A Theoretical and Practical Exposition of 'Participatory' Research Methods

Richard Bowd, Alpaslan Özerdem and Derese Getachew Kassa

Introduction

Participatory research methodologies have, since the 1970s, been used as a tool through which the voices of the most marginalized, impoverished and excluded in society can be heard and thus the garnering of more accurate information about communities in which development practitioners operate can be made possible. In particular the key tenets of participatory research methods, those of participation, teamwork, flexibility and triangulation, make them a valuable set of approaches through which we can better understand communities and therefore design and implement programmes that not only have a more significant impact on those targeted, but that also are locally owned thereby enjoying stronger commitment from these communities.

Whilst participatory research techniques have, in the past, been predominately utilized by development practitioners, their usefulness as a collection of research techniques has been evident in academic disciplines such as politics, sociology, anthropology and economics, among others. Over recent years participatory methods have proven to be advantageous to the researcher and their use for this purpose has increased. However, with its wide range of challenges from accessing populations to the low levels of security and ethical concerns, conducting research in development and post-disaster/conflict environments presents a set of challenges to the beneficial use of participatory research methodologies. More importantly, there lacks any comprehensive study comparing its application in the contexts of development, conflict and disaster.

This gap in the literature represents a particular problem in that the lessons to be learnt for the various applications of participatory research methodologies may be lost. With the increasing use of participatory methodologies as a research toolset it is crucial that the lessons learned and the experiences of researchers using participatory research techniques in different contexts are recorded and, perhaps more importantly, that the methods and processes of participatory approaches evolves as a result of such lessons.

The key objective of this text is, therefore, to assess the use of participatory methods as a research tool in the contexts of development and reconstruction after conflict and disasters through identifying the cross-cutting themes and establishing a comparative lessons learned framework that can help inform future uses of them, both for practitioners and researchers. More importantly, rather than adopting a prescriptive perspective, the aim of this publication is to provide a critical analysis of such methodologies. Specifically, the text benefits from the bringing together of the experiences of those who utilize participatory research methods in different countries and contexts, and from different academic and practitioner perspectives.

This chapter explores the use of the participatory research methodologies by researchers and practitioners. By investigating the theoretical basis of such methodologies, the chapter provides a detailed consideration of the theoretical concepts that underpin participatory methods of research and charts the evolution of these approaches in their use. It addresses the key concepts of participation and power in an attempt to demonstrate ways in which participatory research techniques empower those who engage in them, as well as how they conceal power imbalances and further reinforce the interests of the urban elite in society. It is these contradictions that the chapter aims to tease out, examining both the positive and negative aspects of a much-lauded research approach.

Participatory Methods of Research: An Overview

Unlike most other research techniques, participatory methods place extensive emphasis on the importance of harnessing the non-academic, local knowledge of the people themselves in order to act upon and solve local problems. Power, assumed to rise from the production and control of knowledge, is then transferred from societal elites to those whose voice is often not heard: those on the periphery of decision-making processes. The following definitions of participatory research techniques reinforce these assertions. Chambers (1992: 1) for instance, defines these methods as a 'family of approaches and methods to enable rural people to share, enhance and analyse their knowledge of life and conditions, to plan and to act'. With a more radical stance, Peter Park (1993: 1) describes participatory research as 'a self conscious way of empowering people to take effective action toward improving conditions in their lives. It is a research method that puts research skills in the hands of the deprived and disenfranchised people so that they can transform their lives for themselves'.

Accordingly, participatory techniques are designed to enable the disadvantaged and the poor to critically reflect upon their living conditions, learn the causes of their powerlessness and deprivation, and help them act to redress this power imbalance for meaningful outcomes.

The philosophical roots of the participation literature go far to the works of Karl Marx. According to Hall (1981), Marx, a philosopher and political economist, was an active participant in the French Revolution who then interviewed French factory workers to establish his theory about the commune. Selener (1997) also posits the contributions of Antonio Gramsci, the Italian political activist, to participatory research. Gramsci's tradition is quite distinct from Marx's original accounts on the role and position of the peasantry in capitalist European societies. The latter viewed peasant societies as reactionary forces unable to readily develop class consciousness and revolutionary zeal. Gramsci, however, looked at the rural peasantry as a living political force able to articulate class interests if they were given close scrutiny and political agitation. Organizing and mobilizing the peasantry as an ideological force, for Gramsci, is the prerogative of the 'organic intellectual'. By this Gramsci is referring to intellectuals and change agents born and brought up amidst the oppressed and nourished by the reality of the peasants themselves.

Most importantly, the works of Paulo Freire, the Brazilian philosopher and educator, have had a profound influence on the development of participatory research methods. Known for his famous book, *The Pedagogy of the Oppressed* (1970), Freire stages a critique against a lecture form of education on the basis of it being a form of teaching: a learning process where students sit like empty receptacles to receive wisdom and knowledge trickling down from the teacher. He argues that education should rather be a two way traffic between the teacher and the students that involves critical reflection and conscientization. Conscientization, in Freirian terms, refers to the entire gamut of activities where people participate to identify and critically analyse the social, political and economic factors underlying oppression leading into their organized action for change. According to Freire, knowledge gained through conscientization – experiential learning, participation and transformative pedagogy – brings about structural changes in society by way of empowering the oppressed and the poor. The notion of participation as a learning and empowering instrument is therefore strongly hinged on the works of Paulo Freire (Selener 1997).

Participatory methods explicitly recognize that people have their own local, community based, knowledge systems that researchers from universities, institutes or government departments have not fully tapped. Second, proponents of participatory research techniques state that valid and transformative research could be conducted if people are treated as intelligible partners rather than mere respondents to inquiry instruments. Taking off from here, participatory methods advocate reversals of expert-farmer learning and top-down planning. They also set out to offset biases of what Chambers referred to as rural development tourism by being 'relaxed not rushing, listening not lecturing, probing instead of passing to the next topic, being unimposed than important, and seeking out the poorer people and women, and learning their concerns and priorities' (Chambers 1992: 14).

Participation, Power and Empowerment: The Basis of Participatory Approaches

As a result of the arguments regarding the generation of knowledge espoused by Freire and others, and the apparent need for conscientization, the development of participatory approaches to learning took place. During this period understanding of participation altered: from traditional perspectives of participation being based around people's organizations and cooperatives, community development or animation rurale and guided participation in large-scale projects (Thomas-Slayter 2001), to people-centred perspectives in which the focus lies on power and control. This change in understanding of participation was based on the belief that critical reflection and analysis are not skills solely held by the elite and that ordinary people have the capability to engage in such processes through utilizing their unique local knowledge. Participation, therefore, is crucial to the exploitation of this knowledge and the development of research and policy that can effectuate change. However, increasing and widening participation to enhance research or policy is not as simple as it sounds. Within the people-centred perspective 'inescapably, where development is concerned, participation is about power, an increase in the power of the disadvantaged' (Coady International Institute 1989: 17).

Participatory methods, through the participation of community members, seek to bridge the power relations that exist between researchers and the researched, between practitioners and beneficiaries. In conventional approaches to research and policy development, those being researched or those receiving the benefit of policy are generally not involved in the design process and have limited involvement in the implementation phase. The power held by the researcher or the policymaker ensures that the researched or the beneficiary remain on the margins of knowledge production and dissemination: at least in terms of knowledge that is regarded as legitimate by the elite. Unlike such conventional approaches, participatory methods transfer much of the power typically held in this relationship from researcher to the researched and, through a flexible approach and constructive communication, the researched community becomes empowered in such as way as to enable them to be owners of the research process (Bar-On and Prinsen 1999: 5). As communities have the power to identify problems affecting them, they become empowered to take steps to find a solution.

Empowerment is, therefore, a key objective of participatory research and policy approaches and, as a result of the shift in power, it is argued that participatory approaches enable such a process to occur, to the benefit of those engaged in the process. Specifically, the shift in power facilitates the amplification of the voices of marginalized people in such a way that they are able to articulate their needs and demands and make their contribution to the construction of knowledge. Traditionally marginalized groups such as children, women and the disabled are given a forum through which they can express their views, needs and opinions based on their unique position on the periphery. Additionally, their involvement in the development of knowledge and the development of solutions to community issues through leading the process has significant positive implications for their empowerment.

The development of participatory methods essentially grew out of the recognition and belief that local voices could and should be heard within the process of policy design and implementation. This belief derived from the coalescence of the participation, power and empowerment discussion. As approaches to education and learning changed in the late 1960s and early 1970s, a greater understanding of the power of participation emerged. Participation, seen as a means to a specific end or as an end in itself, grew as a conceptual underpinning of policy development, most fervently in the 'developing' countries of the south but also in the 'developed' states of the north. Under this approach the process of increasing the participation of local voices, by default drove the devolution of power to the holders of those voices. If the value ascribed to local voices went up as a result in changes in thinking vis-à-vis learning, then automatically the owners of those voices have more power. This change in power relations and increased participation led in turn to empowerment of local people. Communities, affected both by poverty and policy, have more control over the direction of their individual and collective lives as can be seen in the following statement from the World Bank's webpage on empowerment:

> In essence empowerment speaks to self determined change. It implies bringing together the supply and demand sides of development – changing the environment within which poor people live and helping them build and capitalise on their own attributes. Empowerment is a cross-cutting issue. From education and health care to governance and economic policy, activities which seek to empower poor people are expected to increase development opportunities, enhance development outcomes and improve people's quality of life (World Bank 2009).

Communities affected both by poverty and policy, through this process of participation, power transfer and empowerment, are able to define their own futures. At least that is how the argument goes; but is this truly the case? Does participation in the development of knowledge result in voices being heard? Whose voice and to what end? Can real participation ever really be achieved? Whilst the benefits of participatory methods espoused by many may indeed eventuate, it is important to consider the opposite case; not least to identify a framework through which 'good' participatory research must be conducted.

Participatory but not Emancipatory

Even though participatory approaches developed as a critique to the formal, expert driven, top-down development projects, the use of participatory techniques has become the new orthodoxy that almost all non-governmental organizations (NGOs), civil society groups, nation-states, and the World Bank claim to secure in their projects. The participation hype that has spread in almost all spheres of the development industry is criticized as having corrupted the original purpose of participation. For many, the incorporation of the participation ideology by the World Bank has handcuffed its radical and empowering aspects. As such, present day critiques against the widespread exercise of participatory techniques are staged at two levels: those that 'focus on the technical limitations of the approach and stress the need for a re-examination of the methodological tools used in PRA, and those that pay more attention to the theoretical, political and conceptual limitations of participation' (Cooke and Khotari et al. 2001: 3). The following section attempts to outline how participation literature has failed to critically discuss power relationships during participatory exercises and the implications this has for participation and empowerment.

A Critique on Binary Models of Power in Participatory Approaches

Power, being the ability to persuade one or more people to comply with one's own interests, often poses conceptual ambiguity. While emphasizing spatial and professional reversals in a bid to decentralize power, participation literature seems to be infested with binary models of power such as the urban elite and the rural poor, the uppers and lowers, the north and the south, academics and practitioners. Power relationships, however, are fluid and do not usually fall into such rigidly stated categories.

Drawing from the works of Michel Foucault (1977), Uma Khotari, for instance, argues that power must be analysed as something that functions in the form of a circulating entity that 'is never localized here or there'. It is a dynamic state of influence and control that emanates from social discourse where people create norms and cultural practices. When these cultural practices and norms accumulate in the conscience of individual interactants they become knowledge. Knowledge is therefore a dynamic, powerful instrument – continuously made and unmade in discourse – that governs the individual. Foucault calls this process 'the subjectification of the self'. Mentioning Foucault's use of Bentham's Panopticon, Khotari argues that power as a control instrument was diffused all over the prison cells and in the psyche of the prisoners themselves: that is, even if there was no prison guard in the Panopticon's control tower. The categorical definition of the poor as resourceless, voiceless and, by extension, powerless by participatory approaches is narrow because it evades the everyday control and power people face in their lives (Cooke and Khotari et al. 2001: 139–53).

Romanticizing 'Community', Disguising the Powerful?

Participation literature is also criticized for essentializing the word community as a homogenous entity where people have egalitarian interests to produce knowledge, work with partners and decide on matters of common good in undisputed manners. In reality however, communities are characterized by protracted ethnic, linguistic and professional cliques and interest groups that make their own rationalizations before any development project becomes operational. There are squabbles and struggles amongst the community members to be elected to community development committees, county councils or work teams that NGOs establish to ensure community participation. The 'myth of community' (Cleaver 1999: 598), which is ubiquitous in the populist slogans of the participation literature, again conceals the everyday, multifarious forms of power struggle within communities. The whole idea of 'community-based ness' to ensure community participation should therefore be contested.

'Local' Knowledge: A Construct of the Powerful?

While asserting the link between power and knowledge, the protagonists of the participatory tradition set out to unearth popular knowledge 'in each individual, collectively reformulated and analysed so that it can be applied in collective actions to benefit a group or community' (Selener 1997: 25). Local knowledge and participatory planning are therefore contrasted to the experts' knowledge and bureaucratic planning of development interventions. Criticisms against these assertions begin positing that local knowledge is 'highly differentiated in terms of who produces it and the different ways of knowing things by rural communities' (Mosse 2001: 19). In other words, what sort of local knowledge one is talking about gets reduced to whose local knowledge one is referring to.

For Mosse, the local knowledge reported as a result of the application of participatory techniques is constructed when powerful project actors shape and dominate what should be discussed, recorded, censored or highlighted in these sessions. More often than not, such reports end up becoming testimonies used to convince donors about the seriousness of a social problem, the perseverance of community A or B, and therefore the relevance of a project in the pipeline. According to Mosse, what is often displayed as local knowledge is little more than an outsider agenda. In other cases, outsider project interests might collude with immediate community interests. Mosse cites an example from India where farmers presented the seriousness of soil erosion and leaching as a problem – when it was not – in order to get paid employment in a reforestation and soil conservation project (Mosse 2001: 16–32). Participation literature has not fully acknowledged the fact that local knowledge is dynamic and vulnerable to various power games within and outside a community.

Local Knowledge: A Faustian Bargain between Modernization and Empowerment?

Not all cultural practices, rooted in local beliefs and knowledge systems, are positive and emancipatory. Some reinforce oppressive hierarchies based on attributes such as age, gender, caste, or ethnicity. While amplifying the importance of harnessing and employing local knowledge in development, participation literature becomes self-contradictory when it meets this dilemma. The dilemma is to either uphold these local knowledge traits as community-based or to dismantle them as oppressive and dysfunctional. Development then becomes a Faustian bargain between empowering the disadvantaged through modernizing local knowledge or to stay put, assuming local knowledge is sacred. According to Francis Cleaver (1999: 597–612), participation literature, which emerged refuting the expert 'we know best' bias in development, is now swinging to another extreme: a local knowledge – 'they know best' – bias.

However some, like Selener, state that 'popular knowledge is by no means the solution for everything or everyone' (Selener 1997: 27). In fact, he argues that participatory research should initiate a dis-indoctrination of the oppressed from local knowledge which might have blindfolded the poor from critical consciousness. Maguire, on the other hand, cautions against the expert-local knowledge dichotomy. For her, participatory research should begin assuming that 'we both know some things, neither of us know everything. Working together, we will know more and we will both learn more about how to know' (Maguire 1987: 37–8).

How Participatory are Participatory Research Exercises in Themselves?

Owing to their public nature, many participatory research sessions have inbuilt group dynamism that might entangle efforts to participate and critically reflect. Bill Cooke (2001: 102–122) draws on findings in social psychology to show how participatory research sessions might become victims of group dysfunction. Three of these malfunctions will suffice as examples: first, group members often tend to take more risks while being in groups; second, members might also conform to suggestions or decisions that they may not personally agree with; third, in some cases, group dynamics might also result in 'group think' – a deterioration of critical thinking and rational choice making. These problems become further compounded if one or two powerful personalities dominate sessions setting the agenda or leading and sanctioning others' opinion.

Participatory Methods in an International Development and Post-Disaster Context

The use of participatory methods gained in popularity in the 1970s and 1980s. Driven by academics such as Robert Chambers, the use of participatory research approaches became mainstream within international development efforts. Participatory techniques, therefore, became a major part of the way in which we developed knowledge and the way we applied that knowledge. Research, whether it be for academic use or to inform the planning and implementation of development interventions, has its foundations in knowledge and as such it is important to consider from where that knowledge originates. Much development policy prior to the 1980s was derived from the legacy of colonial rule in which planning was a top-down conception. A major failure in this approach is that planning did not involve the knowledge of those who were to be affected by the programmes being developed. In the late 1970s came the realization that this approach was indeed a failure with many commenting on the issue. For instance Hatch (1976) stated 'the development profession suffers from an entrenched superiority complex with respect to the small farmer. We believe our modern technology is infinitely superior to his. We conduct our research and assistance efforts as if we knew everything and our clients nothing' (Hatch 1976: 6–7). The 1980s onwards saw the introduction of participatory research methods in which local knowledge is utilized through the participation of those in the recipient community, based on the principles discussed previously.

One such participatory method is Participatory Rural Appraisal (PRA), perhaps the most well known of the participatory techniques, which is based around the five key concepts of empowerment, respect, localization, enjoyment, and inclusiveness (IISD 1995). Empowerment arises when the local community builds confidence through the sharing and generation of local knowledge that has a direct impact on their lives. Respect is derived from the transfer of power from the researcher to the researched who become the teachers of researchers through local knowledge. The PRA process is localized as it occurs in the local community using local resources, thereby avoiding externally driven research. The process of PRA should also be enjoyable for all those involved, often punctuated with jokes, stories and other locally relevant occurrences that contribute to the data collection process. The final concept of inclusiveness is perhaps one of the key concepts as this ensures the voices of the marginalized are heard. By including groups such as women, children, disabled, the destitute, the elderly, and others, data is not only more representative and potentially richer, but the empowerment potential of PRA is also enhanced.

Essentially PRA is a collection of techniques that enable the researcher to quickly ascertain certain features of local communities primarily in order to identify the needs of communities as expressed by those communities themselves so as to be able to design appropriate development programmes to meet those needs (Brockington and Sullivan 2003). Techniques may include wealth rankings, social network mapping, time line variations, institutional diagramming and division of labour analysis. Such techniques can serve as a highly effective research and planning tool that enables academics, policy makers and development organizations alike to acquire the relevant information necessary to understand development needs and contexts. Additionally, they can be utilized by academics to better understand the intricacies and dynamics of local communities and phenomena such as social capital, indigenous social welfare systems and kinship relations. Proponents of participatory methods such as PRA underline the importance of skills such as open-mindedness, the patience to listen and the ability to withdraw once action is initiated, as the values of new professionalism. The ideals, in the literature, ask for strong devotion from the professional and result primarily from a deep personal charge to uphold them sacred. Otherwise participatory research techniques are also doomed to lose their heuristic and empowering essence by faddism, formalism, rushing and routinization (Chambers 1992).

Participatory methods have, for the last three decades or more, been utilized as tools through which to better understand, and act within, the international development context. As with theories of knowledge generation that have shaped the use of participatory approaches, theories of development have also changed over the past 30 years. Beginning from a focus in the 1950s and early 1960s when colonial/post-colonial countries engaged in the 'development' of their former, or soon to be, colonies in order to increase the productivity of the 'peoples of the colonies', maintained influence in the post-colonial era and the imminent Cold War, and instigated a system of governmental management of national economies – the Bretton Woods system – the theory behind international development has come a long way, starting from an economic basis and moving move into human development

During the 1950s and early 1960s, 'the goal of development was growth, the agent of development was the state and the means of development were these macroeconomic policy instruments' (Leys 2005: 110). This modernization theory of development – the idea that undeveloped countries should follow the development path of developed countries in order to effectively modernize – was challenged in the late 1960s and 1970s by Dependency theorists who advocated the pursuit of development within the historical orientated and ethical framework of general development espoused by Hegel and Marx. Dependency theory is based on the notion that the world system, predominately trade and financial systems, serves to enrich wealthy nations at the expense of poor nations by the inequitable transfer of resources from a periphery of poor and underdeveloped states to a core of wealthy states. Based on Marxist analysis of inequality, Dependency theory focuses on how poor countries can best be enriched or developed through a levelling of the playing field.

The 1980s represented the battleground between these two schools of thought with the Modernists, who occupied the Bretton Woods institutions, adopting neo-liberal economic policy and introducing Structural Adjustment Programs (SAPs) which, through currency devaluations, trade liberalization and privatization, sought to reduce the fiscal imbalances of recipient countries. Meanwhile the proponents of Dependency theory promoted bottom-up initiatives to developments such as conscientization and context-based development through focused targeting of programs and resources. It was in this period that participatory approaches to development, heavily influenced by Freire, really became established.

As a result of this impasse eventuating between the two schools, the 1990s saw the development of the Human Development approach by the United Nations Development Program (UNDP). Human Development, influenced heavily by Mahbub ul Haq and Amartya Sen, rather than focusing on economic growth as the sole or primary indicator of development, advocates that development is the:

process of enlarging people's choices. In principle, these choices can be infinite and change over time. But at all levels of development, the three essential ones are for people to lead a long and healthy life, to acquire knowledge and to have access to resources needed for a decent standard of living. If these essential choices are not available many other opportunities remain inaccessible (UNDP 1990: 10).

The advancement in new thinking on the way in which knowledge is derived and imparted, and the development of conscientization through the 1970s and 1980s, proved to have significant implications for the way in which international development was pursued. The change in developmental focus in the 1980s and 1990s to the Human Development model can be seen as a direct result of this rise in new thinking and the development of new tools for knowledge generation. Participatory approaches, so vital for the process of conscientization, became the tools of choice for the development practitioner who, following the human development approach, attempted to empower his/her partners and enable them not only to participate in the investigation and analysis of their oppression, but also in the identification and development of solutions to their situation.

When it comes to conducting research in disaster-affected environments, the research methods utilized would be indistinguishable from those research methods that are applied in a development context or in social sciences in general. However, what makes them different are those circumstances created by the impact of that particular disaster. A number of special characteristics of areas affected by natural disasters bring a number of additional challenges to the application of research, particularly those intending to use participatory methods. First of all, as most natural disasters are a sudden onset of nature such as earthquakes, cyclones and tsunamis, they inflict a huge level of damage on the infrastructure and services which is likely to make the research process an arduous task to undertake. For example, with the devastation of the already limited road and communications infrastructure of most developing countries, logistics in the post-disaster environment are possibly one of the main challenges that researchers have to address in disaster-affected areas. Second, overcoming the challenge of logistics would not mean that researchers could actually reach their target populations as such disasters also cause a huge level of displacement. Populations who have lost their homes and livelihoods overnight may have been dispersed over a wide geographical context. Third, the challenge of resistance from both the individuals and organizations to obtain data and information in a development context is often magnified further in disaster-affected areas, as people may not be emotionally prepared to take part in research and both international and national organizations may obviously be busy with responding to the short and medium term consequences of disasters. This would be the case especially if the organizations and disaster-affected people were not able to see a direct benefit to them in terms of relief and reconstruction assistance (Özerdem and Jacoby 2006).

Research in disaster-affected areas is likely to take place in one of the four main stages of the disaster management cycle. First, the mitigation and preparedness activities to reduce the level of risk that populations might be exposed to because of their socio-economic, political and physical vulnerabilities; second, the immediate aftermath of disasters, which often focuses on impact, losses and relief assistance; third, the rehabilitation of infrastructure and services to return to some sort of normality; and finally, long-term reconstruction activities (Quarantelli 1998). As it would be clearly recognized that each stage would have its own challenges with the undertaking of participatory research, it would be safe to note that the application of participatory methods would be particularly difficult in the second stage.

In relation to those four stages of disaster management, it is also important to categorize populations affected by disasters as this is particularly significant for the primary objectives of participatory research methods. First, there would be those populations directly affected by experiencing physical, material and personal losses from disasters. The second group would be formed by those people who are indirectly affected due to the losses of their families and friends and what they would experience as the post-impact environment. Third, those personnel from social and security services and aid workers who take part in the disaster relief response would be another group who would experience the impact of disaster on their well-being. Finally, there would be people who have had no direct or indirect exposure but still experience distress and uncertainty because of their peripheral location to the disaster (Bolin 1986). Such different population groups in terms of their exposure to disasters would have different strengths and weakness when taking part in the participatory research process, and it would be essential to consider them carefully in the planning and implementation phases.

Participatory Methods in a Post-conflict Environment

Defining the Post-conflict Environment (PCE)

Understanding the specific causes behind a given conflict is crucial to the effective reconstruction of the PCE and participatory research methodologies are very often utilized to gain an increased understanding of these causes. So too is an appreciation of that environment and the impact of the conflict on the society in question. It is only through an accurate comprehension of the challenges that face the reconstruction effort and the threats to such efforts, that any durable restoration can take place and such participatory approaches can be applied in order to achieve a deeper, more nuanced understandings of these impacts on society. Importantly, however, it is crucial to consider this environment in order to ascertain the challenges those implementing participatory methods may be faced with.

The direct and indirect results of civil conflict leave a complex lasting legacy that is difficult to erase. Economies need to be stabilized and developed, infrastructure needs to be rebuilt and institutional renewal or replacement needs to take place. However, arguably the greatest challenge in the removal of the legacy of violent conflict and the reconstruction of the country is the re-establishment of society.

> Societies emerging from war face a range of urgent, interconnected problems on all fronts, not too dissimilar to situations of natural disasters. However, it is the destruction of relationships, including the loss of trust, dignity, confidence and faith in others that proves the most far reaching, potent and destructive problem and the most difficult to address. It has the potential to undermine possible solutions to a wide range of other issues (Barakat 2005: 10).

Education systems are adversely affected by the war, health systems are unable to cope with increasing demands and social institutions become dilapidated or non-existent. However, the challenge of rebuilding these institutions and systems beset by extreme destruction becomes all the more daunting when one takes into account that 'intimate exposure to brutality and subsequent displacement and civil disorder leave individuals psychologically scarred and the intricate network of social interaction deeply torn' (McDonald 2002: 4). As trust is diminished, cooperation and communication reduce and fear increases resulting in the stagnation of societal activity and development. In the absence of communication further fractionalization of society first becomes possible and is then exacerbated as when such division is 'linked with acute social uncertainty, a history of conflict and, indeed, fear of what the future may bring; it emerges as one of the major fault lines along which [society] fractures' (Newland 1993: 191). It is dialogue that is necessary to stabilize and sustain societal relations as 'dialogue is the first step in providing a sense of belonging, for by communication and listening we take the first step toward recognizing our own commonality' (Aboulmagd et al. 2001: 37). However, constructive dialogue in such an environment is difficult to achieve.

The impact of civil conflict on social interactions and systems is evident with community dislocation across many levels being the result. Individual suffering is significant and this has intrinsic implications for the survival of the family, which represents the nucleus of the community. Individuals struggle to rebuild their lives and communities whilst faced with the uncertainty of the future and fear of the past. With everything around them broken, and the causes of the conflict very often remaining, albeit in a latent form, the potential for societal renewal is depleted. Weak social capacity to manage social change and emergent conflict, as evident by the fact that violent conflict broke out, is further undermined and the society's capacity to manage future conflicts in a peaceful way is lessened (Miall 2001). The result of this is a reduced ability to recover from intrastate conflict and an increased probability of conflict renewal.

Researching and Reconstructing a PCE

In order to effectively set priorities in a PCE it is necessary to have accurate information about such communities and the inhabitants of these communities (Colletta et al., 1996; GOM 1995; World Bank 1991). Many research techniques such as surveys and statistical analysis, whilst positively contributing in many ways, may miss information that is crucial to the planning and implementation of reconstruction and recovery programmes or academic endeavour.

Participatory research methodologies can be particularly effective as they make efforts to empower those being researched and challenge the dominance and power of the researcher, thus giving more prominence to the voices of the researched (Gueye 1999). However, they are also particularly useful to use in a PCE as they can ameliorate many of the problems associated with conducting research in a PCE. In terms of the sensitive nature of much research in a PCE, participatory techniques may offer a very useful method through which the negative aspects of such research can be reduced. Because the nature of participatory methods are to examine present day life, questions of the past do not hold as much emphasis as in other techniques and as such the issues that may arise during these techniques are not as prevalent. Additionally, as the process is community-led rather than researcher-led the degree to which sensitive information is presented is very much determined by the community itself and is, to some degree, less in the domain of the researcher. Whilst this may appear to limit the usefulness of participatory methods as a research tool, the primary data derived from participatory techniques is not the only source of data in the process. Body language, the telling of jokes and stories and other events that are socially meaningful tell us something about the dynamics of the society and are as such sources of data.

Although the use of participatory techniques in a PCE can be extremely powerful, they can also present a highly problematic scenario to the PCE. The PCE is characterized by low levels of trust and social cohesion. The differences and divisions that resulted in violent conflict and deepened throughout it may still, to some degree, be evident. In individual interviews the need for researcher sensitivity is so great due to such divisions and even though participatory techniques require a different type of researcher sensitivity, the divisions that remain in a PCE represent a challenge to the researcher, albeit of a different nature. It is the very nature of participatory methodologies to identify, examine and assess differences and divisions within a society or community. Wealth rankings do exactly that. Time line variations present an opportunity for conflict over what happened, when and to whom. Group definition offers the chance to re-engage in a 'them' and 'us' mentality. Social network mapping highlights marginalization and exclusion from the community. Many of the techniques used in participatory approaches, in their attempts to better understand the dynamics within society, can exacerbate the divisions that exist within the society. It is arguable that, in a PCE, such differences and divisions may run along the same lines of division that were evident within the conflict. Therefore by re-examining these differences or identifying new ones, there may be a propensity for conflict to (re)ignite that could result in the outbreak of violent conflict, or for the post-conflict reconstruction process to be damaged. Conversely, however, such techniques within such an environment may serve to augment the conflict management practices and engender reconstruction and reconciliation.

Participatory techniques in a PCE therefore have enormous potential, not only to deliver rich data but also to exacerbate tensions within the PCE that could lead to violent conflict or to aid the transition from a PCE to a peaceful community. Because the use of participatory techniques in a PCE could potentially have long-lasting effects, both of a negative and positive nature, it is crucial that the researcher acknowledges this and plans accordingly.

Conclusion

This chapter sought to engage in an exploration of the development of participatory research techniques, firstly through an exposition of the shifts in theory regarding the creation of knowledge and in parallel, the basis for development, and secondly, through an investigation of development policy changes over the last 60 years. The primary aim of this chapter was to develop a more holistic understanding not only of the theoretical reasons for the emergence of participatory approaches to research and practice, but also a rationale as to why they have grown in importance and become integral components of international development and post-disaster/conflict reconstruction.

Starting from a consideration of the main theoretical debates leading to the emergence of participation as a primary function of knowledge generation, predominantly those of Freire, the chapter developed an appreciation of the changes in the thinking of this time. This was followed by a more in-depth analysis of participation through an examination of power and empowerment. This situated power, participation and empowerment as the conceptual basis for the emergence of participatory approaches to knowledge creation, policy development and programme implementation.

The next section of the chapter then considered the counter-argument to the benefits of participatory approaches. Whilst not discounting the position that participatory approaches have their merits, those taking up the counter-argument do so on the basis of whether the participatory approaches that are followed within research and development practice truly reflect the theoretical presuppositions upon which such approaches are based. Those from this school of thought proffer that whilst the theoretical basis for these approaches may be well intentioned, in practice participation is not an emancipatory exercise for many due to the fact power dynamics within societies and communities are not accurately and comprehensively understood by those who instigate the use of such approaches. Thus local knowledge is a construct of the powerful. However, those who hold power are often not recognized and in any case, power is a fluid concept and so those holding power, and the degree of power they hold, are constantly changing.

After examining the theory behind the development of participatory approaches, the chapter then situated this development within two contexts: international development and post-disaster reconstruction and post-conflict environments. Through considering participatory approaches and international development together it was possible to provide an account of the emergence of participatory approaches to international development in such a way that it reinforced the theoretical exposition earlier in the chapter. This section then moved on to introduce participatory approaches in post-disaster reconstruction research which evolved the discussion in that it was based around a discussion of the nuances that require attention when researching in this unique context. From this point the chapter progressed into a consideration of similar issues within a PCE. The focus here was on the challenges to conducting participatory research in such a context. This reflected issues of trust and confidence that, in a PCE, have been decimated and leave the research context one that is unlike any other.

The remainder of this text is divided into two parts with both parts bringing together the experiences of those who utilize participatory research methods in different countries and contexts, and from different academic and practitioner perspectives, with a view to developing a critical analysis of such methodologies through identifying the cross-cutting themes and establishing a comparative lessons learned framework. Part I is concerned with the conducting of participatory research in the field of international development and post-disaster reconstruction. This includes experience from the contexts of Tanzania, Rwanda, Zimbabwe, Bangladesh and India. Part II examines the experiences of conducting participatory research in a post-conflict environment and includes case studies from Rwanda, Sierra Leone, Liberia, Nepal, Lebanon and Afghanistan, with an additional chapter that is cross-context.

References

Aboulmagd, A.K. et al. (2001), *Crossing the Divide: Dialogue Among Civilizations* (New Jersey: School of Diplomacy and International Relations, Seton Hall University).

Barakat, S. (ed.) (2005), *After the Conflict: Reconstruction and Development in the Aftermath of War* (London: I.B. Tauris).

Bar-On, A.A. and Prinsen, G. (1999), 'Planning, Communities and Empowerment: An Introduction to Participatory Rural Appraisal', *International Social Work* 42(3), 277–294.

Bolin, R. (1986), 'Disaster Characteristics and Psychosocial Impacts', in B.J. Sowder (ed.), *Disasters and Mental Health* (Washington, DC: American Psychiatric Press).

Brockington, D. and Sullivan, S. (2003), 'Qualitative Research', in Scheyvens, D. and Storey, D. (eds) (2003), *Development Fieldwork: A Practical Guide* (London: SAGE Publications).

Brown, M.E. (1993), *Ethnic Conflict and International Security* (Princeton: Princeton University Press).

Chambers, R. (1992), *Rural Appraisal: Rapid, Relaxed and Participatory*, Institute of Development Studies, University of Sussex, Discussion Paper (311).

Cleaver, F. (1999), 'The Paradoxes of Participation: Questioning Participatory Approaches to Development', *Journal of International Development* 11, 597–612.

Coady International Institute (1989), *A Handbook for Social/Gender Analysis* (Ottawa: Social and Human Resources Development Division, Canadian International Development Agency).

Colletta, N.J, Kostner, M., Weidehofer, I. (1996), *Case Studies in War-to-Peace Transition: The Demobilisation and Reintegration of Ex-Combatants in Ethiopia, Namibia, and Uganda* (Washington D.C: The World Bank).

Cooke, B. and Kothari, U. (eds) (2001), *Participation: The New Tyranny?* (London: Zed Books).

Edelman, M. and Haugerud, A. (eds) (2005), *The Anthropology of Development and Globalisation: From Classical Political Economy to Contemporary Neoliberalism* (Oxford: Blackwell Publishers).

Foucault, M. (1977), *Discipline and Punish: The Birth of the Prison* (Harmondsworth: Penguin).

Freire, P. (1970), *Pedagogy of the Oppressed* (New York: Seabury Press).

Gueye, B. (1999), 'Wither Participation? Experience from Francophone West Africa, Drylands Programme' Issue Paper 87, International Institute for Environment and Development, London.

Hall, B.L. (1981), 'Participatory Research, Popular Knowledge and Power: A Personal Reflection', *Convergence: An International Journal of Adult Education* 14(3), 6–19.

Hatch, J. (1976), *The Corn Farmers of Motupe: A Study of Traditional Farming Practices in Northern Coastal Peru, Land Tenure Center*, Monographs No. 1, (Madison: University of Wisconsin-Madison).

IISD (1995), 'Participatory Research for Sustainable Livelihoods: A Guide for Field Projects on Adaptive Strategies, International Institute for Sustainable Development' accessed at http://www.iisd.org/casl/CASLGuide/GuideBook-home.htm, 23 April 2007.

Khotari, U. (2001), 'Power, Knowledge and Social Control in Participatory Development', in Cooke, B. and Kothari, U. (eds) (2001), *Participation: the New Tyranny?* (London: Zed Books).

Kumar, K. (ed.) (1993), *Rapid Appraisal Methods* (Washington D.C: The World Bank).

Leys, C. (2005), 'The Rise and Fall of Development Theory', in Edelman, M. and Haugerud, A. (eds), *The Anthropology of Development and Globalisation:*

From Classical Political Economy to Contemporary Neoliberalism (Oxford: Blackwell Publishers).

Maguire, P. (1987), 'Doing Participatory Research: A Feminist Approach, University of Massachusetts', Centre for International Education, School of Education.

McDonald, L. (2002), 'The International Operational Response to the Psychological Wounds of War: Understanding and Improving Psycho-social Interventions', Feinstein International Famine Centre, Working Paper No. 7.

Miall, H. (2001), 'Conflict Transformation: A Multi-dimensional Task', in *Berghof Handbook for Conflict Transformation*, Accessed at http://www.berghof-handbook.net/uploads/download/miall_handbook.pdf, 12 August 2008.

Mosse, D. (2001), '"People's Knowledge", Participation and Patronage: Operations and Representations in Rural Development' in Cooke, B. and Kothari, U. (eds), *Participation: The New Tyranny?* (London: Zed Books).

Newland, K. (1993), 'Ethnic Conflict and Refugees', in Brown, M.E. (eds), *Ethnic Conflict and International Security* (Princeton: Princeton University Press).

Özerdem, A. and Jacoby, T. (2006), *Disaster Management and Civil Society: Earthquake Relief in Japan, Turkey and India* (London: I.B. Tauris).

Park, P., Brydon-Miller, M. and Hall, B.L. (eds) (1993), *Voices of Change: Participatory Research in the United States and Canada* (Westport: Bergin and Garvey).

Quarantelli, E.L. (1998), *What is a Disaster?: Perspectives on the Question* (London: Routledge).

Scheyvens, D. and Storey, D. (eds) (2003), *Development Fieldwork: A Practical Guide* (London: SAGE Publications).

Selener, D. (1997), 'Participatory Action Research and Social Change', Cornell Participatory Action Research Network, Cornell University, New York.

Thomas-Slayter, B., Barbara, P. and Ford, R. (1993), *Participatory Rural Appraisal: A Study from Kenya* in Kumar, K. (ed.) *Rapid Appraisal Methods* (Washington D.C: The World Bank).

UNDP (1990), *Human Development Report 1990* (New York and Oxford: Oxford University Press).

World Bank (2009), 'What is Empowerment?' June 2009 [online] accessed at http://web.worldbank.org.

PART I
Participatory Research Methods in Development and Post-disaster Reconstruction

Chapter 2

Introduction to Part I: Participatory Research Methods in Development and Post-disaster Reconstruction

Richard Bowd and Alpaslan Özerdem

As discussed in Chapter 1, the development of the use of participatory research techniques in a development and post-disaster reconstruction context has occurred in parallel with, and been influenced by, transformations in thinking regarding the construction of knowledge. With the change in focus from teacher-led knowledge generation and dissemination to conscientization, in which knowledge is gained through experiential learning, participation and transformative pedagogy, the way in which development interventions are designed, planned and implemented has also altered. Post-disaster reconstruction programming has also taken on these changes. As knowledge that informs policy and programming has become based on participatory research, evaluation and assessment, it seems logical that research into international development and post-disaster reconstruction would reflect these changes also. Development, changing from an economic growth model to a human development approach, demands new techniques and approaches to its investigation.

If a community, through their participation, can contribute to the design, development and implementation of a development project or post-disaster reconstruction programme so too can they expect, and be expected, to make contributions to the evaluation and assessments of these projects and programmes. Indeed, it appears entirely reasonable that the techniques and approaches used for project/programme evaluation, whether that be on an academic or applied basis, reflect those used in their design and implementation.

Research in international development and post-disaster reconstruction contexts generally takes place for three key purposes: the gathering of information to enable the development of projects and programmes; the gathering of information to assess projects and programmes; and academic research to further our understanding of the development/post-disaster context. Research that addresses the first two reasons generally makes attempts to be participatory in nature due to the recognition that for development initiatives to be successful, community ownership needs to be in place. A participatory approach to the development of initiatives therefore increases such community buy-in. Research that is of an academic basis endeavours to further our comprehension of various aspects of society, politics and culture within a given context. In this sense, its focus lies in the more nuanced meanings and considerations found within societies and communities.

Regardless of the underlying aim of the research, several factors present themselves to highlight the importance of participatory methods in these contexts. For instance, much feminist writing 'has been devoted to demonstrating that gender relations can be described properly as relations of dominance and oppression' (Wright 1993: 42). Such dominance and oppression is claimed to occur at all levels of society: from the micro-level of domestic violence or the male control of household finances, to the macro-level of unequal gender representation in government or abortion laws passed by male-dominated parliaments. Gender domination and oppression can, under this rubric, be seen to occur at the household level as well at the political. Feminist explanations of social and political domination, despite being highly varied in their ontology and epistemology, centre on the notion of a gender battle.

Looking at participation in the realm of politics, if we take a more traditional institutionalist view of politics as being located in government, it is arguable that such governmental institutions 'have been notoriously resistant to the incorporation of women, their interests or perspectives' (Squires 2004: 123). Participation in the institutions of government has been male dominated and as such this has effects on the output of these institutions. Indeed, 'the laws of state, the structure of labour markets, and the division of labour, to cite several examples, all affect gender practices in significant ways and are shaped systematically by gender relations' (Wright 1993: 47). When we also consider that in many developing/post-disaster contexts the apparatus of government is either weak, corrupt or oppressive, or its capacity has been severely weakened by the disaster, then it is more the informal nature of society that comes into play and is, perhaps, of more importance when focusing on developmental outcomes.

In terms of understanding the lives of women in a development/post-disaster context feminist theory makes two critical contributions. First, at a theoretical level it facilitates a deeper understanding of participation, power and empowerment with community dynamics through viewing such conceptions from a different perspective. When included into policy design this will, for instance, affect the way the provision, and content, of schooling is managed, or how public health provision is linked to economic growth. Second, by placing more emphasis on female participation, and by utilizing such participatory techniques that tease out the views of the often marginalized and oppressed, the voice of women can not only be heard but be heard in such as way that it empowers those who have spoken to continue and encourages those who have not, to do so.

Institutional understandings of political and social life examine the informal rules of life which '– while hard to research – can be every bit as important in shaping actors' behaviour as formally agreed procedures. Informal conventions may reinforce formal rules…a focus on informal as well as formal rules adds breath as well as depth to an understanding of political institutions' (Lowndes 2002: 98/99).

Informal functions are not written down or formalized. They are embedded in culture thus enabling them to permeate through human history. It is informal institutions that facilitate the creation and development of formal institutions. Informal institutions comprise a myriad of political, economic and social relationships and interactions. These may include rites of passage for young men and women in tribal societies, courtship rituals, the way in which people greet each other and provide hospitality, the interaction of students and lecturers in lectures and seminars and the way in which we relate to those of a different gender or age group.

It is these unwritten rules, norms and conventions – institutions – that govern the relationships and interactions we have with other members of society and between societies. When attempting to better understand development/post-disaster contexts which are generally contexts or sub-contexts from which the researcher does not originate: for example, a middle class researcher from a developing country investigating poverty in that same country, participatory approaches can facilitate an understanding of these informal rules of the community/society that may not be possible through the use of other techniques. This is crucial in terms of understanding how power, political, social and economic, is localized.

Leading on from this, a characteristic of many political and social systems in developing countries is power being held by the few who manipulate patrimonial mechanisms to ensure their continued position and privilege. Socio-political domination of this kind is explained by Elite Theory as the contention that the minority ruling classes 'are usually so constituted that the individuals who make them up are distinguished from the mass of the governed by qualities that give them a certain material, intellectual or even moral superiority' (Mosca 1896/1965: 53). Elaborating on this further, Michels develops a logical, linear pattern that emerges due to organizational necessity. First, political organization is required for the successful pursuit of any political objective. Second, the leaders of these organizations will utilize their position to the benefit of themselves and the detriment of the organizations members. Third, the very fact that such leaders control the organizations resources renders the success of such an effort inevitable. Fourth, in the rare event of the leader being ousted their replacement will be a new oligarchy pertaining to the same temptations. Finally, those who are ruled will accept this state of affairs in order to forgo the necessity of organizational involvement (Michels 1915).

In this sense political domination occurs for two distinct reasons. First, hierarchy is inevitable in human society and with that comes dominance and submission. Second, the political ruling class, who arrive at their position due to certain superiorities over the ruled, seek to maintain their position within the ruling class. The ruling class will therefore engage in political endeavour that ensures their survival and such policies can be seen as the exertion of political dominance. Within the context of research in development, much of this is explicitly or implicitly concerned with issues of power: who holds power and how it is wielded. Elite Theories abound within understandings of power in developing countries.

However, whilst they may hold a certain attraction in explaining power within these contexts, they arguably miss the more nuanced understanding of socio-cultural/political/economic dynamics. In order to develop a better understanding of the aspects of a society, whether for academic or practical reasons, participatory research approaches offer useful techniques to derive underlying nuanced understandings that enable better programme design and more in-depth academic investigation.

A key way in which they do this is the offerings they make in terms of reconfiguring power relations within the research process to enable marginalized and peripheral voices to be heard. However, they also go beyond this by increasing research validity through reducing research bias. One of the most problematic issues confronting a researcher is the various biases he or she may face. Research bias affects the validity of research and as such due consideration must be forthcoming. The initial stage of bias mitigation is the identification of potential or actual bias. Chambers (1983) identified six bias groupings that participatory approaches help mitigate: spatial (urban, tarmac and roadside); project; person; dry season; diplomatic; and professional. By providing opportunities for participation and facilitating the empowerment of voices, much of these biases can be mitigated. For example, the elite bias element of person bias refers to the favouring of the less poor and more influential within the village, in this case, in the research. It is the elite within the village who contribute to activities that involve development practitioners, local-level officials and researchers, whereas the 'the poor are often inconspicuous, inarticulate and unorganized. Their voices may not be heard at public meetings in the communities where it is customary for only the big men to put their views' (Devitt 1977: 23). Due to this, research that favours the elite within the village will be skewed and thus cannot claim to be credible. As such, participatory approaches which give voice to the poorer in society help mitigate this bias.

Participatory research methodologies are particularly useful in alleviating these biases through the contributions they make to reflexivity and triangulation. The issue of being reflexive within the research process is crucial as it feeds into the validity debate.

> Reflexivity is the practice of researchers being self-aware of their own beliefs, values and attitudes, and their personal effects on the setting they have studied, and self-critical about their research methods and how they have been applied, so that evaluation and understanding of their research findings, both by themselves and their audience, may be facilitated and enhanced (Payne and Payne 2004: 191).

The need to be reflexive is highly important if claims of validity are to stand. Personal ontology may influence the way in which research is designed, conducted and analysed and it is necessary to be reflexive of these personal biases, belief and views in order to be able stand up to criticism. The very nature of participatory approaches enables a more reflexive perspective within research as they devolve much of the power within the research process to the researched, and thus provide the space for such reflexivity.

Research biases can also be mitigated through the use of triangulation. Triangulation refers to 'the idea that looking at something from multiple points of view improves accuracy' (Neuman 2006: 149) and is derived from navigation and measurement techniques to pinpoint accurate locations. In terms of social research there are four types of triangulation: triangulation of measure – the use of multiple measures of the same incident; triangulation of observers – the introduction of different observers in order to provide alternative perspectives; triangulation of theory – the use of multiple theoretical perspectives during research design and interpretation; and triangulation of method – the mixing of data collection methods. Participatory methods, by virtue of the fact they utilize numerous data collection techniques, enable all four types of triangulation to be addressed.

The following five chapters chart the use of participatory research techniques in very different development and post-disaster contexts and address, in a practical dimension, the theoretical aspects of participatory approaches discussed here and in the previous chapter. Chapter 3 explores the use of participatory research methods in an attempt to work in partnership with active local community researchers in Uchira, Tanzania to analyse collective village life and in particular the operation and impacts of a community-managed water project. With a strong focus on the empowering potential participatory research, Mdee examines the interaction of structural factors and individual agency in shaping who comes to represent the community both in terms of participants of the research and local researchers engaged in the project. Whilst identifying the beneficial aspects of the use of participatory research techniques, the chapter also acknowledges and investigates the limitations of such methods and asks critical questions pertaining to whose voice is being heard. Beginning with an account of the evolution of this research project, the author situates the research within a context and provides a comprehensive, step-by-step guide to the decision-making process that informed the research design. Building on from this, the chapter succinctly introduces each of the participatory techniques used, carefully detailing the strengths and weaknesses of each as experienced through this research: herein lies the strength of the chapter. Finally, the chapter reaches conclusions from the lessons learnt and offers some reflections for consideration.

Chapter 4 is concerned with a demonstration as to the practical use of Participatory Rural Appraisal (PRA) techniques in an economic assessment context in Rwanda as part of the methodology used to research poverty baselines in preparation for the Rwandan Poverty Reduction Strategy Paper (PRSP). Jones develops a practical guide for the participatory researcher, clearly delineating the process of not only conducting economic assessment using participatory methods, but more specifically in the use of such methods to define poverty; a critical contribution of this work. The chapter begins by considering poverty and participation before offering a description of the socio-economic setting of the case country: Rwanda. It then progresses to a comprehensive examination of the use of PRA to define poverty through the eyes of those most affected by poverty before outlining the policy considerations identified as priorities for development by the community. The conclusion then acknowledges the limitations of techniques in research of this nature.

Drawing upon case study research from Zimbabwe in Chapter 5, Burns and Catley review the use of participatory methods in measuring the impact of a drought response livelihoods project implemented by Africare. The chapter describes in detail the systematic use of participatory tools to generate a set of representative qualitative and quantitative data demonstrating project impact, based on the perceptions of project participants. Beginning with a consideration of impact assessments in the context of humanitarian crises, the chapter then introduces the participatory impact assessments (PIA) as an evolution of PRA and a more accurate tool through which to understand the perceptions of those who partook in project design and implementation. The next section provides a justification of Zimbabwe as a case study and details the PIA of the Gokwe Integrated Recovery Action Project in Zimbabwe. The chapter then considers the methodology of the PIA, with a particular focus on participatory tools, before progressing to the results of this assessment. The final section then offers an analysis of the lessons learnt, including the methodological strengths and weaknesses and other challenges.

In Chapter 6, Kanti Paul and Dutt provide details of the first participatory study of the impacts on the environment and people affected by Cyclone Sidr in Bangladesh. The chapter examines the prevalent conditions under which PRA methods were used to collect information from survivors regarding the extent of human deaths and injuries caused by Cyclone Sidr. Attempts are also made to review how participatory research methods have been applied, what the main concerns and challenges in their application were, and how to overcome them. The chapter offers key insights into the beneficial use of participatory techniques in post-disaster contexts, whilst acknowledging their weaknesses at the same time. Starting with a review of disaster and participatory research in Bangladesh, the chapter then considers the application of participatory methods in the post-Sidr context with a key focus on delineating the steps through which the research was conducted. Importantly the chapter then reflects in depth on the challenges associated with participatory research methods in such a context.

In the final chapter of Part I, Jigyasu examines the challenges and opportunities in the context of participatory research aimed at rediscovering traditional knowledge systems for post-earthquake reconstruction in Marathwada and Gujarat in India. Born out of a growing concern at the increasing vulnerability of rural communities to natural hazards such as earthquakes, especially in the context of developing countries, this research aimed at exploring the potential role of local knowledge, resources and strengths of rural communities in India and Nepal for formulating long-term planning and mitigation measures to reduce their disaster vulnerability, especially to earthquakes. From a starting point which justifies the use of the two case studies in question, the chapter moves on to provide a detailed discussion of why participatory research methods are appropriate for research of this nature. The chapter then provides a detailed account of the participatory research process conducted before assessing the strengths and weakness of such approached.

Bibliography

Chambers, R. (1983), *Rural Development: Putting the Last First* (Harlow: Longman).

Devitt, P. (1977), 'Notes on Poverty-orientated Rural Development', in ODI, *Extension, Planning and the Poor*, Agricultural Administration Unit Occasional Paper 2, ODI, London.

Leftwich, A. (ed) (2004), *What is Politics?* (Cambridge: Polity Press).

Lowndes, V. (2002), 'Institutionalism', in D. Marsh and G. Stoker (eds), *Theory and Methods in Political Science*, 2nd ed. (Basingstoke: Palgrave Macmillan).

Michels, R. (1915), *Political Parties* (Glencoe, IL: Free Press).

Mosca, G. (1896/1965), *The Ruling Class*, A. Livingstone (ed.) (New York: McGraw Hill).

Neuman, W.L. (2006), *Social Research Methods: Qualitative and Quantitative Approaches*, 6th ed. (Boston: Pearson Education Inc.).

Payne, G. and Payne, J. (2004), *Key Concepts in Social Research* (London: SAGE Publications Ltd.).

Squires, J. (2004), 'Politics: A Feminist Perspective' in A. Leftwich (ed), *What is Politics?* (Cambridge: Polity Press).

Wright, E.O. (1993), 'Explanation and Emancipation in Marxism and Feminism', *Sociological Theory* 11(1), 39–54.

Chapter 3

Who Speaks For The Community? Negotiating Agency and Voice in Community-based Research in Tanzania

Anna Mdee

Introduction

This chapter explores an attempt to work in partnership with active local community researchers in Uchira, Tanzania combining Participatory Rural Appraisal (PRA) methods with longer-term anthropological approaches. The basis for doing this was to go beyond the quick and dirty application of PRA tools to have a deeper community involvement in the research from inception to final analysis. The project set out to analyse collective village life and in particular the operation and impact of a community-managed water scheme. Through exploring the interaction of structural factors and individual agency in shaping who comes to represent the community, this research built an intensive ethnography of the evolution of collective village processes (Toner 2008). This chapter presents an overview of this research but with a specific focus on the role of local researchers as community mediators and representatives.

The aim was to allow local researchers to be active participants rather than research assistants in an extractive process of data collection. Local researchers were selected and facilitated to gain skills in a range of methods, such as community profiling, life-history interviews, participant observation, transect walks and livelihoods analysis.

The methodology of the research was successful in both building local research capacity and active participation in the research but there were inevitably tensions relating to power, resources and capacity in the interaction, and this chapter reflects further on these.

Two significant aspects of this interaction were methods and money. First, to some extent there was a covert negotiation over methods within the research team which clearly related to the ability and willingness of different researchers to be reflexive and analytical. Second, despite every intention to make the research process as open and participatory as possible, the money for the research came from the UK and was awarded by the Economic and Social Research Council (ESRC) for a specific piece of research. Therefore, it was difficult to achieve fully equal relationships with the research team due to disparity of resources and knowledge and an expectation on the part of the local researchers that the UK researcher should act as a boss.

This chapter explores these tensions further and also examines the evolving relationship of the research team. It considers how knowledge is formed but also the changing nuanced and ambiguous nature of who is an insider and who is an outsider in the research process. Two examples are pertinent to this: first, one of the local researchers who was very critical of local leaders, was framed by them as an outsider; second, I found myself in an ambiguous position in this regard as through the course of the research my own position shifted from being a total outsider: a stranger and a *'mzungu*[1] to becoming the daughter-in-law of the village chairman and often referred to as *Mwenyeji.*[2]

This chapter also considers the question of who speaks for the community? One of my difficulties with PRA is that, despite claims to the contrary, it is often very difficult to see how PRA tools used in short periods of time can capture fully the different voices of the community, considering in particular the dominant discourses and potentially biases of such voices. The research considered the consequences of only capturing those dominant voices which is demonstrated by the community water project that reinforces elite capture and bias despite being a self-proclaimed example of community ownership in action (Toner 2008). The conclusions then reflect on the implications of this interaction for conducting participatory research.

Finding Uchira on the Streets of Cambridge

As an undergraduate student at Cambridge University, I was a member of Survival International, a charity seeking to support the rights of indigenous and tribal peoples. Sometime during the winter of 1995 we held a social event in a café on King's Street. Dr Sybil Mbuya, a medical doctor from Tanzania, happened to be among the party. We got talking and she explained that she had completed her medical training in the UK and frequently came to stay with friends in Cambridge. They assisted her in fundraising for medical projects that she conducted in her home region of Tanzania. She went on to explain that recently she had become involved with a UK charity and with them had succeeded in obtaining a grant of £50,000 from the EU in order to sink a water borehole at her new health centre in the village of Uchira. However, the relationship had soured and she was now excluded from the project but was fighting the matter in court.

Having previously spent four months working as a volunteer on an environmental conservation project on Mafia Island in Tanzania and with a strong and youthful urge to do something to assist Dr Mbuya, I immediately offered to go

---

1   Swahili term referring to a white person but also indicating power, status and even certain attitudes to timekeeping!

2   Local inhabitant/native.

to Tanzania to investigate the situation under the guise of my dissertation project. This study flourished under the care of Ernest Msuya, a member of the Uchira village council who acted as mentor, guide and translator during this development with key informants working in local government, health and education, as well as with a range of village residents. Copies of this report were sent back to the village council and also to local government officials and Oxfam. A key part of this report emphasized the village council plans for an improved water supply system. Members of the council have told me since that they believe this report helped them to eventually receive funding from the Deutsche Gesellschaft für Technische Zusammenarbeit (GTZ) to provide a gravity-fed water supply. A friendship via letter and later email continued with Ernest Msuya and led in 2000 to the creation of a small organization for fundraising in the UK for projects in Uchira. In 2003 this became a UK registered charity named Village-to-Village. I add this detail here in order to better contextualize the participatory research interaction that later develops. Cornwall's (2003) reflection that PRA is about a balance and a tension between action and observation is pertinent to this. The creation of Village-to-Village was a concrete response of the need to offer action.

I did not return to Uchira until 2002 when a research visit for another project, on which I was employed as a research assistant researching sustainable livelihoods approaches, enabled me to return to Tanzania.[3] That research had left me frustrated as to how little development practitioners and policy-makers actually knew about the impact of their work at the micro level and the untested assertions being made concerning the validity and possibilities of populist approaches to development intervention (Toner 2003; Toner and Franks 2006).

In 1996 Uchira had significant problems with adequate supplies of drinking water, but GTZ had since funded the rehabilitation and expansion of the existing piped water system. This intervention emphasized community ownership and the possibilities for community-based management as a system for the delivery and management of services. Given my already strong links to this village and the availability of some longitudinal data, Uchira seemed to offer an ideal opportunity to further explore some of the questions and frustrations I had with notions of people-centred and bottom-up development, and to explore some of the theoretical ideas which shape current practice.

This study began not with a particular participatory project or intervention, although this is one component, but with the residents of the village of Uchira itself in order to examine the relationship between individual participation, collective action and change in community-driven development. The methodological foundation was an advocated actor-centred (Long and Long 1992; Arce and Long 2000). It recognizes the importance of individual agency in shaping collective

---

3 'Goodbye to Projects' was a three year DFID-funded study exploring the application of sustainable livelihoods approaches in development interventions in Tanzania, Uganda and South Africa, for more information see: http://www.bradford.ac.uk/acad/dppc/research/poverty/projects/goodbye.

action due to the fact that an actor-centred approach acknowledges the negotiation between the individual and the social-economic context in which they live. It also recognizes that actors are only 'partially enrolled in the projects of others' and consequently reinterpret such projects (Arce and Long 2000). Therefore, actors are able through their own agency to subvert and reinterpret external interventions, whether it is globalization or a water supply rehabilitation project (Hickey and Mohan 2004). Some actors are able to exert more agency than others with agency being shaped by 'social networks, lifeworlds and experience' amongst other factors (Lister 2004; Hilhorst 2003). Hilhorst (ibid.) applies this approach to produce an anthropological account of the evolution of a non-governmental organization (NGO) in the Philippines. I wished to apply a similar approach to this case study of individuals, collective activity and institutional change in development in Uchira village, the aim of which was to produce an intensive[4] ethnographic account of the interfaces of individual agency and collective action at the micro-level (Sayer 2000; Berg 2004).

Producing an Ethnography of Development and Change in Uchira

Coming from a background of social anthropology my inclination tends towards participant observation as a means of constructing ethnographic research. However, personal circumstances prevented me from following the Malinovskian path of disappearing to the field for a couple of years and re-emerging to produce and construct my account of this time (Malinowski 1922). There is quite an extensive literature detailing the process of adapting and applying the benefits of anthropological techniques to the development field (Okely and Callaway 1992; Pottier 1993; Gardner and Lewis 1996; Moore 1997; Arce and Long 2000; Eriksen 2001; Panayiotopoulos 2002; Bebbington, Dharmawan et al. 2004; CDS 2004; Olivier de Sardan 2005; Booth, Leach et al. 2006).

I wanted to explore a means of producing ethnography through cooperation and collaboration with local researchers and using short but intensive periods of immersion in the field, similar to Booth (2003). The aim in this case is that data and analysis are emergent from this interaction (Gonzalez 2000). However, in practice the co-production of an ethnography with local researchers was not an easy process given differences in background, education and resources, and I reflect on this below.

Once funding had been obtained for research in Uchira I was able to return in December 2003 and recruited Ernest Msuya, my guide and instructor in 1996, to work with me. My idea was that we should work closely together during my

---

4   I use the word 'intensive' in the sense that this is a focused study of one particular village, as opposed to an extensive study that might compare a number of villages. This draws on the distinction between 'intensive' and 'extensive' research employed by Sayer (2000).

periods of residence in Uchira, but that he would be able to continue with the fieldwork when I was back in the UK. Ernest's knowledge of the local political scene and his good connections enabled him to negotiate the acceptance of this research locally. However this also meant that I was to some degree dependent on him and his networks. If people wanted to talk to me very often they would first approach Ernest to ask him to facilitate this, and he seemed to enjoy this role as gate-keeper cum minder, but it did come to cause tensions.

Ernest initially wanted to undertake all of the data collection on his own and I had to persuade him that the size of the project would necessitate some additional assistance. As my own networks in the village were poor at that time I asked Ernest to find two suitable secondary school leavers to assist us. We discussed that they should be of different genders and religions so that we could not be seen to be biased towards any group, although this hope may have been slightly naïve.

Whilst it was my intention to allow the research to be actively shaped by the local research team, it was unavoidable that I would be imposing many of the parameters on the work. I wrote the research proposal, secured funding in partnership with colleagues in the UK and paid the salaries and in that sense such a partnership is by definition unequal (Erikson Baaz 2005). I was required and expected by the research team to act as the boss, and they made it clear that they wanted clear guidance and structure; something I now think reflects the hierarchical culture of village life in Tanzania. The team would even say to people, as they introduced me, 'our boss is in town', but our relationship was always relaxed and friendly. This also has echoes of the reinterpretation of PRA noted by Fiedrich (2003) in which he recounts how PRA was delivered by one trainer in Uganda as a more linear and structured process than intended but in a manner which better fitted the 'hierarchical codes of power in Africa'. Whilst I had the power in terms of paying salaries and guiding research questions and activities, the local researchers still held considerable power over me in terms of who they could decide to interview, what questions they would concentrate on, what methods of data collection they preferred, and how they would transcribe and translate data. However, this diminished as my command of KiSwahili improved.

As a research group we also began to take on a more active agency in the village through repeated engagement with local officials and the staff of the Water Users' Association. This also shaped the research to some extent. For instance, it kept being repeated during interviews that even the poorest in the village could afford to pay contributions to various organizations, be it primary school or membership fees for the Uchira Water Users' Association (UWUA). This led us to conduct livelihoods interviews with selected respondents that we classified as have-nots, those who are getting-by and the big-shots. The analysis of these interviews allowed the local researchers to respond to officials making such comments, who in return often produced more considered responses. This follows a reflexive dialogical model embracing the interplay of theory and practice; as well as structure and agency (Mikkelsen 1995).

During my period of contact with Uchira my status and relationship with the community evolved considerably. In 1996 I was a young student pursuing a first degree on a youthful mission to change the world and by 2007 I was married to the son of the current village chairman. Whilst having become less of an outsider in the village neither am I fully an insider, although my changing status and increasing language skills have allowed me growing access to the dynamics of family and collective village life in the course of this period. During the fieldwork people tended to see me as 'that Mzungu who got some money from people in the UK to build a health centre', referring to the work of Village-to-Village, the charity of which I was Chair of Trustees. Mention of the health centre often seemed to encourage people to agree to be interviewed and Ernest liked to use this in his introduction of me rather than emphasizing my status as an academic. He wanted to reinforce that I was giving something to Uchira and so people should give their time for the research. Therefore, I can make no pretence of being a neutral outside observer of village life. I am part of networks of family and civil life in the village, and actively engaging in processes of collective life. This chimes with the reflections of Swantz (2003), also on her engagement in Tanzania, when she says 'I did these things as a member of the village'. She is clear that this type of research necessitates that it is also has an action-oriented role.

Multiple Methods of Data Collection

Several methods of data collection were employed in the course of the research in order to generate the range of information required to answer the research questions. For instance, in order to further understanding of the local-national institutional relationships and to construct a profile of community-life in Uchira, semi-structured interviewing, supported by the collection of documentation, was undertaken with a range of key informants. Intensive social research techniques including interpretive biography: life history interviewing and diagramming, autoethnography: local interpretation through diary keeping, observation and analysis, in-depth interviewing and participant observation were used to make inferences about the influence of individual agency in collective action, and in turn the shaping of change.

Additional methods were used to study the process of institutional evolution in the UWUA including process documentation, institutional mapping, participant observation, interviewing, and a review of institutional records and documents. Researchers observed water collection at public water points and collected data on water usage in Uchira, in addition to recording official processes, such as meetings of the water management committee, as well as observing other sites of collective activity in the village such as village assemblies, religious and political meetings, football matches and cultural events.

Table 3.1 presents an overview of the three areas of investigation in this study. As is reflected above, the multiple methods used collected a wide

Table 3.1   Overview of research methods

	Methods	Sampling	Scale	Recording	Strengths	Weaknesses
Individuals	Life-histories	Purposive sample (following community-profiling) according to age, gender, ethnicity and wealth.	41 (2004)	Life timelines Family mapping	Revealed extent of individual participation in collective activities. Provided detail on types of agency used by individuals in shaping their lives.	Interviewees and local researchers needed much encouragement to be reflective and describe more than a simple succession of events. My assumption that reflection is easy and automatic.
	Livelihoods interviews	Purposive sample by local researchers covering 3 categories of well-being.	67 (2004)	Interview notes	Provided a locally-appropriate wealth-ranking used to make sense of how wealth can shape individual agency and collective action.	Estimates of income and expenses were highly inconsistent but the number of interviews combined with the local knowledge of researchers assisted in interpreting this data.
	Peer research	Purposive sample – population under 30, covering range of gender, ethnicity, religion.	25 (2004)	Interview notes	Provided data on how age (particularly youth) shapes individual agency. This group did not respond well to life-history interview by main research team and thus peer research proved more effective.	Data could be quite patchy and unreflective. Additional interviewing of local researchers improved process of analysis. My assumption that local researchers could do this with limited training.
	Participant observation/ Autoethnography	N/a	2004-6	Field diaries	My personal field diary was a vital record of interactions, observations and interviews. Local researcher's diaries and spoken reflections very valuable in interpreting data – particularly where interviews were patchy or incomplete.	Local researchers somewhat reluctant to complete written records and to spend time translating them. Again my assumption that local researchers could do this without more training.

Table 3.1 (continued)

	Methods	Sampling	Scale	Recording	Strengths	Weaknesses
Collective activities: interface of structure and agency	**Interviews**	Key points – water pumps, dispensaries, church, markets.	200+ (2004/5)	Interview notes	Useful source for community-profiling especially when compared to 1996 interviews.	Notes by local researchers were unreflective and unquestioning. Required further discussion and elaboration for analysis.
	Participant observation	Engagement in political, religious, and social gatherings.	2004-6	Field diaries photographs	Field dairy was a vital source of data in this respect but local researchers observations were better accessed through interview/conversation.	Data was very patchy depending on the researchers involved.
Instit. Evolution: processes of change	**Process documentation**	Key stakeholders – UWUA, Village Council, Ward Office, political meetings.	2004-6	Summary notes	Captured evolution of process of collective action – also allowed us to identify those individuals most able to shape collective actions.	Notes by local researchers could be too unreflective and unquestioning.
	Interviews/ secondary data	Key informants in relevant institutions.	Snowball process starting from known sources and repeated on several occasions 2004-6	Interview notes	These interviews often revealed tensions in the implementation and differential understandings of policy. Enhanced understanding of translation of policy from macro to micro level. Such interviews also formed a useful dialogue on findings.	Views and research findings were sometimes sensitive and controversial and dialogue with some actors had to be carefully handled.
	Water point survey	Timed surveys at range of water points.	12/24 (2004)	Charts recording customer details, price paid, consumption, distance travelled	Captured very well local evolution of collection mechanisms, water pricing and motivations of tap attendants. Data provided a good baseline to track evolution.	Water Office used this information to enforce pricing rules without considering implications.

range of data that enabled me to piece together an ethnography of change and development in Uchira. I reflect here on the most challenging aspects: life-history interviewing, autoethnography and longitudinal tracking of village evolution. The most significant challenges in this regard were the need to adapt intensive anthropological techniques to be conducted by a collaborative team of researchers and my lack of opportunity to spend significant periods of time in the field. Similar to Mosse (2003), I think on balance that whilst not being an equal replacement for an intensive and protracted stay in the field, such a methodology proved good enough for the purposes of this study.

Life-histories

Over 40 initial life history interviews were conducted in July/August 2004. The selection of participants tried to reflect a spread of respondents representing different ethnic groups, gender, age, economic status, and religion as identified through the community profiling activities undertaken: key informant and livelihoods interviews. Interviews usually took place at interviewees homes, inside or outside according to the type and amount of seating available in the household. In wealthier homes we were invited in to sit on comfortable armchairs and offered some refreshments. In less wealthy homes we would perch on low stools or any available rocks. Some life-history interviews were conducted at public water points or within business premises. Many, but not all, of the interviews took place in the presence of other family members and we took careful note of who was present in interviews.

Some experimentation with method was necessary. It was found most productive to produce visual timelines of people's lives and generational charts. Some questions advocated in the literature on biographical methods, such as asking people to reflect on the times of their lives when they were most happy (Atkinson 1998), caused bemusement and confusion to interviewees and were dropped by the research team in favour of a more structured approach. This structured approach asked people to reflect on their lives in a chronological pattern, but particularly focused on when and why people had participated in collective activities outside of the family. We also completed family kinship and network charts in order to make sense of kin connections, and linkages within and without Uchira. This revealed interesting data concerning networks of family support but also patterns of migration, employment and marriage. It also highlights how the process of reflection actually requires further explanation as it is not something people automatically do.

Field Diaries and Autoethnography

All researchers were asked to keep a personal reflective record of the research processes. I found a research diary to be an effective means of reflecting on the developing research experience particularly during intensive periods of fieldwork and in charting my personal relationship with the research which has much in common with McGee (2002). The proposed use of autoethnography was a largely experimental element in the research and intended to examine how local researchers could be facilitated to produce accounts of development activity. Harrison (2000) explores the use of diaries as a research tool in understanding the reinterpretation of development work in a project in Zambia, and this research intended to build on this experience. However, the local research teams were not as enthusiastic and, as discussed above, only Rhoda actually used her diary. The team preferred to reflect on events through stories and gossip. As I became more immersed in the minutiae of life in Uchira I also found that my capacity for interpreting and accessing such gossip increased. I think also that I was naïve to assume that local researchers could, and would, produce critical and reflective questioning and accounts without more intensive support and training to be able to do so. Therefore, many of the weaknesses identified in the table above are not the fault of the local researchers, rather the blame lies with my over expectations of their capacity to do this without more support.

Ethnography is usually thought of as being produced by an outsider. However, in working in cooperation with a team of local researchers there is also space to explore the production of autoethnography produced by insiders (Reed-Danahay 1997). Following periods of training in the research methods local researchers were encouraged to direct and shape the research in response to the issues raised in the profiling, life-history interviewing and organizational mapping. This method also incorporates the local analysis of data. As detailed above a reflexive process of analysis took place during the joint translation of interview data. Ernest Msuya also wrote his own independent analyses in relation to the operation of the UWUA and other aspects of life in Uchira. The capacity for reflection by the research team did grow with time but there were certainly different preferences for the expression of such reflection.

Peer Research

During the collection of data in life-history interviews the reticence of the young to talk openly was noted. Very often they were shy, fearful of not knowing answers or did not appear to have any opinions, or felt that their lives had been short and that not a great deal had happened to them. In discussion with the research team it was decided that a separate study of youth perceptions should be carried out, as it appeared that Ernest's position as an older and well-connected man made younger participants unwilling to express themselves. I had already been approached by a Form 6 leaver with a place at university for some employment on the project and he seemed to be the obvious person to conduct the study. Together we discussed the basis of such a study, selection criteria of respondents and the scope of the questions to be asked. I allowed him some discretion to develop interviews as necessary. He worked over a two-week period assisted by another Form 6 leaver. They undertook the transcription and translation of interviews and also produced their own synthesis report. This work produced some interesting data on the views and position of younger people in the community. In particular it highlighted tensions within their identities regarding their own perceptions of traditional and modern life. Both individuals involved in this part of the study had higher levels of education and seemed to some degree to be more comfortable with being encouraged to attempt their own analysis and reflection.

Longitudinal Research

One of the opportunities presented in returning to Uchira to undertake this research was the opportunity to consider how the village had changed in the period between 1996 and 2004–5, and to achieve a more complete profile of the community. The 1996 study constructed a basic archaeology of previous and current development activity in Uchira and this current, and more detailed, study offered a rare opportunity to examine what had changed and how during this period. This work also enabled us to identify the linkages between international/national policies and their interpretation and implementation at the local level. Ernest Msuya had worked with me on the original study and therefore we aimed to re-interview key informants and re-visit key locations in order to update the 1996 village study. This enabled us to produce comparative maps of the village in 1996 and 2004 which illustrate changing influences in the provision of services. The 1996 study had also identified several influential individuals within the village and this study re-engaged with them to understand the dynamics of their participation in collective village life.

One of the emergent themes of the research was a need to quantify poverty in the village. Dialogue with regional officials and some UWUA staff and the village council often resulted in denials that some people had difficulties in paying for water or making contributions to village development projects. From community profiling we had already produced a qualitative wealth ranking but as a research team we felt the need to quantify some aspects of wealth. Livelihoods interviews which were semi-structured around questions of income and consumption, then led to a quantification of typical expenditure in different wealth groups. This part of the research facilitated much deeper discussions on issues of ability to pay for services such as water, and demonstrated that some of the very poorest were using up to 30 per cent of their cash income to pay for water, and was a necessary baseline of primary data that informed interaction with some individuals and agencies. Similar dialogical needs are found in the work that reflects on the World Bank Study *Voices of the Poor* (Brock and McGee 2002). However, this also led to some villagers, individuals with power within UWUA, trying to assert that local researchers were not interested in the community and they simply wanted to cause trouble. This again highlights the need to disaggregate the community to understand the power dynamics at play. A short intensive PRA exercise would have difficulty in recognizing such dynamics.

Making Sense of the Data

The process of data analysis took place in two ways: first, as an on-going interaction with the local researchers in Uchira. As mentioned above, this process produced comparative maps of the villages, wealth rankings and descriptive data relating to the evolution of institutions and mechanisms for the delivery and payment of water. All of this data provides a baseline for the more analytical element of this research. The second part of the data analysis involved textual and discourse analysis of interviews. This was based on an interactive and iterative process of coding the data in order to produce a typology: for instance, of differential participation in collective action, and then returning to further sort and categorize the data, before further refining the typologies (Laws, Harper et al. 2003; Mikkelsen 2005). The categories and typologies used to analyse the data are hence emergent from it but also based on existing analytical frameworks. Analysis of data happens on different levels and both interpretation and expression of research findings is a process of negotiation and reflects the positions of the different actors and institutions in a co-production of knowledge. The life-history interviews formed one element of the research but became one of the central points of analysis. Life-histories were recorded in diagrammatic form using a life line that charted significant events in the life of an individual, a family network chart and a range of significant observations and opinions made by the individual during the interview. These charts were then used to identify differential forms of agency that people had employed in their lives using a typology developed by Lister (2004). They were also coded in relation to different social relationships which had enabled or constrained the action of the individual. This analysis offered an insight into how community identity and voice is shaped and also revealed the structural barriers, in particular to the poor, women and young people in shaping their community. However, more significantly it also showed when individuals had been able to overcome such structural constraints. My conclusions from this data which were drawn up in the UK were extensively discussed with local researchers in subsequent visits.

At this point the research became far less interactive; both practically and out of necessity as I was no longer able to spend longer periods of time in Uchira. Therefore, the interpretation of data in the study was largely my own and consequently cannot claim to be a co-production of knowledge with active local researchers. I have come to understand that such a co-production would require a far higher investment of time and resources than was possible in this research. It is also recognition that the research had to be packaged for an audience beyond the village. Knowledge gained from the research has been used locally in building up the NGO 'Village-to-Village' and in challenging some of the problematic aspects of the water project, particularly in relation to the ability of the poorest to pay for water. Beyond the village, the research has an academic and policy audience and requires an exclusive and specialist language. Again to pick up on Swantz (2003), this is not a problem, and it is simply that we are using the language and knowledge that we have to take action on the behalf of others.

Conclusion

This chapter considered an attempt to marry PRA tools with anthropological methods to produce research in a collaborative manner with one village in Tanzania. The experience of this research shows the necessity of not assuming that concepts such as reflection are automatically transferable. It also shows that the relationship and dynamics of the research team and the encounter itself shape the interaction between researchers and the researched. Absolute equality in the process is an impossibility given imbalances in knowledge, power and resources, and it is not helpful to pretend otherwise. Chambers (2005) has argued on several occasions that we should not instruct too closely but should hand over the stick. This was certainly my intention as I embarked on the research but it was very clear that people may not want the stick, feel it is appropriate that they should have the stick, or have the resources to use the stick.

My own reflection on this period of research finds strong connections with the experience of Swantz (2003) and Cornwall (2003): that research and action should be inextricably linked. However, the process of participatory research and action is not as easy as is sometimes asserted. I tend to agree with Alumasa's (2003) assertion that tools are just tools, and that in this sense participation, and with it PRA, has been commercialized. This is symbolized by the merchants of participation who go from one workshop to another.

Jassey (2003) also makes a vital point that PRA tends to produce similar responses to all problems and I have certainly seen this in previous research (Toner 2003). It is not helpful necessarily to see the poor as experts on their own poverty. This position is dangerous in the sense that it leads to the exclusion of proper consideration of the broader structural conditions that shape poverty.

For me then, the value of PRA and participatory research and action in general is more concerned with a philosophy of respect and humility, a way of accessing specific local knowledge and of beginning a long-term interaction of reflection and action that necessarily must extend beyond the boundaries of a particular community. It is much less about formulas and rules and more about flexibility, creativity, diversity, contextual fit and hybridization (Dale 2004). It is about starting a conversation of many voices, and starting to find ways of enabling those with small voices to be better able to make themselves heard.

References

Alumasa, J. (2003), 'Hanging on the Edge of a Cliff: My Loud Thoughts as I Walk Along the Winding Path of Participatory Development in Kenya', in Cornwall, A. and Pratt, P. (eds) *Pathways to Participation: Reflections on PRA* (Rugby: ITDG Publishing).

Arce, A. and Long, N. (eds) (2000), *Anthropology, Development and Modernity: Exploring Discourses, Counter-tendencies and Violence* (London: Routledge).

Atkinson, R. (1998), *The Life Story Interview* (London: Sage Publications).

Bebbington, A., Dharmawan, L. et al. (2004), 'Village Politics, Culture and Community-driven Development: Insights From Indonesia' *Progress in Development Studies* 4(3), 187–205.

Berg, B.L. (2004), *Qualitative Research Methods for the Social Sciences* (Boston: Pearson).

Booth, D. (2003), 'Bridging the 'Macro'-'micro' Divide in Policy-oriented Research: Two African Experiences', in D. Eade (ed.) *Development Methods and Approaches: Critical Reflections* (Oxford: Oxfam Publishing), pp. 44–59.

Booth, D. and Leach, M. (2006), *Experiencing Poverty in Africa: Perspectives From Anthropology* (Toronto: University of Toronto).

Brock, K. and McGee, R. (eds) (2002), *Knowing Poverty: Critical Reflections on Participatory Research and Policy* (London: Earthscan).

CDS (2004), *Participatory Ethnographic Evaluation and Research* (Swansea: Centre for Development Studies).

Cornwall, A. (2003), 'Winding Paths, Broken Journeys: Travels With PRA', in A. Cornwall and G. Pratt. *Pathways to Participation: Reflections on PRA* (London: ITDG Publishing), pp. 47–53.

Dale, R. (2004), *Development Planning: Concepts and Tools for Planners, Managers and Facilitators* (London and New York: Zed Books).

Eriksen, T.H. (2001), *Small Places, Large Issues: An Introduction to Social and Cultural Anthropology* (London: Pluto Press).

Erikson Baaz, M. (2005), *The Paternalism of Partnership* (London: Zed Books).

Fiedrich, M. (2003), 'Maps Turning to Minefields: Local Knowledge of PRA in a Ugandan Village', in A. Cornwall and G. Pratt (eds) Pathways to Participation: Reflections on PRA (London: ITDG Publishing), pp. 68–74.

Gardner, K. and D. Lewis (1996), *Anthropology, Development and the Post-modern Challenge* (London: Pluto Press).

Gonzalez, M.C. (2000), 'The Four Seasons of Ethnography: A Creation-Centered Ontology for Ethnography', *International Journal of Intercultural Relations* 24(5), 623–50.

Harrison, E. (2000), 'Men, Women and Work in Rural Zambia', *European Journal of Development Research* 12(2), 53–71.

Hickey, S. and G. Mohan, (eds) (2004), *Participation: From Tyranny to Transformation?* (London: Zed Books).

Hilhorst, D. (2003), *The Real World of NGOs: Discourses, Diversity and Development* (London: Zed Books).

Jassey, K. (2003), 'PRA From the End-user's Perspective', in A. Cornwall and G. Pratt (eds) *Pathways to Participation: Reflections on PRA* (London: ITDG Publishing).

Laws, S. and Harper, C. et al. (2003), *Research for Development* (London: Sage Publications).

Lister, R. (2004), *Poverty* (Cambridge: Polity Press).

Long, N. and Long, A. (1992), *Battlefields of Knowledge: The Interlocking of Theory and Practice in Social Research and Development* (London and New York: Routledge).

Malinowski, B. (1922), *Argonauts of the Western Pacific* (London: RKP).

McGee, R. (2002), 'The Self in Participatory Poverty Research', in K. Brock and R. McGee (eds) *Poverty Reduction: Critical Reflections on Participatory Research and Policy* (London: Earthscan), pp. 14–43.

Mikkelsen, B. (2005), *Methods for Development Work and Research: A New Guide for Practitioners* (New Delhi: Sage).

Moore, J.D. (1997), *Visions of Culture: An Introduction to Anthropological Theories and Theorists* (Walnut Creek: AltaMira Press).

Okely, J. and H. Callaway, (eds) (1992), *Anthropology and Autobiography* (London: Routledge).

Olivier de Sardan, J.-P. (2005), *Anthropology and Development: Understanding Contemporary Social Change* (London: Zed Books).

Panayiotopoulos, P. (2002), 'Anthropology Consultancy in the UK and Community Development in the Third World: A Difficult Dialogue' *Development in Practice* 12(1), 45–58.

Pottier, J. (1993), *Practising Development: Social Science Perspectives* (London and New York: Routledge).

Reed-Danahay, D. (ed.) (1997), *Auto/ethnography: Rewriting the Self and Social* (Oxford and New York: Berg).

Sayer, A. (2000), *Realism and Social Science* (London: Sage Publications).

Swantz, M.-L. (2003), 'My Road to Participatory Action Research', in Cornwall, A. and Pratt, G. (eds) *Pathways to Participation: Reflections on PRA.* (London, ITDG Publishing), pp. 196–202.

Toner, A. (2003), Exploring sustainable livelihoods approaches in relation to two interventions in Tanzania. *Journal of International Development* 15(7), 771–81.

Toner, A. (2008), 'Who Shapes Development? An Ethnography of Participation in Collective Village life in Uchira, Tanzania', in Cornwall, A. and Pratt, P. (eds) *Pathways to Participation: Reflections on PRA* (Rugby: ITDG Publishing).

Toner, A. and T. Franks (2006), Putting Livelihoods Thinking into Practice: Implications for Development Management' *Public Administration and Development* 26(1).

Chapter 4

Poverty Assessment in Rwanda through Participatory Rural Appraisal

Richard Jones

Introduction

This chapter aims to practically demonstrate the use of Participatory Rural Appraisal (PRA) techniques for economic assessment in post-conflict Rwanda. This technique was used as part of the methodology for researching poverty baselines in preparation for the 2001 Rwandan Poverty Reduction Strategy Paper (PRSP).

The chapter initially outlines the use of participation to inform strategies for poverty reduction, the socio-economic setting of Rwanda and the role of PRSPs. This establishes the context for a practical example of using PRA techniques to establish perceptions of wealth from the perspective of different Rwandan communities. Finally some words of caution of such an approach will be offered.

Participation and Poverty Reduction

In order to achieve sustainable poverty reduction, the identification of the role of the socio-economic needs of the poor must be undertaken. The perception of poverty from the communities' viewpoint is critical to this. It is not a particularly recent concept. In 1998 the Development Resources Centre Africa (1998: 5) clarified that participation and empowerment of the poor and exploited people in the development process is implicit in the wider process of social transformation. This contention was further supported by the World Bank's Learning Group on Participatory Development (2000: 4) which defines empowerment as 'a process, through which stakeholders influence and share control over development initiatives, discussions and resources which affect them'.

The Socio-economic Setting of Rwanda

Any participatory poverty assessment of Rwanda has to be informed by the socio-economic setting. Prunier (1998) and Omaar and de Wall (1995) provide an in depth analysis of events leading up to the genocide and the genocide itself (April–July 1994)[1] which led to the Rwandan Patriotic Front (RPF) taking control of Kigali by the end of July 1994. One of their first priorities was to start to reconstruct the Rwandan economy. Over 177,000 shelters were rehabilitated/constructed to house the returnees and displaced, as well as the rebuilding of basic infrastructure. The challenge to reconstruct Rwanda and its economy was and remains daunting, although in the 14 years since the end of the genocide the government has against great odds achieved relative economic and social stability.[2] However, there remain many challenges that emanate from the structural poverty evident in Rwanda and the region, as well as the poverty resulting specifically from the genocide.

The Government of Rwanda (2001: 8) cites that poverty in Rwanda is due to the economic structure which reflects a failure to achieve productivity increases in a context of a large and growing population. A very weak export base of US $16 per capita compared to an average of US $100 in sub-Saharan Africa and vulnerability to external price shocks are some macroeconomic challenges that Rwanda faces, whilst low agricultural productivity, environmental degradation and high levels of subsistence farming are particular microeconomic challenges.

Any poverty assessment must also be informed by the profound effects of the genocide on the population of 8.1 million.[3] Over 500,000 have missing limbs, over 100,000 females are coping with the trauma of rape, 300,000 people have disabilities from wounds sustained during the genocide, 2 million people have experience of being refugees living in chronic conditions in refugee camps and 300,000 have been displaced, 85,000 households are child-headed as both parents were killed, 45 per cent of all households are female-headed and 13.5 per cent of the population have AIDS.

---

1 Prunier, G. (1998). *The Rwanda Crisis – History of a Genocide.* London: Hurst & Company and Omaar, R. and de Waal, A. (1995) *Rwanda: Death, Despair and Defiance.* London: African Rights.

2 Articles commemorating the tenth anniversary of the genocide are generally reflective of this, but many contain words of caution, referring to the way Rwanda under President Kagame has in the words of some commentators 'brushed things under the carpet,' – the real problems of the increasing pressure on the land and the persistence of resentments and negative perceptions shared amongst a significant number of the population have yet to be addressed. The BBC online has many articles to mark the 10th anniversary of the genocide. The themes of brushing the past/negative perceptions/ tensions under the carpet are described in detail. See www.bbc.co.uk/world/africa/35 (2004).

3 Source: Government of Rwanda PRSP (2001), New Times (2002) and Des Forges (2004).

Strategies for Poverty Reduction in Rwanda

The main vehicle for poverty reduction is the national PRSP. It is implemented in the context of the need to reduce poverty, as a way of reducing the possibility of renewed conflict.[4]

The main focus is on gradual structural transformation that will eventually decrease the pressure on the land. Thus national income will be derived from commercial, IT, agro-processing, tourism, mining, exporting of skills and garment manufacture. This is achieved through the development and commercialization of the agricultural sector so farmers can grow crops such as maize, bananas, potatoes and tea/coffee for the international/regional market. The increasing income from the crops will mean that farmers will be increasingly purchasing from the secondary sector which in turn will increase aggregate demand for the goods/services and the need for ever more people to be employed in the secondary sector. This strategy requires significant government intervention in the form of infrastructure development, fertilizers, extension services, social capital support to vulnerable groups and subsidies as well as commitment to reduce inflation, curb money supply, reduce budgetary deficits and improve the balance of payments. In recognition of the economic and social damage of disease, low educational attainment and cultural barriers to development, there are additional specific interventions to reduce incidences of malaria, HIV/AIDS, improve literacy and raise the status of females. Past inequalities are being overcome by attempting to mainstream the income distribution to all sectors of the economy and close the urban-rural gap.[5]

Defining Poverty through PRA

The objective of the PRA exercise in Rwanda was to define poverty from the prospective of different communities primarily in terms of perceptions of wealth. The findings then informed the preparation of the PRSP. In preparation for the exercise two prior activities had to be undertaken: 1) a resource mapping exercise to inform the validity of the bases chosen and 2) an assessment of the household baseline and community life. The standard procedure for each base was to initially work with the translator and key informants: typically the councillor, elders or other administrative officials such as the cellule leader initially to validate the bases, develop research methods and then collect data to define perceptions of wealth.

---

4   For more information on the poverty context of Rwanda and the poverty reduction programme, see Jones, R. (2006), 'No Alternative: Post-war Poverty Reduction as Structural Transformation in Rwanda'. *Journal of Conflict Security and Development* 6(2), June 2006.

5   The Rwandan PRSP (2001) cites how the level of inequality has risen since the mid-1980s, the gini coefficient increasing from 0.27 to 0.455, mainly because of the widening urban-rural gap.

Table 4.1 Community baselines

Parameter	Muyumbu	Runda	Gicumbi	Nyamata
Province	Kigali Ngali (north)	Gitarama	Byumba	Kigali Ngali (south)
Geographic Location	North	South	North	South
Distance from Kigali and major towns	Kigali: 20km	Kigali: 25km Gitarama: 25km	Kigali: 45Km Byumba: 20Km	Kigali: 45km Nyanza: 20km
Distance from paved road	6km	4km	10km	30km
State of road from trunk route	Unpaved murram track Good condition	Unpaved murram track Good condition	Unpaved track, poor condition, too narrow for cars/trucks	Unpaved road, very poor condition
Population; Population (<14); Population (>14)	8000 3500 4500	10000 5000 5000	4076 1000 3076	12000 8000 4000
Ethnic Group Ratio	Hutu 70% Tutsi 30%	Hutu ? Tutsi ?	Hutu 95%	Hutu 80% Tutsi 20%
Locals: Refugees	Mixed	Mixed	Locals only	Mixed
No. Primary schools	1	1	1	1 (very large)
Water supply points	1 (7km away)	1 (3km away)	1 (5km away)	4 (in town)
Latrines	One per household	One per 5 households	One per household	One per household
Poorest months	August–December February–May	September–December March–June	October–December March–June	September–December March–May
Common crops	Matoke, bananas	Matoke, cassava	Matoke, sorghum	Matoke, beans, sweet potatoes, bananas

Table 4.2   **Similarity of research bases**

Province	Research Bases	Gini coefficient	Incidence of food poverty	Incidence of extreme poverty
Kigali-Ngali	Muyumbu, Nyamata	0.411	74%	52.8%
Gitarama	Runda	0.346	61.8%	35%
Byumba	Gicumbi	0.417	65%	45%

Source: Rwandan PRSP (2001: 27). Adapted by author.

Resource Mapping and Base Validity

Places and facilities of strategic importance to the community were established; such as the water supply point, administration office, dispensary, pub, shops, fields, tracks, roads, forest and, if present, the primary school, health clinic and market. Participants were asked about the routes of importance, between shelters to fields, the water supply point and the forest for wood collection, and this enabled common routes and journeys to be defined.

As with any form of research care was taken to ensure that the research bases were valid in order to be able to extrapolate the findings on a regional or national level. Research was undertaken to assess the appropriateness of potential research basis and eventually four were chosen, two in Northern Rwanda: Gicumbi (Byumba) and Muyumbu (Kigali-Ngali – north) and two in Southern Rwanda: Runda (Gitarama) and Nyamata (Kigali-Ngali – south). This assessment had clarified the community baselines of the locations as described in Table 4.1.

Any appraisal of economic indicators highlights the similar standard of living that is a feature of all the regions in the Great Lakes. Table 4.2 indicates the general similarities between the research bases.

Poverty Indicators in Research Bases

Further, in collaboration with the Ministry of Finance it was established that the research bases of Muyumbu, Runda, Gicumbi and Nyamata were reflective of typical post-conflict Rwandan communities throughout the country because of high levels of general poverty, high population growth rate, high levels of subsistence farming: at 95 per cent of population it was reflective of the national average, presence of returning refugees, ethnic balance: Hutu 85 per cent, Tutsi 14 per cent and Twa 1 per cent of the population which was reflective of national average and lack of arable land: 874 people per km^2 of arable land (World Bank 2001).

Table 4.3   Positive and negative aspects of life in research

Positive Aspects of Research Bases	Negative Aspects of Research Bases
Muyumbu: There is not much erosion of the land as ditches are dug and plots are terraced. The road here (up from the main road) is good. If people have money they can buy more food in the market. There are many trees for wood and fuel (charcoal).	**Muyumbu:** There is not enough land for locals. There is not enough land for returning refugees. There is tension (between returning refugees and locals) over land. People eat only once a day (a meal of poor nutritional value). The land is poor and decent crops cannot be grown. There are no jobs. There are too many people. No one (from Kigali) cares. Diseases (malaria, diarrhoea, worms). Water collection is 7km away. Water is bad. Primary school is too expensive.
Runda: Close to health centre (5km). Close to main road. The road to Runda is in good condition. There is a primary school in the settlement.	**Runda:** The soil is poor – yields are low. There are no fertilizers. There is not adequate land to grow enough food to sustain the household. Refugees coming back also need the land but there is not enough for us all. There are tensions between the returning refugees and the established locals. Medicines for malaria and worms are too expensive. There are too many people living in too small an area. There are no jobs. People are hungry. The water is bad.
Gicumbi: The air is fresh as Gicumbi is at a high altitude. Malaria is not as bad as lower down. The school is 6km away.	**Gicumbi:** The land is not fertile. There is bad erosion, as terracing has to be used. There is not enough land to grow food. There are no fertilizers. People are always hungry. Medicines are too expensive. The water is bad and the well is 5km away. There are no jobs. The track to the main road is in bad condition. All items are expensive, as they have to be carried here. People are cold in their houses, as they cannot afford decent material. There are security problems and many thieves. The location of the settlement is remote.
Nyamata: There are several NGOs providing basic needs such as housing and water (4 wells at least in town); there is a health centre in the town, the market is well stocked and there are several schools.	**Nyamata:** There are many people who committed violent acts during the genocide who are still living in the area they have not been brought to justice. Many refugees are coming back, some are helped by the NGOs others are not. There are too few jobs.

Table 4.4   Access to community resources in research bases

Community Resources	Problems
Water supply points and sanitation	M: The one well in the settlement does not work. People have to walk 7km to fetch water. The water is bad. The latrines are poorly constructed. R: The well is down in a very steep valley about 3km away and carrying the water back up is difficult (especially as it's the women and children carrying the water). There are not enough latrines and they are dirty. G: The well is 5km away; the water is bad and causes worms. Many people can't afford the charcoal to boil the water so they become ill. The latrines are poorly constructed and as soil is so hard, they are not very deep N: the wells are close but the quality of the water changes sometimes good sometimes bad.
Primary Schools	All: All schools within 40mins walking distance. Parents cannot afford to send all their children to the school (especially the younger ones and/or girls); at the poorest times of the season when there is not much cash, parents have to keep their children at home as they cannot afford school fees/equipment.
Land	All: Most people have a plot of land within 12Km of the settlement. M/R: There is not enough fertile land, the plots are not big enough. Recently returned refugees get no land as there is none left to share. G: There is not enough fertile land, much of the land is eroded, there are no fertilizers and the plots are not big enough for households to eat properly.
Shelters	All: Most shelters constructed out of mud bricks with thatch roof or tarpaulin sheeting. M/R: Poorly constructed, with leaking roofs. Cramped and do not provide any security when all are out working in the fields. G: Poorly constructed and do not offer much protection from the cold (especially at night).
Food	All: Matoke and beans (occasionally cabbage/rice). All: Poor nutritional quality and insufficient quantity.
Health Services	All: Most people cannot afford the medicines. M: Dispensary in settlement: Stocking Fansidar (for malaria) and panadole. R: Health centre/dispensary 5km away stocking medicines for malaria and panadole. G: Nearest dispensary is 25km away in Byumba Ville it is well stocked. N: There is a well stocked health centre but prices are high.

Notes: M = Muyumbu, R = Runda, G = Gicumbi, N = Nyamata.

The Household Baseline and Community Life

To establish primary concerns and perceptions, all respondents were asked to define both the positive and negative aspects of life in the research bases as Table 4.3 demonstrates.

Access to Resources   Once primary community resources were clarified the level of access to these resources was established. Participants were then able to identify possible reasons why their access to resources and the quality was either good or bad. Table 4.4 illustrates the findings.

Reasons for Poor Resources   To gain further clarification of how the participants viewed their own situation, they were asked why they thought that they lacked these resources.

In addition to the similar socio-economic profiles, the four research bases also had other underpinning similarities captured as follows:

1. There are too many people here.
2. The returning refugees want land and there is none left, so we cannot sell produce from our land and make money to buy goats and improve our shelters.
3. People in Kigali have told NGOs (and UNHCR) not to come here as they think we did bad things in 1994.
4. The land is not fertile so we cannot grow enough to sustain our families and sell surpluses to pay for other things.
5. There are many tensions within the community and arguments over land, refugees and other resources often cause arguments and resentments stemming from the genocide and people's roles within it so people fear to talk about their problems.

Many of the above issues are summarized from direct quotes. A female from Nyamata observed that:

> There are tensions here because we are so poor and there is not enough rain. We are a growing population, there is too much pressure on the land now and in the future it will be worse. No one wants land by the river because its bad and dirty, even though UNHCR have built the umudugudu [shelter] which we are thankful for they cannot make Rwanda bigger! Land is the main cause of our tensions because of our poverty...

Whilst a male from Muyumbu pointed to the people queuing to see the local official:

Look at those waiting to complain about us, they say we take their land, but we have no land – nothing ... and we are hungry. They queue to see the Bourgmestre everyday, last week, last month and they will queue also tomorrow when you have gone and next week and next month. But maybe one day soon they will tire of queuing to complain about us because they have to share the land and we have a right to cultivate the land too ... it is the nature of the Rwandese to put up with bad things quietly only for so long and then what will happen? – it will be like in 1994 they will kill us or force us run away.

Defining Characteristics of wealth

On the basis of the above and the sometimes rambling nature of the data collected the final stage of the process was to define characteristics of wealth in a two stage process.

Defining characteristics of wealth (stage 1)   The key informants were then asked to define characteristics of the richer and poorer people within the settlement. In all cases the primary wealth indicators were centred on the type, size and construction of shelter and number of goats owned. It is interesting to note the differences between settlements researched (Table 4.5, summary), particularly between the extremes of Muyumbu and Nyamata. A person in Muyumbu is poor if they have two goats or less whilst in Nyamata a poor person has six goats or less. Conversely, even the richest person in Muyumbu is likely to have fewer goats than the poorest in Nyamata. Whilst richer people have corrugated iron roofs in Muyumbu this is a characteristic of poorer people in Nyamata. The rich in Muyumbu and Runda can only afford to send the majority of children to primary school whilst it is the poor of Gicumbi and Nyamata who are constrained in the same way.

During the research it became apparent that goats played an even more important part in the micro economy than had originally been thought. If people had money it was perceived that the money is primarily invested in the shelter, children's education and then goats. However, the assessment highlighted that people invested in goats before their shelter and even children. Therefore the number of goats owned and the value over the year became a critical proxy indicator of community wealth, and proved the usefulness of the initial pilot studies.

Whilst there were variations, there were no extremes of wealth, which confirmed the already established economic indicators that indicate all people may be classed as suffering from chronic poverty. Even within the chronic poverty bracket there were subtle variations of wealth.

Defining characteristics of wealth (stage 2: the social map)   By this stage the team had a sound appreciation of the physical and economic characteristics of the settlement as defined by the key informants. It was then necessary to take the wealth ranking exercise further and build upon the established facts with participants from across the settlement.

People were then selected on a basis of the above characteristics in roughly equal numbers to participate in further workshops, focus groups, semi structured interviews and individual interviews. This ensured from the outset that as representative a sample as possible was constructed. The participants were asked to rank different types of livelihood; in most cases there were 5–6 different categories:

1. Rich with money and food: very happy;
2. Rich with food and other resources but not money;
3. Well off, comfortable: can survive;
4. Poorer than average (3). Not eating properly: only once a day, shelter in need of repairs, take longer to recover from illness;
5. Very poor, not enough food: eat once a day, shelter in a poor condition, frequent illness, land exhausted, only marginally productive;
6. Miserable: extremely poor, not enough to eat, no money, no land, have to work for others, bare survival, hand to mouth existence, do not know if such a person will be alive tomorrow, if illness occurs the result is death.

No. of Goats

As the key informants had confirmed that the main wealth differential was the type of shelter and levels of goat ownership, an additional exercise was undertaken to further define wealth: and therefore poverty. This was undertaken by combining the established wealth variables with the perceptions of the categories of the poverty that the poor themselves had defined. Such an exercise built upon all the stakeholders' contribution within the settlement and aided triangulation of the research. It was necessary to use the following props: stone represented a shelter; leaf represented a tin/corrugated iron roof: both characteristic of richer people; grass represented a thatched roof: characteristic of poorer people.

These three props were combined with the established wealth ranking indicators. The format of the exercise was to lay a long piece of wood on the ground and let the community members take a stone, as their shelter, and either a leaf or some grass to represent their shelter roof. The participants then had to choose a number from 1–6 that defined most accurately their livelihood characteristics. They would then place their characteristics against the stick. At the end of the exercise the numbers would be grouped together and this showed the characteristics of the majority of people within the village which allowed a scale to be drawn up.

In most cases the majority of participant's characteristics were defined as stone, grass 4/5/6: poorer than average to miserable bare existence. This was validated by the construction of their shelters with grass roofs indicating higher levels of poverty. This exercise was especially useful as it enabled some form of comparison to be made between the other research bases and it reflected the other

Table 4.5 Wealth indicators for Rwandan research bases

Parameter	Muyumbu	Runda	Gicumbi	Nyamata
Daily income	300RwFr	300/400RwFr	400/500RwFr	500RwFr
Average cost of a goat in poor months	5000RwFr	6000RwFr	6000RwFr	8500RwFr
Average cost of a goat outside poor months	8000RwFr	9000RwFr	9000RwFr	11500RwFr
Wealth indicators used	Type of shelter (size, roof and construction material), no. of goats, meals per day	Type of shelter (size, roof and construction material), no. of goats, meals per day	Type of shelter (size, roof and construction material), no. of goats, meals per day	Type of shelter (size, roof and construction material), no. of goats, meals per day
Principal characteristics of 'richer' people	4–5 goats Corrugated iron roofs Larger shelters More fertile land 2 meals a day Majority of children in primary school	4+ goats Tiled roofs Larger shelters with bricks and cement plaster More fertile land 2 meals a day Majority of children in school	7+ goats Tiled roof Larger shelter with bricks near the main track More fertile land All children in school 2 meals a day	15–20 goats Tiled roofs Larger shelter with brick Metal doors Can employ others to work on their land Shelters in a compound All children in school 2 meals a day More fertile land Possible ownership of a motorbike
Monthly earnings of richer people	10,000RwFr	10,000RwFr	12,000RwFr	20,000RwFr

Table 4.5 continued

Parameter	Muyumbu	Runda	Gicumbi	Nyamata
Principal characteristics of 'poorer' people	0–2 goats Grass roofs Smaller shelter Less fertile land 1 (often small) meal a day Majority of children not in primary school Higher incidences of illness Recent returnees	0–2 goats Tarpaulin for doors/roofs mud brick shelter Grass roofs Less fertile land Recent returnees 1 (often small) meal a day Majority of children not in primary school	0–3 goats Smaller shelter (poorly constructed) Corrugated iron roof Fields are far from home Less fertile land 1 meal a day Some (not majority) of children not in primary school	2–6 goats Smaller shelter (poorly constructed) Corrugated iron roofs (leaking) Possible ownership of a bicycle 2 meals a day (smaller portions) Some (not majority) of children not in primary school Less fertile land
Majority of people (on scale)	4,5,6	4,5,6	3,4	2,3,4
Parameter	Muyumbu	Runda	Gicumbi	Nyamata
No. of goats in 'poorer' households	0–2	0–2	0–3	2–6
No. of goats in 'richer' households	4–5	4–5	7–10	15–20
Cost of a branch of matoke (15–20 bananas)	250RwFr	300RwFr	400RwFr	425RwFr
Cost of a bottle of Primus beer	250RwFr	300RwFr	300RwFr	320RwFr

Parameter	Muyumbu	Runda	Gicumbi	Nyamata
Common risk coping mechanisms	Consume less food, sell goats (if owned), take children out of school, work longer hours, sell assets (housing material), rely on others kindness, steal, do not take medicine if ill	Consume less food, sell goats (if owned), take children out of school, cook with less charcoal (water is not boiled – disease)	Consume less food, sell goats (if owned), take children out of school, walk further for work, prayer	Consume less food, sell goats (if owned), prostitution (females), non investment in shelters
Main priorities for the community	Land availability reform Refugee integration Improve security Improve quality of water (and reduce dependence on beer) Provide more materials for shelter improvement and mosquito netting Non farm income generation activities Address need for fertilizers	Land availability reform Refugee integration Improve water supply Address need for fertilizers	Land availability reform Projects (goat breeding) Improve security Improve water supply Address need for fertilizers	Road improvement Land availability reform Projects for personal development Refugee integration Construction of a tank reservoir Address need for fertilizers

poverty parameters that were highlighted as a result of the previous assessments. As can be seen in the summary table of wealth indicators (Table 4.5), there was a correlation between daily incomes, goat cost, wealth indicators defined and scale values. The differences in community wealth are also clarified by other proxy indicators such as the cost of matoke[6] and a bottle of beer.

In addition there was also a correlation between levels of poverty and status in terms of being a local resident or recently returned refugee. The recently returning refugees do not get access to decent land, they often return with little money/valuables and until they build up some modest wealth through working for others, at a cheaper rate than the established locals, are living at the more extreme end of the poverty bracket: 5 and 6 on the scale. Many of the respondents claimed to have lived in this bracket since their return, even if that was five years ago.

Furthermore, the levels of wealth were also triangulated by the subsequent risk coping mechanisms that people adopted. Robb (2002) defines risk coping mechanisms as 'mechanisms that people use to deal with their prevailing livelihood characteristics'. As Table 4.5 shows, the poorer the community the more severe the risk coping mechanism.

Wealth Indicators

Gender Variations

Throughout the exercises it was found that there were some subtle gender variations in the responses. Males tended to place more emphasis on the physical parameters of wealth: the quality of the soil in the fields, the number of goats owned, the construction and size of the shelter and the amount of beer richer men consumed every night. Females tended to emphasize social parameters as being determinants of wealth such as receiving greater respect, having better-dressed children and the decreased likelihood of becoming ill. However, there did not appear to be any significant difference between males and females over access and use of resources other than the usual differences:

1. Women and children fetch the water.
2. Men go out drinking.
3. Women have to queue for the medicines.
4. Women get paid less to cultivate the land although they do the same day's work as men.
5. Men build the shelters if they are present.

---

6   Matoke (savory bananas) is a staple food in the Great Lakes. A branch of matoke is a standard form of payment for many casual labourers.

In the absence of men, women assume the role of the man and undertake the same tasks although often getting paid less. Both groups in the all the research bases were certain however, that the primary wealth differential variables were the shelter – type/construction, number of goats and the number of meals eaten a day. The latter variable was not used extensively for the purposes of the research as the other variables were easier to identify. All participants agreed that it was better to own a plough or goat as a means of production/wealth asset rather than consumer durables like a radio. Such gender variations and emphases on increasing means of production are common features of any rural participatory process in areas of chronic poverty.

Priorities for Change

On the basis of the above exercises the communities were asked to summarize ways in which their livelihood could be improved. These priorities are correlated to the general points raised throughout the research especially in the poorer research locations of Muyumbu, Runda and Gicumbi. They were ranked as follows:

More land/fertilizers Without exception, all the participants stated that the most pressing issue to be resolved was that of land. People are only eating once a day because they cannot grow sufficient crops to enable two daily meals to be consumed. The soil is so exhausted yields are low, that fertiliser distribution should be viewed as a priority. Directly related to this, is the need to:

Tackle the refugee problem The participants stated that the government should stop more people coming into Runda and Muyumbu and taking their land and making them poorer. When pointed out to them that most of the people who are returning are originally from this community the consensus was that the situation has changed. All have suffered and the status quo can only be maintained so long without violence.

Income generation activities The participants stated that they have a desire to undertake other work besides subsistence farming. It was the responsibility of the government/international community to provide them with employment such as goat/cattle breeding initiatives, infrastructure development and small business initiatives.

Improve security There are high occurrences of petty crime and violence and this coupled with the existing tensions causes a climate of general insecurity to prevail. The security problems can, according to the participants, be overcome by equipping responsible people with guns to maintain order.

Improving water supply and quality Many of the female participants had strong views on this priority. Due to the water being so bad men only wash with water and only drink it occasionally. Drinking the locally distilled banana beer, which is very potent, was generally used to quench men's thirst. As such men often become drunk and abusive towards their family members. Men need to be sensitized to the danger of alcohol abuse and more importantly the water must be improved so men do not have to drink banana beer out of necessity and the disabling effects of water related infections are minimized.

Better material for shelter/mosquito nets   Shelters are basic and most are in need of some form of repair, but no one can afford the materials. The government/NGOs should provide tarpaulins, corrugated iron sheets, bricks etc. The most common cause of death is malaria so people would live longer if they had mosquito nets.

Conclusion

Throughout the research it became apparent that there were some issues associated with the wealth ranking techniques that had to be considered and the implications factored into the exercise.

Influence of Key Informants

As far as realistically possible, it was ensured that the key informants did not unduly influence or bias the establishment of the wealth differentiation variables. It was necessary to work with the key informants first to gain a broad understanding and then work with the rest of the community to gain an in-depth knowledge of perceptions and physical and social manifestations of wealth as well as the broader livelihood characteristics.

Consequences of Being a 'Mzungu'[7]

The communities researched were often remote and far away, in Rwandan terms, from the larger provincial towns and the capital. Many of the participants had not conversed with a *mzungu*. Many had the perception that their problems could be immediately resolved due to the large amount of money that white people inevitably have and carry around with them. It was this mindset, no doubt confirmed by the people's experience as refugees in Goma, which was one of the largest humanitarian efforts ever seen, in which the international community sustained over a million people. Thus people had a tendency to exaggerate circumstances to suit, and this usually meant making the situation sound even worse so that more help could be forthcoming. However the translator, key informants, and when necessary personnel, all of them Rwandan, from the Ministry of Finance were

---

7   East African/Great Lakes Region term for 'white man'.

able to redress some of the more wild statements which had been made. The key in such circumstances is to triangulate what is being said.

Participants Reluctant to Show off Relative Wealth

There were a few participants who were reluctant to clarify their status in front of others, presumably not wishing to arouse jealously. However, this was predicted and some individual participants were followed up with questions about their livelihood and assessments were made of their shelters to ensure that there was a correlation between what they determined their position to be on the wealth ranking exercise and their real poverty. In the majority of cases there was a correlation as the participants had identified themselves correctly using the determined scale.

Usefulness When Differences in Wealth of Community are Negligible

The wealth ranking exercise was a very useful way in which to differentiate wealth within the community and clarify perceptions of poverty that could inform national strategies for poverty reduction. Nevertheless, in Muyumbu as the poorest community there were very few real differences in perceptions and characteristics of wealth, and therefore the corresponding relationships to the physical differences of shelter and goat ownership. The participants for the sampling frame were chosen on a basis of what were minute differences in terms of shelter construction and type. Thus decisions were being taken to assess whether the occupants were relatively well-off or not on a basis of how many holes were present in the roof of the shelter! However, it was still beneficial to the overall Rwandan research as the results proved to be useful in making comparisons between other research bases.

References

Development and Resources Centre Africa (1998), *A Profile of Poverty in Sub-Saharan Africa: Some Critical Issues* (Johannesburg: Development Resources Centre).

Government of Rwanda (2001), *Rwandan Poverty Reduction Strategy Paper. (2001). Ministry of Finance and Economic Planning* (Kigali: Government of Rwanda).

Jones, R. (2006), 'No Alternative: Post-war Poverty Reduction as Structural Transformation in Rwanda', *Journal of Conflict Security and Development* 6(2), June 2006.

Omaar, R. and de Waal, A. (1995), *Rwanda: Death, Despair and Defiance* (London: African Rights).

Prunier, G. (1998), *The Rwanda Crisis – History of a Genocide* (London: Hurst & Company).

Robb, C. (2002), *Can the Poor Influence Policy?* (Washington: World Bank Publications).

World Bank (2000), *World Development Report 2000/1 Attacking Poverty* (Washington: World Bank Publications).

World Bank (2001), *Development Indicators* (Washington: World Bank Publications).

Chapter 5

Participatory Approaches to Impact Assessment: Experiences from Humanitarian Interventions in Zimbabwe

John Burns and Andrew Catley

Introduction

Impact Assessment and Humanitarian Crises

Despite the huge and growing level of funding dedicated to humanitarian assistance globally, very little is known about the impact of emergency programs on the lives and livelihoods of crisis-affected people. Although humanitarian assistance is often directed at short-term projects lasting only a few months, some parts of the world are affected by protracted crises or complex emergencies and are subject to repeated, back-to-back emergency programs over many years. Various reviews examine the evaluation of humanitarian assistance, the reasons why impact assessment is rarely conducted, and when used, why impact assessments often fail to produce convincing evidence (Hofmann et al. 2004; Darcy 2005).

In part, weaknesses in impact assessment of humanitarian programs have been attributed to the methodological challenges of measuring impact in a humanitarian context. Issues such as weak or lack of baseline data, the difficulty of attributing impact to a specific project or project activity, and the ethics of using control groups in a humanitarian setting are often cited as justification for not measuring impact (Hofmann et al. 2004; Watson 2008). In addition to methodological challenges are a set of institutional and organizational factors. For example, conventional monitoring systems and project evaluations focus on measuring project implementation or service delivery as opposed to the real impact of a project on the lives of the intended recipients. Increasingly, this focus relates to more stringent financial accountability and the need for organizations to justify expenditure to donors against measurable, delivered items (Hoffman et al. 2004).

In terms of participatory approaches to impact assessment, humanitarian agencies are often weak at involving local people in defining, measuring or attributing impact. Where attempts to assess impact are made, they tend to be based on proxy indicators of impact which are identified by the implementing organization or donors. In other words, success is defined by the external agencies and service providers as opposed to the clients. Where client opinions are used to demonstrate impact, these opinions are most commonly collected in the form of ad hoc interviews and case studies with selected community members. This information is often presented as success stories by humanitarian agencies and accompanied by eye-catching images. In terms of evidence-based approaches, these case studies are selective and anecdotal, and provide very limited evidence of impact.

Despite the challenges to impact assessment in humanitarian situations, it is generally accepted that the involvement of local recipients of emergency aid should be a fundamental aspect of project evaluation, accountability and improvements to future, programming. For example, the *Humanitarian Charter and Minimum Standards in Disaster Response* (commonly known as the Sphere handbook) is a set of international standards and guidelines underpinned by international humanitarian and human rights conventions and laws. A common standard in this document is the principle of participation. 'The ultimate test of humanitarian action is not what was intended by humanitarians, but whether the results are judged positive by the beneficiaries themselves and sustained by them. People are the best safeguard for keeping the "human" in humanitarian' (Minear et al. 1991).

It seems that many humanitarian practitioners are aware of the importance of participation, but struggle to apply this principle in relation to the systematic assessment of interventions.

Participatory Impact Assessment in Humanitarian Crises

Various development and research organizations began to develop the concept of Participatory Impact Assessment (PIA) from the mid 1990s and viewed it as a natural extension to the use of approaches such as Participatory Rural Appraisal (PRA) during project design. It was argued that if local people could be assisted to design and implement their own projects, based on their priorities, then they should also play a key role in evaluating these projects and learning how to improve them. Methodologically, PIA included simple but important adaptations to participatory methods, such as measuring changes over time and exploring causal relationships (Guijt 1998). Agencies such as ActionAid began to use participatory assessment approaches in post-conflict but politically unstable areas such as Somaliland (ActionAid 1994), and these approaches were later adapted for the humanitarian contexts of southern Sudan (Catley 1999; Hopkins and Short 2001; Hopkins 2003; Catley et al. 2008) and southern Somalia (Hopkins 2002; 2004). In these areas, one strand of methodological adaptation was the repetition of standardized participatory methods with different groups of informants, and the use of simple nonparametric statistical tests to summarize and analyse the results (Catley 1999). In part, this approach helped to overcome the concerns of policy makers and academics about soft participatory approaches by presenting qualitative data in a numerical form.

From 2005 the Feinstein International Center at Tufts University, Boston, Massachusetts, US began to apply and further adapt PIA for the assessment of humanitarian interventions in two main programs in Africa *viz.* the *Pastoralist Livelihoods Initiative* and the project *Impact Assessment of Innovative Humanitarian Projects in Sub-Saharan Africa*. The Pastoralist Livelihoods Initiative used PIA to examine the impact of drought-related interventions in pastoralist areas of Ethiopia. These PIAs were part of a multi-stakeholder policy process convened by the Ministry of Agriculture and Rural Development, and aiming to develop a national guideline for emergency responses. The general approach is described by Abebe et al. (2009), and included specific PIAs of commercial de-stocking (Abebe et al. 2008), livestock vaccination (Catley et al. 2009) and emergency livestock feed supplementation (Bekele and Tsehay 2008).

The project *Impact Assessment of Innovative Humanitarian Projects in Sub-Saharan Africa* aimed to develop and test a participatory assessment toolkit to measure the impact of a number of livelihoods projects being supported by the Gates Foundation under a separate grant, the Sub-Saharan Africa Famine Relief Effort. This initiative involved seven projects being implemented by Africare, CARE, Save the Children USA, Lutheran World Relief and the International Medical Corps in Southern Sudan, Mali, Niger, Malawi and Zimbabwe, and included two final impact assessments in Zimbabwe described by Burns and Suji (2007a and 2007b) and two in Niger described by Burns and Suji (2007c) and Burns et al. (2008). This chapter focuses on the use of PIA in Zimbabwe under this project. It explains why Zimbabwe was viewed as a humanitarian crisis, and the approach and lessons learned from the PIA process.

Why Zimbabwe?

The cholera outbreaks in Zimbabwe in late 2008 represented the latest chapter in the country's decline into a complex humanitarian crisis. Since 2000, the worsening economic situation was defined by high unemployment, hyperinflation, declining food production and a breakdown of social services (USAID 2009). The humanitarian situation was further intensified by corruption, political violence, detrimental government policies and the effects of HIV/Aids (USAID 2009). Between 2000 and 2006 Zimbabwe went from being ranked 130 to 151 on the United Nations Human Development Index. By 2005, it was estimated that 2.9 million Zimbabweans would be unable to meet their food needs for the following year (ZimVac 2005), and by December 2008 the United Nations estimated that 5.5 million Zimbabweans were in need of food assistance (USAID 2009). Like most other countries and areas where we had previously used PIA, Zimbabwe was affected by political instability and major humanitarian interventions. However, it also differed from our previous PIA experiences in at least two key areas. First, there were very high levels of education and literacy in Zimbabwe, raising questions of how participatory methods would be perceived and how they might be adapted. Second, a major symptom of political and economic turmoil was hyperinflation, raising questions about how to measure the value of livelihoods assets in relation to project inputs and the rapidly declining value of local currency.

Participatory Impact Assessment in Zimbabwe: A Case Study

This chapter reviews experiences from a PIA the Gokwe Integrated Recovery Action Project, a drought recovery and famine mitigation intervention implemented by Africare in four wards of Gokwe-South district in the Midlands Province of Zimbabwe. Traditionally a commercial cotton producing area, farmers would rely on cotton sales in order to purchase food and agricultural inputs. However, a number of recent shocks, including depressed cotton prices on the world market, rising inflation in Zimbabwe, and three years of inadequate rainfall effectively depleted this source of income for farmers in the district (Africare 2005). In response, farmers intensified maize production in order to meet their household food needs (Africare 2005). However, given maize's low nutritional value and poor resilience to drought, this strategy had little impact on the food security or nutritional status of the project communities.

In response to this contextual evaluation, the project was designed to provide income and nutritional benefits to 10,000 drought affected people by improving production, utilization and marketing of crops. The project objectives and the activities attached to them also aimed to improve household food security and nutrition, and reduce people's dependency on income generated from cotton and maize. Some of the crops promoted by the project, such as groundnuts, sweet potato, cassava and sorghum were traditionally grown in the area, but had declined in importance with the expansion of commercial cotton production. The only new crop type introduced by the project was soybean. The agro-processing activities were included to complement the crop production activities and these were anticipated to add value (taste and marketability) thereby facilitating nutritional and income transfers to households participating in the project. Each of the project activities included a training component. The Project started in December 2005, and the impact assessment was conducted seventeen months after the project started.

This chapter summarizes the goals and objectives of the PIA. Specifically, it aims to describe:

1. How a participatory approach can be used to measure the real impact of a project using indicators of impact defined by project participants.
2. How participatory tools can be used to produce representative results on project impact in the absence of any meaningful baseline data.

Participatory Impact Assessment Methodology

The Questions

The impact assessment was carried out by project staff, extension officers affiliated with the project and researchers from the Feinstein Center. The study covered the four geographical areas (wards) where the project was implemented, although for the purpose of analysis these wards were aggregated into two areas, Nemangwe and Njelele. The definition of impact used for the assessment was 'those benefits and changes to people's livelihoods, as defined by the project participants, and brought about as a direct result of the project'. Community defined indicators of project impact had been collected from project participants during an earlier visit to the area. This was done by simply asking participants what their expectations of the project were, and what livelihoods benefits if any, they expected as a result of the project. Participants consistently identified project derived food and income benefits as the most important indicators of project impact. These indicators were then used to develop the following research questions which formed the basis of the assessment:

1. What impact has the project had on the food security and the nutritional status of the assisted communities?
2. What impact has the project had on income (and savings) of the assisted communities?
3. What impact has the project had on the livelihoods of the assisted communities?

Informants and Sampling Issues

The assessment included 16 focus group discussions with both project and non-project participants, and 262 household interviews exclusively with project participants. The sampling frame for the household interviews was the 10,000 community members (2,000 households) participating in the project. Participation in the assessment was based on voluntary attendance in pre-arranged meetings in the different project locations. These meetings were used as a starting point for the focus group discussions, during which project participants would be asked to volunteer their participation in the household interview component of the assessment. These volunteers were then randomly selected, but stratified by gender to ensure at least 50 per cent of the participants were female. The focus group discussions were structured around a set of participatory exercises designed to collect qualitative data on community level perceptions of project impact. The household interviews were structured around a set of standardized participatory exercises designed to collect numerically representative data on individual perceptions of project impact at the household level. With the objective of saving time, the household interviews were carried out with a group of up to as many as nine participants at a time. Typically a participatory exercise and the corresponding questions would be explained to the group as a whole. Following this, each individual would be randomly asked to carry out the exercise until each member of the group had completed the exercise and answered any relevant questions pertaining to it.

The assessment also included 16 key informant interviews. These were used to collect specific contextual information on the project area, and to cross check

Table 5.1   Summary of methods used

Method	Use/Issue	Sample Njelele	Sample Nemangwe
Impact scoring	To determine the relative importance of different project benefits at the household level	117	145
Simple ranking	To determine the relative importance of project benefits at the community level	8	8
Before and after scoring	To measure: • relative changes in the importance of food sources within the household food basket • relative changes in food sources • relative changes in income sources • relative changes in expenditure	117	145
Before and after scoring against a nominal baseline	To measure relative changes in: • the volume of the household food basket • production (yields) of existing crops • household income	117	145
Scoring of household food security	To determine the duration (number of months) of household food security for project and non-project participants	8	8
Focus group discussions	To: • collect qualitative community level perceptions of project impact • to triangulate data from household interviews • collect data on the perceptions of non-project participants • collect data on the perceptions on the projects strengths, weaknesses, opportunities and threats (SWOT analysis)	8	8
Key informant Interviews	To: • develop project maps and timelines and seasonal production calendars • cross check information	8	8
Individual case studies	To: • collect richer qualitative data on project impact at the household level	-	-
Semi-structured interviews	Used to collect: • community defined indicators of project impact • information on household coping mechanisms Used with all methods to determine attribution, cross check information and clarify responses	117	145

Source: Burns and Suji 2007.

information from the focus group discussions and household interviews. More specifically, these sessions were used to develop community maps of the project area, and historical timelines. These were used to define the geographical and temporal boundaries of the project with the aim of ensuring that data collectors and participants alike understood the limits of the area being assessed, and the time period in which impact was supposed to take place. The historical timelines were used as a reference tool throughout the assessment, and were useful in helping to reduce recall bias. Seasonal crop and activity calendars were also collected during these sessions to provide background information on the project area.

Participatory Methods

The primary data collection tool used during the assessment was a semi structured interview. For the household component of the assessment, these interviews were organized around a set of scoring exercises designed to capture perceptions of relative change in household food security, household income, and household expenditure. Table 5.1 provides a summary of the different methods used.

Given the limited baseline data on indicators of food, income and expenditure, before and after scoring exercises were used to establish a retrospective baseline. This was done by using the project timelines as a reference point. Participants would be asked to recall a scenario from before the project started, and using a set number of counters, they would be asked to give a numerical representation of that particular scenario. They would then be asked to give an after representation of the same scenario indicating the situation at the time of the assessment.

For example, before and after scoring exercises on household food sources were carried out, with the objective of understanding changes in household food security. This was done by asking a group of participants to list all their existing sources of food. The data collectors and participants would then jointly assign a visual aid to each food source. These visual aids might consist of locally available materials or cards with pictures or symbols on them representing each of the different food sources. Once all the participants were clear on what each visual aid/indicator represented, the first participant would be asked to assign a score to each indicator based on their perception of the importance of that particular food source with regards to its contribution to the household food basket during the agricultural year before the project started (April/May 2004–April/May 2005). This was done by asking the participant to distribute 25 counters amongst the visual aids with the greatest number of counters being allocated to the most important indicator – food source, and the fewest number going to the least important. The data collectors would emphasize that all 25 counters be used but that if an indicator – food source – had not contributed to the food basket during that period, or that it was not considered important it did not have to be assigned a score. Once the participant was happy that the scoring accurately represented their perceptions, the data collectors would record the results. The participant would then be asked to repeat the exercise to represent the contributions from different food sources for the agricultural year after the project started (April/May 2006–April/May/2007). This was done using the same indicators and the same number of counters. If any changes were observed between the before and after project scenarios, the data collectors would ask the participant to explain the reasons for these changes, and these would be recorded.

A similar process – using before-and-after scoring – was used to look at changes in income and expenditure. For income, the seven most frequently mentioned income sources were used as indicators for the exercise. Changes in income utilization were captured using five key household expenditures. Most of these expenditures, or at least an improved ability to cover them had previously been identified by participants as additional indicators of project impact. For example, the ability to invest in livestock or farming implements using project derived income had been proposed as useful indicators of project impact.

Although the before and after exercises were effective in capturing relative changes, they did not indicate if there had been an actual increase or decrease in household food or income. With the objective of capturing actual as opposed to just relative changes, participants were asked to show changes in food and income against a nominal baseline. This was done by placing ten counters in a basket representing household income before the project. The participants were then given another ten counters and asked to show any relative changes in household income by either adding counters to the original basket of ten, or removing them. For example if someone were to add three counters to the original basket this would represent a 30 per cent increase in income. Alternatively if they were to remove two counters it would represent a 20 per cent decrease in income. The participants would then be asked to account for these changes. The same exercise was carried out to assess actual changes in the volume (quantity) of the household food basket. A similar exercise was conducted to assess changes in crop production (yields) with the objective of isolating changes pertaining to the crop production and agronomy training activities of the project.

After each scoring exercise, participants were asked to explain and give reasons for any observed changes. These reasons were classified as either project or non-project factors, and tallied to provide an attribution score. The reasons given and the corresponding scores for improvements in food security and income were largely attributed to project related factors. If anything, external factors such as inadequate rainfall and rising inflation in all likelihood mitigated the impact of the project.

A simple scoring exercise was also used to compare the relative importance of different project benefits. This was done by asking participants to score a set of six frequently mentioned benefits in order of importance by distributing 25 counters between the six indicators. The indicator with the highest number of counters represented the most important project benefit, and the one with the lowest number of counters represented the least important benefit.

Participatory methods are often criticized for not providing representative data. This is because people often only do an exercise once, or repeat it a limited number of times. However, if these methods are standardized and repeated in a systematic way, numerically representative results can be derived from them. With the objective of collecting representative data on project impact, the scoring methods for the household interviews described above, were repeated 262 times during the assessment. This was done systematically, using the same indicators, the same number of counters, and framing the questions in exactly the same way. The data was then tested for normal distribution, and a comparison of mean scores from the before and after exercises was calculated at ninety-five per cent confidence interval. This was done using Statistics Package for Social Sciences (SPSS) software.

A variety of participatory tools were also used during the focus group discussions. Participants were asked to share their perceptions on the project through a Strengths, Weaknesses, Opportunities, and Threats (SWOT) analysis. These discussions were also used to collect community definitions of food security and information on common coping strategies employed during periods of food insecurity. A simple ranking exercise of project benefits was also carried out using benefits that had been identified by the focus group participants, some of these benefits had been classified as opportunities and strengths during the SWOT exercise. A simple ranking of project activities was also conducted to provide a comparison of the different types of interventions being implemented under the project. An exercise to compare the duration of household food security between project and non-project participants was also performed. This was done using 25 counters representing a household's post-harvest cereal balance. Each group would then distribute the counters along a 12 month calendar starting during the maize harvest in April, with the distribution of counters representing household utilization of maize per month until depletion. The results from these exercises were all based on group consensus.

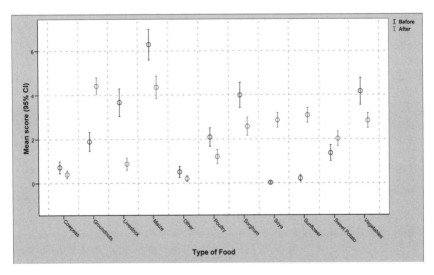

Figure 5.1   Changes in household food basket, Nemangwe

Table 5.2   Attribution table explaining changes in the importance of different food sources

Factors	Number of responses	
* Represents project related factors	Njelele (n=117)	Nemangwe (n=145)
Availability of new (drought tolerant) seeds from Africare*	10	40
Decrease – crops were affected by drought/ floods	8	39
Variety of food crops introduced- reduced dependence on maize*	22	24
Training in agronomy led to better crop production and higher yields*	10	24
I had no draught power and was unable to till as much land as I did in 2005	4	3
In 2005, inputs were delivered late; early delivery in 2007*	9	-
I had to subdivide my land to introduce the new crops – led to lower production for some	-	10

Source: Data was derived using semi-structured interviews following the before and after scoring exercise on food sources.

Note: Factors scoring below 2 per cent of the overall responses were not included in this table. Some people gave more than one response others gave none (number of responses Njelele, 70; Nemangwe, 145) (Source: Burns and Suji 2007).

Table 5.3   Perceived changes in the volume (quantity) of the household food basket

Location	Variable	Mean Score (increase) 95% CI
Njelele (n=117)	Changes in Household (HH) food basket (volume)	16.4 (15.8, 16.9)
Nemangwe (n=145)	Changes in HH food basket (volume)	14.3 (13.5, 15.1)

Note: Data derived by scoring a total of 20 counters against a given baseline of 10 counters.

Source: Burns and Suji 2007.

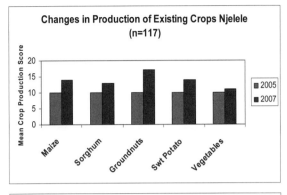

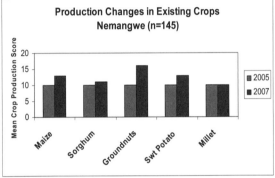

Figure 5.2   Perceived changes in household production (yields) between 2005 and 2007

*Note*s: Data derived by scoring with 20 counters against a nominal baseline of 10 counters.

Source: Burns and Suji 2007.

Triangulation of assessment data was done in a number of ways. First, the results from the focus group discussions, household interviews, and key informant interviews were compared for consistency. Second, the results were cross checked with the projects Monitoring and Evaluation records and progress reports to ensure that project implementation and service delivery corresponded with any assessed impact. For example, if the results showed an increase in the importance of soybeans in the household food basket in 2006, did the project actually deliver soybean seeds as planned in time for the 2006 planting season?

A third method of triangulation used was a comparison of the results of the different scoring exercises to identify patterns and trends that concurred. For example if one exercise revealed that household food crop production had improved, it follows that an exercise on expenditure should show a decrease in the proportion of household income spent on food over the same period. This would then be cross-checked with the results from the attribution exercises collected

Table 5.4   Attribution table for changes in the overall quantity of the household food basket

Factors	Number of responses	
*Project related factors	Njelele (n=117)	Nemangwe (n=145)
Diversity of crops means that there is more food available in the HH*	39	54
New skills and knowledge in agronomy – higher production*	25	35
Agro-processing (no need to spend limited income on processed foods)*	49	27
Decrease due to unsuitable soil-type and drought	2	35

Note Data was derived using semi-structured interviews following the before and after scoring exercise on food basket changes. Factors scoring below 2 per cent of the overall responses were not included in this table. Some people gave more than one response others gave none. (Number of responses Njelele, 115, Nemangwe, 152).

Source: Burns and Suji 2007.

Table 5.5   Attribution for changes in production of existing crops being promoted by the project

Factors	Number of responses	
Project related factors*	Njelele (n=117)	Nemangwe (n=145)
Overall decrease due to drought	9	51
Decrease due to late planting because of late seed delivery	2	5
No fertilizer	4	1
Lack of Draught Power (decrease)	3	1
Increase due to getting more and a variety of new adequate seed on time*	53	62
Training in agronomy*	1	28
Early planting resulted in better harvest and higher yield	-	10

Note Data derived using semi-structured interviews following the before and after scoring exercise on production changes. Factors scoring below 2 per cent of the overall responses were not included in this table. Some people gave more than one response others gave none. (Number of responses Njelele, 106, Nemangwe, 170).

Source: Burns and Suji 2007.

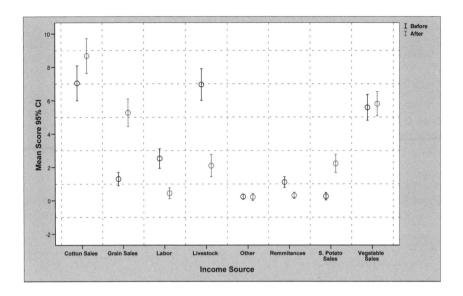

Figure 5.3   Changes in household income sources, Nemangwe

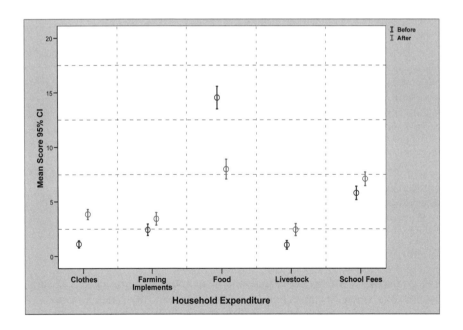

Figure 5.4   Changes in household expenditure, Nemangwe

Table 5.6   Changes in household income

Location	Variable	Mean Score (increase) 95% CI
Njelele (n=117)	Changes in HH Income	16.3 (15.9, 16.8)
Nemangwe (n=145)	Changes in HH Income	15 (14.3, 15.7)

Note: Data derived by scoring a total of 20 counters against a given baseline of 10 counters.

Source: Burns and Suji 2007.

Table 5.7   Attribution table for changes in household income (increase/ decrease)

Factors	Number of responses	
*Project related factors	Njelele n=117	Nemangwe n=145
Decrease – Poor yields due to drought	–	14
Increase – marketing new crops (soya beans, sunflower, sweet potato)	69	66
Value addition to crops – fetching better prices	16	26
No change in income – but I make savings on food purchases	30	32
Cotton did well in 2007 and price per kilo was good	3	1

Note: Data was derived using semi-structured interviews following the before and after scoring exercise on income changes. Factors scoring below 2 per cent of the overall responses were not included in this table. Some people gave more than one response others gave none (number of responses; Njelele, 118, Nemangwe, 140).

Source: Burns and Suji 2007.

during the household interviews. In many ways, the interpretation and analysis of the results from the household interviews involved a comprehensive process of triangulation.

Results from the PIA

The overall results from the before-and-after exercises were able to illustrate significant changes in the relative contributions from the different sources of household food and income that had taken place since the project started. Changes in the relative importance of crops that had been introduced or promoted by the project such as soybean, sunflower, and groundnuts were clearly captured in the results. A relative decrease in the importance of maize was also captured, explained by the corresponding increase in the importance of the other food sources (crops) promoted by the project; suggesting an impact against the stated project objective of reducing people's dependency on maize. A reduction in the importance of contributions from food sources that are typically expanded on during periods of drought was also captured, indicating an overall improvement in household food security. Similarly an increase in the relative importance of income derived from project crops was captured. The results also showed a reduction in the importance of income derived from economic coping strategies such as on-farm wage labour, and the sale of livestock assets.

The before and after household expenditure exercises showed changes in the relative proportion of income spent on clothes, farming implements, and livestock, and in one of the project areas there was also a significant increase in the proportion of income spent on education related expenses. These changes were offset by a relative decrease in the amount of income spent on food, explained by an increase in the proportion of food needs being met through self production. As mentioned, the ability to cover schooling costs, purchase clothes, and invest in livestock and farming implements had been identified by participants as indicators of project impact. These, with the possible exception of clothes purchases, also represent important livelihoods investments.

Lessons Learned

Methodological Strengths, Weaknesses and other Challenges

The participatory impact assessment methods used during this research demonstrate a number of strengths and advantages over more conventional evaluation approaches. Most donor and non-governmental organizations (NGOs) monitoring and evaluation systems tend to over emphasize the measurement of process as opposed to impact. Performance benchmarks based on the implementation of project activities and delivery of inputs are frequently used as proxy indicators of impact, but in reality tell us very little about the real impact of the project on the lives of the participating communities and households. Consistent with this, most agency monitoring and evaluation systems emphasize external indicators as opposed to community defined indicators of project success. This can largely be explained by the fact that it is much easier to measure easily quantifiable indictors such as the number of people trained, or the quantity of seeds distributed. One of the strengths of the assessment approach demonstrated in this case study is that it measures the real impact of the project on the livelihoods of the participants, and it does this using their own indicators of project impact. By acknowledging that aid recipients are capable of identifying their own indicators of change, this approach emphasizes the principles of local ownership, control and capacity building. In contrast to more traditional top down approaches to project evaluation, PIA fits well with the growing demand for greater downward accountability in the humanitarian and development sector.

In most cases where agency evaluations do try to look at the real impact of a project on people's lives, there tends to be an over emphasis on anecdote, ad hoc interview, and staff or consultant opinion. Not only is this type of evidence unlikely to convince donors and other stakeholders of project impact, being non-representative, it often has little value in informing future programming. The reliance on this kind of impact analysis can partly be explained by the fact that understanding impact requires an iterative process of dialogue with participants. Impact indicators are often qualitative in nature and collecting this information in a systematic and representative manner, and presenting it in an easily digestible format can be challenging and time consuming.

This study demonstrates how a numerical value can be assigned to an impact indicator allowing it to be easily measured. One of the strengths of this approach is the systematic use of participatory methods to collect statistically representative data. This kind of data provides convincing results of project impact which can and have been used to improve programming and inform policy and best practice in the development sector (see Behnke et al. 2008). The approach is also flexible, and can be adapted to different projects, contexts and indicators. It is also accessible to practitioners, and with a minimum amount of training, it can be carried out by NGO staff with little or no technical oversight.

Another advantage of the approach is that it does not rely on the existence of baseline data. In many humanitarian contexts, the lack of any meaningful baseline data is a major constraint to measuring impact. This approach demonstrates how participatory methods such as before and after scoring exercises and scoring against a nominal baseline can be used to develop a retrospective or proxy baseline against which to measure impact.

In spite of some of the comparative advantages of PIA, as with all methods and approaches, it does have its limitations. In terms of evidence, it is certainly not as rigorous as a randomized case control impact study. Conversely, the time involved in collecting numerically representative data implies that less time is spent on collecting richer more qualitative information from project participants. This often may imply that the views of some sub groups within a community may not be well captured during these types of assessments.

This particular assessment faced a number of challenges and involved a number of methodological compromises. For example, in order to achieve the desired sample size within the given assessment timeframe, the decision was made to interview up to nine household participants at a time. This innovation may well have resulted in peer bias whereby one participant's response might influence the rest of the group. In an attempt to minimize the risk of peer bias during the participatory exercises, the data collectors would change the order in which people carried out each exercise, and they would make sure to clear all the counters away before asking a new participant to carry out the exercise.

Another challenge faced during the assessment was the obvious expectation of continued assistance from the project participants. It is possible that this may have influenced the responses to certain questions. In response to this challenge, the research team had to continuously explain the purpose of the assessment, and its independence from any future funding or donor support. However, in spite of these efforts, it was virtually impossible to convince people that an impact assessment could be de-linked from future assistance or a second phase of the project.

The results from the participatory exercises carried out during the focus group discussions, while interesting and useful for triangulation, were based on group consensus and could hardly be considered rigorous or representative. The exercises to compare household food security between project and non-project participants during the focus group discussions might also be considered a simple control. However, a certain amount of caution should be applied to this assumption as the same criteria that excluded the control group from project participation raises questions about their reliability even as a simple control group.

The objectivity of the research team might also have been an issue during this assessment. Aside from the Tufts researchers, all the data collectors involved in the assessment were project staff or extension workers affiliated with the project.

Although the inclusion of Africare managers and project staff in the assessment process may have compromised objectivity, it certainly added value to the overall exercise. Prior to the assessment, Africare had understood the role of the Tufts led impact assessment as an external evaluation linked to future funding decisions. As such it was understandably viewed with a certain degree of skepticism. The participation of Africare in the assessment effectively changed this outlook to one of a joint learning exercise. The tools and approach were quickly picked up by the assessment team and the results were easily understood and accepted by senior managers in the Zimbabwe country office. The transfer of impact assessment skills was also an important by-product of the decision to include Africare in the assessment process, and project managers have since indicated that they intend to continue using and adapting the approach to some of their other projects in Zimbabwe. At the field level, project staff suggested that this was the first time they had been involved in this type of exercise, and they appreciated the opportunity to be able to assess the actual impact of their work.

With the objective of saving time, more innovative methods for assessing attribution were excluded from the study. For example matrix scoring exercises have been effectively used to compare service providers against indicators of convenience, reliability, affordability, effectiveness and trust (Admassu et al. 2005) and to score different types of drought interventions against a variety of indicators of impact (Abebe et al. 2008). However, these types of matrix scoring exercise are time consuming, and while they might have added a stronger element of attribution to the focus group discussions, they would have been a cumbersome addition to the 262 household interviews. Nonetheless, the simpler attribution method that was applied does not illustrate attribution of project and non-project factors as clearly and effectively as these other methods.

During the initial assessment training workshop, Africare had expressed reservations about the appropriateness of using participatory tools, the concern being that participants might be offended considering Zimbabwe's high levels of education and literacy. During the assessment, care was taken to explain that the scoring tools were used to give a visual representation to help the data collectors understand and interpret the results by providing an easy visual reference point for the follow up questions. It was also mentioned that if there were participants who had not had the same education opportunities as the rest, that these tools would give them an equal voice. Although there was no indication that any offence was taken to the use of participatory tools during the assessment, sensitivity and caution should be applied when using these tools in certain contexts, and indeed in some communities they may not be appropriate.

While the systematic use of scoring exercises provided a numerical representation of project impact, the overall participatory approach also provided additional information on the project which might be useful for future programming and decision making. Specifically, the identification and use of community indicators of impact allowed for a more comprehensive understanding of project impact and a prioritization of community perceptions of impact. For example, the scoring exercises on project benefits revealed that in some areas, the skills and knowledge transfers provided by the project outweighed some of the more tangible resource transfers such as the provision of agricultural inputs or agro processing equipment. Therefore, if Africare were to continue operating in the project area on a limited budget, consideration might be given to a stronger emphasis and focus on training activities as opposed to the procurement and distribution of inputs. Furthermore, the questions and discussion on impact and attribution following the scoring exercises shed light on how people utilized the projects asset transfers in this particular context. This was particularly important in the context of Zimbabwe where impact measured in terms of investments in livestock assets and livelihoods diversification resulted as a direct response to hyperinflation, where cash income devalued overnight. In some respects this suggests that in spite of recent successes of cash based responses in emergencies (Harvey 2007); cash interventions may not be an appropriate response in the context of hyperinflation.

Overall, the strengths of the approach and methods used outweigh the weaknesses. In many ways the limitations of these methods are what give them the flexibility and advantage over more conventional approaches. The approach tries to find a balance between practicability, participation, and scientific rigor, and an over emphasis on one of these comes at the expense of one or more of the others. Nevertheless, what it does provide is a systematic, accessible participatory approach which can produce convincing evidence of impact on the lives of project participants.

References

Abebe, D. et al. (2008), 'Livelihoods impact and benefit-cost estimation of a commercial de-stocking relief intervention in Moyale district, southern Ethiopia', *Disasters* 32:2 June 2008 (Online Early).

Abebe, D. et al. (2009), 'Using Participatory Impact Assessment (PIA) to inform policy: Lessons from Ethiopia', in Scoones, I. and Thomson, J. (eds), *Farmer First Revisited* (Rugby: Practical Action Publishing), pp. 269–300.

Abebe, D. (2005), 'Participatory review and impact assessment of the community-based animal health workers system in pastoral and agropastoral areas of Somali and Oromia Regions' (Addis Ababa: Save the Children US).

Admassu, B. et al. (2005), 'Impact assessment of a community-based animal health project in Dollo Ado and Dollo Bay districts, southern Ethiopia', *Tropical Animal Health and Production* 37:1, 33–48.

ActionAid (1994), *ACTIONAID Somaliland Programme Review/Evaluation*, (London: ActionAid).

Africare (2005), 'Gokwe Integrated Recovery Action: Proposal submitted to the Bill and Melinda Gates Foundation, October, 14th 2005' (Harare: Africare).

Alinovi, L., Hemrich, G. and L. Russo (eds), *Beyond Relief: Food Security in Protracted Crises* (Rugby: Practical Action Publishing).

Behnke, R., Kervan, C. and Teshome, A. (2008), *Evaluation of USAID Pastoral Development Projects in Ethiopia* (Addis Ababa: Odessa Centre Ltd. and USAID Ethiopia).

Bekele, G. and Tsehay, A. (2008), 'Livelihoods-based Drought Response in Ethiopia: Impact Assessment of Livestock Feed Supplementation' (Addis Ababa: Feinstein International Center and Save the Children US).

Burns, J., Suji, O. and Reynolds, A. (2008), 'Impact Assessment of the Pastoralist Survival and Recovery Project, Dakoro, Niger' (Medford: Feinstein International Center). <https://wikis.uit.tufts.edu/confluence/display/FIC/Impact+Assessment+of+the+Pastoralist+Survival+and+Recovery+Project+Dakoro%2C+Niger>.

Burns, J. and Suji, O. (2007a), 'Impact Assessment of the Gokwe Integrated Recovery Action Project, Zimbabwe' (Medford: Feinstein International Center). <https://wikis.uit.tufts.edu/confluence/display/FIC/Impact+Assessment+of+the+Gokwe+Integrated+Recovery+Action+Project>.

—— (2007b), 'Impact Assessment of the Zimbabwe Dams, and Gardens Project' (Medford: Feinstein International Center). <https://wikis.uit.tufts.edu/confluence/download/attachments/14553652/Burns--Impact+Assessment+of+the+Zimbabwe+Dams+and+Gardens+Project.pdf?version=1>.

—— (2007c), 'Impact Assessment of the Chical Integrated Recovery Action Project, Niger' (Medford: Feinstein International Center). <https://wikis.uit.tufts.edu/confluence/display/FIC/Impact+Assessment+of+the+Chical+Integrated+Recovery+Action+Project%2C+Niger>.

Catley, A. (1999), 'Monitoring and Impact Assessment of Community-based Animal Health Projects in Southern Sudan: Towards participatory approaches and methods. A report for Vétérinaires sans frontières Belgium and Vétérinaires sans frontières Switzerland' (Musselburgh: Vetwork UK). <http://www.participatoryepidemiology.info/userfiles/Southern-Sudan-Impact-Assessment.pdf>.

Catley, A. et al. (2009), 'Impact of Drought-related Livestock Vaccination in Pastoralist Areas of Ethiopia', *Disasters*, forthcoming.

Catley, A., Leyland, T. and Bishop, S. (2008), 'Policies, Practice and Participation in Protracted Crises: The Case of Livestock Interventions in South Sudan', in Alinovi, L., Hemrich, G. and L. Russo (eds). *Beyond Relief: Food Security in Protracted Crises* (Rugby: Practical Action Publishing).

Darcy, J. (2005), 'Acts of Faith? Thoughts on the Effectiveness of Humanitarian Action' Humanitarian Policy Group Discussion Paper prepared for the Social Science Research Council seminar series The Transformation of Humanitarian Action New York 12 April 2005 (London: Overseas Development Institute).

Guijt, I. (1998), 'Participatory Monitoring and Impact Assessment of Sustainable Agriculture Initiatives', SARL Discussion Paper 1 (London: International Institute for Environment and Development).

Harvey, P. (2007), 'Cash-based Responses in Emergencies', Humanitarian Policy Group Report 24 (London: Overseas Development Institute).

Hofmann, C.A., Roberts, L., Shoham, J. and Harvey, P. (2004), 'Measuring the Impact of Humanitarian Aid: A Review of Current Practice', Humanitarian Policy Group Report 17 (London: Overseas Development Institute).

Hopkins, C. (2003), 'Community Participatory Evaluation of the OLS Livestock Programme, A Community Based Animal Health Project Implemented by VSF Belgium, Bahr El Ghazal, South Sudan' (Nairobi: VSF Belgium).

Hopkins, C. (2002), 'Emergency veterinary relief programme, Gedo Region, Somalia – Participatory impact assessment' (Nairobi: VSF Suisse).

Hopkins, C. (2004), 'Participatory Impact Assessment and Evaluation of the Pastoral Assistance Program (PAP III), Gedo Region, Somalia' (Nairobi: VSF Suisse).

Hopkins, C. and Short, A. (2001), 'Participatory impact assessment and evaluation of the OLS livestock programme. A community based animal health project implemented by VSF Suisse, Western Upper Nile Region of South Sudan', (Nairobi: VSF Suisse).

Minear, L., et al. (1991), *Humanitarianism Under Siege: A Critical Review of Operation Lifeline Sudan* (Trenton: Red Sea Press).

Scoones, I., Thomson, J. and Chambers, R. (eds.) (2009), *Farmer First Revisited* (Rugby: Practical Action Publishing)

USAID (2009), 'Zimbabwe Complex Emergency, Situation report #2, Fiscal Year (FY) 2009, USAID, Bureau for Democracy, Conflict and Humanitarian Assistance (DCHA)' (New York: Office of U.S. Foreign Disaster Assistance). <http://www.usaid.gov/our_work/humanitarian_assistance/disaster_

assistance/countries/zimbabwe/template/fs_sr/fy2009/zimbabwe_ce_sr01_
10-28-08.pdf> accessed 6 January 2009.

Watson, C. (2008), *Impact Assessment of Humanitarian Response: A Review of the Literature* (Medford: Feinstein International Center).

ZimVac (2005), *Zimbabwe Rural Food Security and Vulnerability Assessments, June 2005 Report* (Harare: Zimbabwe Vulnerability Assessment Committee).

Chapter 6

Applications of Participatory Research Methods in a Post-disaster Environment: The Case of Cyclone Sidr, Bangladesh

Bimal Kanti Paul and Sohini Dutt

Introduction

Applications of participatory methodologies to record victim assessments in a post-disaster situation in Bangladesh have not received much attention among hazard researchers. A careful examination of the relevant literature reveals that only a few researchers (Sommer and Mosley 1972; Chowdhury et al. 1993; Ikeda 1995; Thompson and Sultana 1996; Choudhury et al. 2004) have applied Participatory Rural Appraisal (PRA) methods. These methods include Rapid Rural Appraisal (RRA), focus group discussions, semi-structured interviews with local people, open group meetings, and careful field observations. Some of these PRA methods have been used to collect both qualitative and quantitative information regarding various aspects of disasters in Bangladesh during the last three decades. These methods have been applied to study several types of disasters, such as river and flash floods (Thompson and Sultana 1996; Choudhury et al. 2004), and cyclones (Chowdhury et al. 1993; Ikeda 1995).

Since the devastating cyclone of 1991, no hazard researcher has explicitly applied PRA methodology to collect information from cyclone victims in Bangladesh. The occurrence of Cyclone Sidr, which made landfall in southwestern coast of Bangladesh on 15 November 2007, provided an opportunity to apply PRA techniques to study its impacts on the environment and people of the affected areas. This high-end category 4 storm caused 3,406 deaths and over 55,000 people sustained physical injuries. It caused damage and losses worth US $1.7 billion, an amount which represents about three per cent of the country's gross national product (GOB 2008).

The objective of this chapter is to document the prevalent conditions under which PRA methods were used to collect information from survivors regarding the extent of human deaths and injuries caused by Cyclone Sidr. Attempts are also made to review how participatory research methods have been applied, what the main concerns and challenges in their application were, and how to overcome them. Among the PRA methods utilized, the focus of this chapter is on group interviews.

A brief outline of participatory techniques used in disaster research in Bangladesh is presented followed by the main section regarding how PRA methods were applied in the context of Cyclone Sidr. Challenges confronted with the PRA methods employed in this study are then discussed.

Disasters and Participatory Research in Bangladesh: A Brief Review

Sommer and Mosley (1972) were the first to apply PRA methodology to collect disaster related data in Bangladesh after the devastating cyclone of 1970, which killed nearly 500,000 people. They conducted two population-based surveys – one immediately after the cyclone and the other two months later. For the first survey, they used a variant of PRA methods to assess the immediate medical needs of the areas impacted by the event. The second survey was designed to serve as the basis for long-range relief and recovery planning and it was much more detailed than their first survey. One of the important purposes of the second survey was to validate the findings of the first survey, as well as to determine its efficacy as an independent survey tool (Sommer and Mosley 1972). In their second survey they interviewed 2,973 households from 79 unions of the nine most affected thanas. A thana is the third largest administrative unit in Bangladesh and consists of several unions. A union, on the other hand, comprises of 20–30 villages.

Although not explicitly stated, it appears that Sommer and Mosley (1972) chose to use PRA methodology for two reasons. Prior to the 1970 cyclone, coastal Bangladesh was not well connected with paved roads and the cyclone partially or totally damaged most of the existing roads. Because of difficulties in transportation and communication encountered during the first survey, the research team had to fly daily from Dhaka by US Army STRICOM helicopter to impacted areas (Sommer and Mosley 1972). Since this journey took about four hours, members of the research team could not stay more than five hours in each of the 18 survey sites. Aerial transportation is costly so completion of the field survey had to be completed as quickly as possible. The Bangladeshi government as well as domestic and foreign relief agencies urgently needed relevant data for planning relief operations.

A series of surveys was conducted by both domestic and foreign agencies to collect relevant data following Cyclone Gorky in 1991. For example, the Bangladesh Rural Advancement Committee (BRAC) sponsored four separate studies and, nearly one year after this cyclone, a field survey was conducted by a research team organized by Japanese Overseas Corporation Volunteers (JOCV). The first survey sponsored by BRAC used rapid interviews as a PRA method and was conducted approximately three months after the cyclone to assess the extent of human loss and the risk factors associated with those fatalities (BRAC 1991). The Japanese team also used a simplified version of RRA to collect information from cyclone victims. The team organized 18 group discussions where between four to six participants took part in each discussion (Ikeda 1995). These discussions were held in nine localities. Each locality had two group discussions, one for women and the other for men. The total number of participants was 90–45 males and 45 females (Ikeda 1995).

Thompson and Sultana (1996) reported distributional and socio-economic impacts of flood control projects in Bangladesh and made their evaluations based on RRA and Project Impact Evaluation (PIE) techniques. The latter method was used to measure project impacts by comparing the area affected by flood control projects with a control area not under jurisdiction of any such projects. This method made use of a questionnaire survey to collect information from 24 villages: 12 each from affected and control – non-affected – areas. The study attempted to highlight the effects of the project on employment, women, income, landholdings, housing, losses related to floods, and social conflicts.

Except for the study by Sommer and Mosley (1972), it is not clear under what circumstances local and foreign researchers have used PRA methodologies to collect data from disaster victims. Were such methodologies used because of a shortage of time and/or resources? What was the composition of research teams? Familiarity of team members with the study area, their past fieldwork experience, and their willingness to freely interact with participants are key factors for successful employment of PRA techniques (Chambers 1980). It is also critical in PRA research to address any unequal power relations between participants and researchers. These and other challenges faced by researchers who have used PRA techniques after the 1970 and 1991 cyclones have also not been documented. Similarly, these researchers did not mention anything regarding how any challenges encountered were resolved. This information is valuable for researchers who wish to apply PRA methodology in future studies not only in Bangladesh, but elsewhere as well.

As noted, nothing is mentioned regarding the quality of data collected from disaster victims, or how much enthusiasm was shown by participants of PRA methods employed in post-disaster situations in Bangladesh. However, a careful comparison of data collected through PRA and non-PRA techniques after the 1991 and 2007 cyclones suggests that both types of techniques provided a reasonably high quality of data. For example, the mortality rates calculated by Sommer and Mosley (1972) on the basis of data collected through the first and second survey are consistent with each other. As expected, mortality rates were higher for the second survey compared to the first survey. The second survey included cyclone-related deaths caused weeks after the cyclone, while the first survey was not able to include deaths which occurred after the cyclone. A similar consistency was also observed between mortality rates collected through PRA and non-PRA methods after the occurrence of Cyclone Gorky in 1991 (Chowdhury et al. 1993; Ikeda 1995). This is an important finding for researchers who wish to apply PRA methodology. Often researchers express doubt regarding the accuracy of data collected through PRA methods simply because data are collected from the field over a relatively short period (McCracken et al. 1988; Thompson and Sultana 1996).

Applications of PRA Methods in the Post-Sidr Situation

Since no one has exclusively studied the extent, nature, and causes of cyclone injuries in Bangladesh, the November 2007 Cyclone Sidr has provided a valuable opportunity to accomplish this task. Similar to many developing countries, there is no provision in Bangladesh for keeping medical reports and/or records for persons killed or injured by extreme natural events or for any other events. For this reason, it was decided to collect relevant data directly from sample households impacted by Cyclone Sidr. A decision was also made to quickly travel to Sidr-affected areas to capture perishable data. Such data are often more accurate and usually more insightful than data collected years after the occurrence of a disaster.

It took almost two months to complete all formalities pertaining to the study, such as preparing the questionnaire, securing a return air ticket, and getting approval from the Committee for Research Involving Human Subjects (IRB), Kansas State University (KSU), Manhattan, Kansas, USA, where Bimal Kanti Paul is employed. Both the university and the funding agency require such approval prior to administration of any survey and/or interview involving human subjects. Generally it takes no more than two weeks to get such approval. In the present case, it took longer because the application was submitted near the end of the fall 2007 semester, an unusually busy time for the university.

Because of constraints in time and financial resources, the decision was made to complete the field survey during the winter break, which generally lasts about five weeks from the second week of December until the third week of January of the following year. Because of circumstances beyond the control of Kanti Paul, field work began the first week of January 2008 instead of the second week of December 2007, as originally planned. Kanti Paul left the study area after three weeks to resume faculty duties at KSU, while the two other team members remained in the field until the data collection was completed. With the employment of additional field investigators, it would have been possible to complete fieldwork by the third week of January 2008, but no such attempt was undertaken due to constraints on time and financial resources.

As noted, field work was completed within a relatively short time period. In doing so, however, no compromises were made regarding the quality and accuracy of the data collected. Relevant data were collected using four methods: individual interviews with a structured questionnaire, semi-structured group interviews with local people, informal discussions with local leaders, governmental officials and workers of non-governmental organizations (NGOs), and through field observations. The last three methods of data collection are important components of PRA methodology.

Research Team

One important characteristic of PRA techniques is to work with a multidisciplinary team. Chambers (1980) maintains that a PRA research team should not be composed of only one experienced and well-informed person (also see Beebe 1985). At the same time, it is recommended that this research team should not be composed of too many individuals; an interview conducted simultaneously by several researchers can intimidate the participants. Moreover, too many researchers may hinder research and/or the interaction and participation of all members of the team. A small team of two or three members is considered the ideal size of a research team using PRA techniques (Chambers 1980). Considering this, a three-member research team was formed for this study. One of the two other team members was a geography graduate student at the University of Dhaka, Bangladesh. The other team member has an undergraduate degree in veterinary medicine. Both of them are citizens of Bangladesh.

As indicated, the first author, also a member of the research team, has been living in the United States for more than two decades. All members of the research team have participated in and/or conducted formal field surveys in rural Bangladesh in the past. First as a graduate student then as a faculty member at the University of Dhaka, the first author has conducted many field surveys in rural Bangladesh in the 1970s. While a graduate student in Canada and the United States, as well as a faculty member at KSU, the first author also conducted fieldworks in rural Bangladesh. Thus, the research team was composed of people familiar with the study area, its problems, and culture.

Questionnaire Survey

Using a structured questionnaire, core information was collected from households affected by Cyclone Sidr. Because of road conditions which restricted access to all cyclone-impacted areas, individual villages were selected on the basis of a purposive sampling procedure. Waiting for improved access would have restricted the collection of ephemeral data on cyclone-induced injuries. A total of 13 villages were chosen from four severely impacted districts: Bagerhat, Barguna, Patuakhali, and Pirojpur. Among all cyclone-affected districts, the Bangladesh government identified these four as the worst-affected accounting for about 88 per cent of all fatalities caused by Cyclone Sidr (GOB 2008). All of the selected districts are located on or near the seashore, with intersecting rivers emptying into the Bay of Bengal. All the selected villages experienced storm surges and these surges entered the villages through estuary channels. Storm surges ranged from 15 feet (4.5 metres) in the Barguna sites to ten feet (three metres) in the Patuakhali, Pirojpur, and Bagerhat study sites. Among four study sites, the Barguna site is closest to both the landfall location and the coast of the Bay of Bengal.

For the questionnaire survey, an individual household was considered the primary sampling unit (PSU). A complete list of all households in the selected villages was not available prior to conducting the questionnaire survey. This situation compelled the use of a systematic sampling procedure to select respondents for the survey. Prior to survey administration, it was decided that the number of households to be selected from each village should be proportional to village size. From each selected household, the household head was interviewed in his/her residence. If the household head was unavailable, a senior member from the household was interviewed. It took about 30–40 minutes to complete a questionnaire survey. A total of 277 respondents were successfully interviewed for this study.

As indicated, the information was collected through a pre-tested, structured questionnaire administered by the research team. Some minor changes were made in the questionnaire on the basis of feedback received from pilot testing. The questionnaire recorded details regarding cyclone warning messages and evacuation orders, household response, and other pertinent information. The respondents' socioeconomic and demographic characteristics, survival status of family members, number of deaths and injuries in each household, and other relevant information were also collected through the questionnaire.

The questionnaire survey reveals that two-thirds of all respondents were landless. Although this figure is about 28 per cent higher than the national proportion, the reported percentage does represent the land ownership patterns in the coastal regions of Bangladesh. Consistent with landlessness, average landholding size (0.85 acres) is also lower than the national average. Slightly over one-fourth of all respondents owned a small holding (up to 2.5 acres or 1.0 ha), and the remaining respondents owned between 2.5 and 7.49 acres (1.0 and 3.0 ha).

The survey further shows that fishing was the primary occupation for 35 per cent of all respondents, followed by farming (19 per cent). Thirteen per cent of the respondents were engaged in business and the overwhelming majority of these businessmen were associated with the buying and selling of fish. The same was also true for the day labourers. Thus, nearly two-thirds of all respondents surveyed were employed, directly or indirectly, in fishing-related jobs – not a surprising finding for people living in a coastal area. With respect to respondent level of education, nearly 6 per cent of all respondents had studied beyond the 10th grade.

The low level of education and relatively high illiteracy rate (39 per cent) among respondents surveyed is typical of people living in the coastal regions of Bangladesh. All the socioeconomic characteristics of the respondents included in this study clearly indicate a higher level of poverty and a lower level of education in the coastal areas studied than in the rest of Bangladesh. Thus, these coastal residents are more vulnerable to any natural disasters, particularly cyclones, compared to people in other parts of the country.

Semi-structured Group Interviews

The primary reason for conducting group interviews was to gain a clear understanding of the circumstances accounting for injuries and public response to care for injured persons. Another reason for utilizing semi-structured interviews was to verify and corroborate injury-related information gathered from the questionnaire survey. Both the face-to-face questionnaire survey and the semi-structured interviews were administered approximately three months after the cyclone and it took nearly two months to complete data collection. Individual and group interviews were conducted at about the same time to facilitate immediate cross-checking and verification of data.

Semi-structured group interviews were carried out in the form of a group discussion between six to ten local people and at least one member of the research team. As noted, all members of the research team had participated in and/or conducted formal field surveys in rural Bangladesh in the past. For this reason, it did not take much time to build rapport and trust with Sidr victims. All group meetings were conducted in Bengali – the vernacular of Bangladesh. The dialect used by the people of Sidr-impacted study areas is a somewhat different from those used by the team members, who come from the central part of the country. However, this did not create any serious problems between team members and participants of the group meetings.

Group meetings were held in six different localities: one each in the Patuakhali and Bagerhat districts, and two each in the Barguna and Pirojpur districts. No separate group meetings were held exclusively for women and women participated in three of the six group meetings. All the group meetings were led by one or more members of the research team, none of whom were female. This apparently did not discourage women from participating in the discussions (Figure 6.1). In fact, the team observed that women were more enthusiastic to talk in discussions than the men. The total number of participants in group discussions was 50–35 males and 15 females. Each group meeting lasted between 60 and 90 minutes. The research team did not use an audio tape recorder or a video recorder, but carried a digital camera.

Participants of group meetings were carefully chosen. They represented members of all socio-economic classes, age groups, occupational categories, and families with and without cyclone-injured members. Some families experienced both death and injuries among their members due to Sidr. It appeared that many of these families had returned to a relatively normal state and were willing to participate both in questionnaire survey and group discussions. Unsolicited persons, particularly children, were also present at these meetings, which were held in roadside tea stalls and courtyards of local families (Figure 6.1). No one appeared to be reluctant to speak at these sites. None of these meetings were held in work places and/or private or public offices. Prior to each group meeting, prospective participants were asked whether they were willing to take part in the meetings.

A similar approach was also taken for face-to-face individual interviews, where respondents of the questionnaire survey were ensured anonymity. Survey questionnaires were kept secure with the first author and were not shared with anybody other than for research purpose. In both types of interviews, no one declined participation. Before commencing interviews, verbal informed consents were obtained from the participants. The verbal informed form was read to both participants and respondents. After their consent, they were briefed regarding the purpose, consequences, and benefits of this research. They were also informed

Figure 6.1   Interviewing a group of disaster-affected people

that they would not receive cash or other type of rewards for participation, their participation was strictly voluntary, and that they had the right to withdraw from the study at any time without any compensation. Further more, it was also explained that they were free to refuse answers to any questions if they felt uncomfortable.

Informal Discussions and Participant Observation

These traditional methods were applied to gain an in-depth understanding regarding the various aspects of injuries caused by Cyclone Sidr. These were also used as additional tools for validation, that is, to confirm or refute the data collected through interviews and group discussions. Although the members of the research team did not stay for an extended period of time in the field, informal discussions and observation provided valuable insights regarding the topic of interest of this research. Since all members of the research team are Bangaldeshi in origin, an extended period of stay in the field for field observation was not necessary.

Informal discussions were conducted with participating emergency responders, local leaders, school teachers, government officials, and NGO workers. In each of the study sites, research team members informally discussed a variety of subjects, including, but not limited to, number of deaths and injuries, organizational response, cyclone warnings and evacuation, sheltering, and personal behaviours and relevant issues coastal residents experienced during Sidr. The time spent with each respondent ranged between 15 minutes to an hour. All participants were enthusiastic to provide information on the cyclone.

Challenges with Participatory Research Methods

In administering both questionnaire survey and group meetings, the research team confronted several challenges which are classified into four groups.

Expectations of Sidr Victims: Additional Emergency Aid

First, when villagers found out that the research team included a faculty member of an American university, most wanted to be included in the study as respondents and/or participants of group meetings. Although no question was asked to report monetary damages caused by Cyclone Sidr, most villagers felt that the team was sent by the American government to enquire how much damage was caused by Cyclone Sidr and who was affected by the cyclone.

Some of the villagers knew that American medical teams came to the areas affected by the cyclone and provided valuable medical assistance to the injured. Several villagers reported that US Navy ships distributed potable water, food, medical supplies, and other much-needed aid to Sidr victims. Three villagers also stated that a US naval task force came to Bangladesh following devastating cyclone in 1991, which killed some 140,000 people (Paul 2008a). Many villagers, however, sincerely thought that the face-to-face interviews and group meetings were a continuation of the American government's willingness to help the cyclone victims in Bangladesh. They came to the conclusion that whatever amount of additional disaster assistance the Bangladesh government receives from the US government would depend on the report of the research team.

Prior to conducting the field survey, the research team members suspected that after hearing the composition of the team, respondents of questionnaire survey might inflate the number of deaths and injuries in an effort to gain more US assistance. It is noteworthy that no question was asked to the respondents on damage caused by the 2007 cyclone and participants of group interviews were not asked to provide number of deaths and injuries in their households. To overcome the inflated number, the team members first listed names of all household members and then asked the respondents to identify the dead and injured persons from the list. In the case of death, the team members also requested to see the location of graveyard for the deceased person. After cross-checking with local key personnel, government officials, and other sources, the number of deaths and injuries reported by the respondents proved to be accurate.

However, several villagers admitted they thought members of research team brought relief aid in their microbus and might donate it to respondents who had completed the questionnaire survey and/or participated in group meetings. Others suspected that survey respondents and participants of group meetings would

Figure 6.2   Disaster-affected people gathering around interview sites

receive aid later, after the research team returned to Dhaka. Many villagers of the study area were confident that talking with a member of the research team would guarantee them receiving American relief aid. Therefore, they wanted to be included in the questionnaire survey and/or group interviews.

Despite their request, it was not possible to include all household heads residing in the selected villages in the questionnaire survey, nor was it possible to include one member from each household in group meetings. To overcome these problems, the research team members decided to record the names and addresses of all household heads not selected for questionnaire survey and/or for participation in group meetings. In addition, they were also asked to form a queue and then one of the team members took their pictures with a camera (Figure 6.2). The news of recording names and taking photographs spread quickly. As a result, lot of people gathered around group interview sites and they were insisting the research team record their names and take their photographs.

Considering the size of the gatherings, team members advised some villagers to come the next day; otherwise they would have to wait an hour or more. Surprisingly, they preferred to wait for an hour or often longer rather than coming back on the following day. It was not clear whether these villagers believed that the team would be present next day – and this may have impacted their decision to wait. In all the sites, at least one Sidr victim asked how long the team would stay at that site. Team members were unable to answer this question exactly because their stay in each site depended on how much progress they made each day.

Although team members did not say anything other than recording the names and addresses of non-selected household heads, and asking them to pose for a picture, most villagers seemed happy and stopped requesting they be included in the questionnaire survey and/or in group meetings. However, five people in three different sites were obviously desperate to participate in the group meetings, and ultimately were included as participants.

All of them belonged to lower socio-economic class and they thought the research team ignored them because of their socio-economic status. Members of the research team strived to create an equal relationship between the researchers and the respondents of questionnaire survey and participants of group meetings. As a powerful research method, the research team has used reflexivity to ensure successful completion of the fieldwork.

Sidr Victims' Inquiries about US Immigration

In all group meeting sites, dozens of people asked the first author of this chapter how to immigrate both legally and illegally to the United States. They are familiar with the diversity visa (DV), also called the lottery visa. Under this program, the United States has allowed more than 6,000 Bangladeshis entry into the country as immigrants every year beginning in the early 1990s. In recent years, this number has been reduced to nearly 4,000 (Paul 2008b). Several villagers asked how to apply to study in the United States; each have sons and intend to send them to the United States to further their education.

As indicated, several persons were interested in how to illegally enter into the United States. The first author clearly explained the procedures for obtaining both DV and student visas, but expressed ignorance regarding how to enter illegally. Although the answer to the issue of illegal entry was not liked by those who raised this issue, team members abstained from providing inaccurate information. While the team members at times compromised their dietary restrictions, they were not flexible on the entry issue. Several Sidr victims requested the telephone number of Kanti Paul. They were provided with the number and all of them called the author while he returned to Dhaka. They asked how to illegally enter the United States. The author clearly told them that he had no knowledge about the matter. Two of them hinted that they would provide any amount of money for this purpose.

Hospitality of Sidr Victims

Like their experience in previous fieldwork, the research team was amazed by the warmth and hospitality shown to them the villagers and participants of group meetings. They offered food, tea, sweets, and coconut water, which is good for the stomach. It is worth mentioning that coconut trees thrive in coastal areas of Bangladesh and nearly every house in the selected villages has coconut trees.

However, it was not possible to accept all such offers. Although refusing hospitality is considered offensive to the host/hostess in rural Bangladesh, team members randomly accepted a few such offers and apologized for their non-acceptance of others. Two members of the research team were following a strict diet advised by their doctors. This was explained to villagers who then understood the reason for not accepting all offers of food items. Still, responding to these offers slowed the progress of both the questionnaire survey and group meetings.

It was clear to the research team that the hospitality shown by Sidr survivors, even from the poorest households, was not due to any desire to please the team in order to secure emergency relief aid. Rather, this behaviour reflects a sincere generosity that villagers typically extend toward guests. A similar conclusion was also reached by other social science researchers who have conducted fieldwork in rural Bangladesh (see Sultana 2007).

Other Challenges

The number of people gathered around the research team consistently increased as the day advanced. This gathering sometimes interfered with tasks assigned to each team member. These people often spoke loudly and talked with the participants of group meetings. Participants also asked questions to the team members which were not related to the subject matter of discussions. Answering and discussing topics beyond the research questions took a considerable amount of time. This delayed completion of questionnaire survey and group meetings by four to five days. It would have been more than that, if members of research team had not frequently steered respondents and participants back to the research questions. Another reason for delay in completing this project was that a large number of people, particularly children, constantly followed team members. Team members were always calm, and did not express anger or rudeness toward them or any one.

Conclusions

This chapter presented an application of participatory research methods in a post-disaster context. It briefly discussed the methods utilized to collect information on the circumstances that caused deaths and injuries during Cyclone Sidr, which made landfall across the southwestern coast of Bangladesh on November 15, 2007. This chapter also explained the challenges confronted by the methods employed and how these challenges were overcome. Despite alleged shortcomings of participatory methodology as a tool for data collection, this methodology was employed in order to collect relevant data quickly, cheaply, and effectively with no significant reduction in reliability.

This study has demonstrated that rich and accurate information can be gathered in a post-disaster situation through the application of PRA methods. A considerable amount of both qualitative and quantitative data were collected, most of which are relevant to the research in question. It was possible to do so because of the experience and knowledge of the team members both regarding the topic and the study area. The research team was able to analyse the data collected with this methodology without significant difficulty.

Members of research team suspected that the topics discussed in group meetings could revive the pain of some participants, particularly those who had lost one or more family members or where one or more members sustained serious injuries. Fortunately, this possibility never materialized, probably because of the timing of these meetings, which did not occur immediately after Sidr's landfall. Participants also had the option to stop if they became distressed during these meetings, but no one left these meetings before they were over.

A common criticism of the use of PRA methods is that the information gathering does not always follow a thoroughly scientific process and thus any data collected are less valuable. Such criticisms are probably not true for this study. Members of the research team sincerely believed that the research subjects were freely and openly discussing topics relevant to this study. Collected information is therefore accurate and reliable. Furthermore, respondents of the questionnaire survey and participants of group meetings trusted team members; this aided the conducting of interviews and assured meetings ran smoothly and in a friendly environment. Because all team members are from Bangladesh and each had conducted prior field surveys in rural Bangladesh, security and access were not issues they encountered while conducting their fieldwork in Sidr-impacted areas.

Some researchers, such as Smith (1999), noted that indigenous communities prefer outside researchers based on the deeply held view that indigenous people are not knowledgeable enough for such activities or that they have a hidden agenda. This was not observed by members of the research team in the field. Rather, after experiencing a tragedy of great magnitude, team members were not expecting the congenial way in which Sidr victims treated them. The interviews were conducted both in a cordial and learning environments. The team members carefully listened to the respondents and participants of individual and group interviews, and members respected their view and opinions.

Acknowledgements

We wish to thank the Natural Hazards Center at the University of Colorado at Boulder, CO, USA; and Dean's Office, College of Arts and Sciences and Provost Office, Kansas State University, Manhattan, KS, US for finding this study. We would also like to thank Munshi Khaled and Bankim Rakhit for participating in the field survey in Bangladesh.

References

BRAC (Bangladesh Rural Advancement Committee). (1991), *Cyclone '91: A Study of Epidemiology* (Dhaka: BRAC). Beebe. (1985), *Rapid Rural Appraisal: The Critical First Step in a Farming Systems Approach to Research* (Gainsville, FL: University of Florida).

Chambers, R. (1980), *Rural Development: Putting the Last First* (London: Longman).

Chodhury, N.Y. et al. (2004), 'Impact of Coastal Embankment on the Flash Flood in Bangladesh: A Case Study', *Applied Geography* 24, 241–58.

Chowdhury, A.M.R. et al. (1993), 'The Bangladesh Cyclone of 1991: Why So Many People Died', *Disasters* 17(4), 291–303.

GOB (Government of Bangladesh). (2008), *Cyclone Sidr in Bangladesh: Damage, Loss and Needs Assessment for Disaster Recovery and Reconstruction* (Dhaka).

Ikeda, K. (1995), 'Gender Differences in Human Loss and Vulnerability in Natural Disasters: A Case Study from Bangladesh', *Indian Journal of Gender Studies* 2(2), 171–93.

McCracken, A. et al. (1988), *An Introduction to Rapid Rural Appraisal for Agricultural Development* (London: International Institute for Environment and Development).

Paul, B.K. (2008a), 'Bangladeshi American Response to the 1998 Status of Forces Agreement (SOFA): An Assessment', *The Professional Geographer* 57(1), 495–505.

Paul, B.K. (2008b), 'Bangladeshi Americans', in Schaefer (ed.).

Schaefer, R.T. (ed.) (2008), *Encyclopedia of Race, Ethnicity, and Society* (Thousand Oaks, CA: SAGE Publications).

Smith, L.T. (1999), *Decolonising Methodologies: Research and Indigenous Peoples* (London: Zed).

Sommer, A. and Mosley, W.H. (1972), 'East Bengal Cyclone of November 1970: Epidemiological Approach to Disaster Assessment', *The Lancet* 2999, 1029–36.

Sultana, F. (2007), 'Reflexivity, Positionality and Participatory Ethics: Negotiating Fieldwork Dilemmas in International Research', *ACME: An International E-Journal for Critical Geographies* 6(3), 374–85.

Thompson, P.M. and Sultana, P. (1996), 'Distributional and social Impacts of Flood Control in Bangladesh', *The Geographical Journal* 162(1), 1–13.

Chapter 7

Rediscovering Traditional Knowledge for Post-disaster Reconstruction through 'Participatory' Research Methods in India and Nepal

Rohit Jigyasu

Introduction

This research was encouraged by the growing concern at the increasing vulnerability of rural communities to natural hazards such as earthquakes, especially in the context of developing countries such as India and Nepal. Various initiatives towards earthquake preparedness, mitigation and rehabilitation in rural areas by public, semi-public and non-governmental agencies have failed to produce significant difference in their vulnerability situation. Therefore, this research aimed at exploring the potential role of local knowledge, resources and strengths of rural communities in India and Nepal for formulating long term planning and mitigation measures to reduce their disaster vulnerability, especially to earthquakes.

The past and present status of local knowledge, skills and capacity of rural communities were investigated to understand the key issues and challenges for their role in reducing disaster vulnerability, which is seen not only as a pre-disaster condition but also as a continuous process, which is influenced by the overall development context and various response decisions taken during the post-disaster situation.

To get an integrated and dynamic perspective on how local knowledge and capacity and disaster vulnerability influence each other, three case studies were investigated: Marathwada region in Maharashtra, India; the Kutch region in Gujarat, India; and the Kathmandu Valley in Nepal. While the first case looked at the impact of post-earthquake rehabilitation eight years after the 1993 earthquake, the second case investigated the immediate transition phase from relief to rehabilitation within a span of one year after the 2001 quake. The third case of the Kathmandu Valley in Nepal explored various transformation processes in rural communities, which created conditions for pre-disaster vulnerability. A detailed understanding of these processes also helped in identifying the changing scope of local knowledge and capacity and the resulting impact on vulnerability.

The Marathwada case provided an excellent opportunity to study the impact of post-earthquake rehabilitation process over a long time. While a number of extensive studies had been conducted assessing the rehabilitation process immediately after the earthquake, no study existed on assessing its long-term impact. The case study area included around 50 villages, which had borne the brunt of the earthquake and had been either relocated or reconstructed *in situ*. In a few villages the retrofitting option was also tried for the first time in the country. The reconstruction was mainly contractor driven, although in some cases an owner driven approach was also adopted. The research required appropriate techniques to assess these approaches to understand the extent to which these took into account local knowledge and capacity and were able to reduce vulnerability in the long run, seven years after the earthquake.

The Gujarat case provided an opportunity to look at the immediate aftermath of the earthquake and also the complex processes that created the setting or context for a disaster of such immense proportions, just before the earthquake. It also gave an opportunity to assess the post-earthquake rehabilitation process and compare it to the one followed in Marathwada. Comparative analysis was possible since the earthquake affected region in the Kutch district of Gujarat consisted of many villages of similar size as in the case of Marathwada. Also, various approaches for reconstruction were tried here as well, most of which were owner driven based on the lessons learnt from the reconstruction process followed in Marathwada. In fact, the Gujarat case proved to be the largest initiative in an owner driven reconstruction ever attempted in India. In the third case of the Kathmandu Valley, links between post-disaster reconstruction and the pre-disaster vulnerability situation were analysed through detailed study of physical, social and economic transformation processes in rural communities. Due to very similar social, cultural and developmental contexts, these conditions were assumed to throw more light on the vulnerability situation in the South Asian subcontinent in general and the other two case areas in particular. Moreover, the pre-disaster vulnerability situation of all the three areas could well be linked to the underlying reasons for the loss of local knowledge and capacity. Such an analysis would require an in-depth study of the social and physical structure of the village from an external perspective of a researcher as well as that of the inhabitants in order to understand the changes in an holistic and dynamic manner.

The three case studies were analysed for various underlying structural and non-structural causes that create negative conditions in which the disaster vulnerability of these communities is increasing because of weakening local knowledge and capacity. Needless to say, in all the three cases, various sections of the local community such as house owners, craftsmen and farmers became the central subjects of research.

Why Undertake Participatory Research?

The Scope and Nature of Local Knowledge

Local knowledge is constructed mainly at two levels of perception; as perceived by the researcher or a professional (the external worldview) and as perceived by the local community (the internal worldview). In order that the internal worldview of the community and the external worldview of the researcher coincide to produce a comprehensive understanding of local knowledge, it will be useful, at the start, to distinguish between direct, personal knowledge, based on the experience of the knower with the facts at hand, and indirect, or processed, knowledge, which is based on the measurements and systematic observations of the researcher. Processed knowledge in the form of models must be connected to personal knowledge so that both complement each other. While the former can be gathered through various analytical tools of scientific research, the latter can be best deciphered through participation between the researcher and the bearers of this knowledge.

The process of knowledge generation can very well be a matter of luck: chance discovery, a reflection-on-action: self-learning through re-tracking back and forth or through mutual learning: through sharing experiences. Therefore, no knowledge should be considered absolute as something given and external to humans. Instead it evolves over time through continuous dialogue and discussion among various stakeholders. Therefore, such knowledge is inter-subjective rather than objective, based on mutually accepted meanings and beliefs. Moreover, in most cases, local knowledge for disaster mitigation and preparedness is not consciously designed for the purpose; rather it is part of holistic multi-purpose actions and therefore the bearers of knowledge may not be aware of its full potential. Such an inter-subjective, holistic and sub-conscious knowledge needs participation between the researcher and the subjects of his research.

Scientific Method for Rediscovery of Local Knowledge and Capacity

Local knowledge cannot be accumulated merely by the deductive scientific method. Rather it works both vertically and laterally, like a matrix with various inter-relationships that give different meanings to a given set of variables. In that sense, it is very complex for which there can be no standard instrumental mechanism of scientific research.

For recovering the internal world view of the bearers of this knowledge, it is very important to understand the life experience of the respondents. Such a description helps the researcher to obtain a comprehension of how people immediately experience their situation and their physical environments and evolve mechanisms to deal with them. This may come under a phenomenological tradition, where what is focused on is the immediate, direct experience of the physical environments as they appear to the individual (Næss 1995).

Moreover, research engaging in traditional knowledge should not only explain what is already known but also the hidden meanings in the present settings and old meanings which have disappeared or have been changed in the present and have not been understood by users. (Nooraddin 1996). However the understanding of meanings, particularly spiritual and social ones, by the researcher could be oversimplified or distorted if one does not have a thorough understanding of local knowledge which controls perceptual reactions (Clifford 1983). Therefore, an important aspect of research into the rediscovery of local knowledge is the use of hermeneutics for interpreting meanings behind various sets of information.

This kind of research may fall within the anthropological field of study. Pike (1954) has differentiated between *emic* and *etic* approaches in the anthropological field of research (Pelto and Pelto 1970). Emic approach refers to the approach that deals with the insider's view of culture usually held by the natives, while the etic approach deals with the researcher's view, who is not part of the culture. The former approach would be more suitable for research on the nature of local knowledge as it requires cultural behaviour to be studied and categorized in terms of the views and perceptions of the local community. Accordingly, the primary research method of the emic approach would be in-depth interviews in the native language, while for the etic approach it is the observation of behaviour. Additionally, the intent of the former is to identify categories of meanings, as nearly as possible in the ways the natives define things, while for the latter, it is to seek patterns of behaviour, as defined by the observer, who is the researcher in this case.

Knowledge development is a very dynamic phenomenon. Therefore, knowledge at a particular point in time is dependent on its immediate context that may or may not be relevant at another point in time. Vulnerability itself is a process and thus it is appropriate to consider the changing nature and status of local knowledge and its consequence on the changing vulnerability of rural communities in South Asia. In order to understand this changing nature, one needs to assess the changing social, cultural, political and economic context and resulting transformation processes. One also needs to consider the changing behaviour, attitudes and perceptions of various stakeholders, including various sections of the local community, that govern various decisions taken to reduce disaster vulnerability in future.

Therefore, the main objective of such research is not to make a static database of knowledge for mitigating the impact of earthquakes. Neither is it related to the assessment of physical vulnerability, nor to the assessment of earthquake impact. The issue at hand is to assess current practices in disaster management, to understand how much they build on local knowledge and capacity, and to discuss their impact and effectiveness in reducing disaster vulnerability of rural communities. An important aspect considered here is that assessment of the impact of disaster management cannot overlook the broader developmental context that creates vulnerability in the first place. It is an investigation that demands careful follow-up study of both short-term effect and long-term impact of the vulnerability process on individuals, communities and their living environment.

This dynamic nature of such a research, which seeks to assess the current status and potential future role of local knowledge in reducing disaster vulnerability, necessitates participation of the community which bears this knowledge in the first place. This requires the application of a range of data collection strategies and diversified sources of evidence, which can only be gathered through participatory research methods that are described in the following section.

Participatory Research Process

Participatory research process was initiated in all the case study areas so as to get a comprehensive perspective on the role of local knowledge and capacity in post-disaster reconstruction by taking into account views and perceptions of all the stakeholders including the local community. The research findings were intended not only to fulfil the academic obligations by answering the research question set forth by the researcher but also to disseminate these findings to the research subjects, especially various organizations and vulnerable communities before or after the disaster with the hope of improving the reconstruction practice. Various participatory methods that were employed during the research are briefly described below.

Interacting with Key Stakeholders

The first step in the fieldwork was mainly to acquaint myself with various public, semi-public and non-governmental organizations (NGOs) that are working in the field of disaster management in India and Nepal. Additional to this, the views of various professionals and academicians were also taken into account on different social, economic and technical aspects related to disasters in general and earthquakes in particular.

In the case of Marathwada, I interacted through the district commissioner's office, which helped me with my first reconnaissance visit to the relocated villages and explained the official position on the reconstruction process as well as provided me with the maps, documents and statistics relevant to the rehabilitation process. During my first visit to these villages, I was accompanied by a staff member of the commissioner's office, who showed me various projects undertaken by the government as part of the reconstruction process. Later, I also interacted with various non-governmental and civil society organizations, which were engaged in the reconstruction process and various development activities in the region. This provided me with a comprehensive overview of the situation on the basis of which I could frame my future research strategy.

The case study of Gujarat was added only after the earthquake hit the region in January 2001. Preliminary reconnaissance of the situation immediately after the quake helped me to get in touch with government agencies at national and state level, non-governmental and civil society organizations, professionals such as engineers, architects, development practitioners, and academics from local institutions and understand their views on the situation in the immediate aftermath of the disaster. As in the case of Marathwada, preliminary assessment in Gujarat was undertaken through informal visits to the affected villages and interviews with various stakeholders. Most times, I accompanied the members of civil society organizations involved in the reconstruction process during their missions to the areas of their operation. This helped me develop initial rapport with key stakeholders, notably non-governmental organizations, who were engaged in the reconstruction process. It is noteworthy to mention here that both in Marathwada and Gujarat it is this initial contact with various stakeholders that put me in touch with organizations, in whose activities I participated later as part of my research process.

In the case of Bungamati village in Nepal, I interacted with leaders of various sections of the local community as well as representatives from the local village development office and various local community based organizations from the village.

Field Observations through Participating in the Activities of Local Organizations

It is often difficult for a researcher, with the status of an outsider, to approach the community directly and seek its participation in his or her research activities. Therefore, one of the main sources of primary data for my research was field observations to gain in-depth insights into the local dynamics and processes by directly or indirectly participating in various activities in the field. In most cases, the medium of local NGOs and community based organizations (CBOs) was used to gain access to communities. Importantly, I did not approach the local communities individually as a researcher; rather I submersed myself in the normal activities of these NGOs and made detailed observations in this process.

In Marathwada, I participated in the activities of an NGO called the Ahmedabad Study Action Group (ASAG). This NGO had been involved in implementing low cost strengthening and retrofitting techniques in the region since 1993, and had built up a valuable database on the rehabilitation process as well as a rapport with the local community. While participating in their activities, I also interviewed the volunteers who were working for this NGO since the earthquake struck and ascertained their views on the rehabilitation process. Some volunteers from ASAG also accompanied me during another visit to the region and showed me their work and other areas of interest. They also introduced me to local community members in a few villages. Additionally the views of other NGOs and CBOs, whom I came across during various activities, were also noted through various interviews.

Much like in Marathwada, local NGOs like Abhiyan, Veerayatan and Unnati provided the medium to access communities in Gujarat and assess their views on post-disaster rehabilitation. These NGOs were involved in various aspects of rehabilitation and reconstruction such as providing temporary and permanent shelter and livelihood regeneration. Therefore, I volunteered to participate in some of the activities of these NGOs during which visits were paid to their project sites, the work done by them was observed, and views of various stakeholders were gathered.

The same process was repeated while carrying out fieldwork in the village of Bungamati in the Kathmandu Valley. Here access to the community was made through the active help of a local community based organization named Rotary Patan West. This organization put me in touch with the local Village Development Committee (VDC), who further introduced me to the local ward, the smallest administrative unit within the village, committees and the volunteers of local CBOs.

Scale of Investigation and Inductive Research Process

An important decision concerned the scale of this research and whether detailed investigation should be undertaken at the village level or for the entire region. In the cases of Marathwada and Gujarat, initial participation in the activities of non-governmental and community based organizations engaged in post-disaster reconstruction helped me in understanding various issues at the regional level. Moreover, participating in the activities of these organizations made me realize that the impact of rehabilitation was different in different villages, not only depending on their category for rehabilitation but also within various villages belonging to the same category. Therefore, an attempt was made to take into consideration the villages where different approaches towards reconstruction were being followed. These included villages with full-scale contractor driven reconstruction, NGO facilitated reconstruction and villages with total self-help houses. Due to the enormous geographical size of the Marathwada and Gujarat regions, and the diversity of reconstruction approaches, it was much more interesting and informative to make a general assessment of the situation in the entire region and cite cases from individual villages to bring forward various issues and approaches.

In the case of the Kathmandu Valley, initial rapport with local VDCs and Rotary Patan West in Bungamati village helped in limiting the scope of the study to a detailed assessment of rural transformation processes in this traditional village and its immediate environs. Therefore, initial participation in the activities of NGOs helped me to decide on the scale of investigation for all the three cases.

Another consequence of participatory research was that the fieldwork was conducted in an inductive way. Therefore a clear chalked out plan for data collection was not made. Rather, things took shape as the research progressed. Therefore, I did not limit myself to researching on one issue but engaged in a holistic assessment of the situation while participating in the activities of NGOs. This enabled me to draw the inter-relationships of various findings into my research question. For example, I first decided to work at the village level but when I investigated the Marathwada case I found out that one or two villages did not tell the whole story. The whole set of information was enriched by taking a macro perspective. Even the case study in Gujarat was included as part of this inductive approach to research. In Gujarat too, I initially wanted to focus on one or two villages. However, I later discovered that the dynamics of the developments over nine months were so interesting that I decided instead to focus at the macro level on the dynamics of the transition from the immediate aftermath to the post-disaster rehabilitation phase.

In both cases, I gathered information by assuming the role of a journalist, collecting, checking and cross-checking information from various sources, not to establish the truth but to understand diverse perspectives of various government, non-government and individual stakeholders. The participation of the local community was vital in this activity. For example, during one of my field visits, I got to know from an NGO that in one of the reconstructed villages in Gujarat, a certain underprivileged landless group of artisans had not received any support from the government and were left behind in their damaged houses amidst the rubble. On the other hand, some wealthy groups from the same village, who owned large chunks of land, were able to receive compensation packages from the government and managed to get themselves relocated. However, when I posed this query to the public agency in charge of reconstruction, this charge was strongly refuted. In order to cross-check this allegation, I met a journalist who had covered this issue in one of the stories for a weekly journal. He threw some more light on the situation of this village. Having armed myself with various points of view, I decided to visit this remote village and gathered useful insights of the situation, which I found to be partially true. However in this process, I gathered interesting information that helped me analyse the process of increasing social vulnerability of certain communities in the post-disaster context.

Semi-structured Key Informant Discussions and Life Stories

Rather than a standard questionnaire, spontaneous semi-structured discussions were conducted for primary data collection. One of the main reasons for this was that it enabled the views of different stakeholders, including NGOs, CBOs, government organizations, traditional craftsmen, academics, professionals and various sections of the local community, including earthquake victims, to be gathered and to assess their issues and problems in the shortest possible time. As a starting point, various respondents, which included sections of the community especially the marginalized – most vulnerable – groups, officials from government agencies at various levels, leaders, representatives and volunteers from various NGOs, specific groups of people like craftsmen, contractors and architects, were identified through participation in various reconstruction and development activities undertaken by NGOs. In most cases, these were identified while I progressed with my research so the list was updated as per the developments in the field. All these stakeholders became key respondents for the research and in many instances provided important contacts of other potential respondents.

The discussions primarily aimed at understanding the views of respondents on various aspects of the rehabilitation process. These discussions were held by me directly since the villagers could understand my language. It is important to mention here that rather than preparing standard questionnaires, I conducted semi-structured discussions with the primary aim of assessing peoples' views on the rehabilitation to appreciate how it has affected them. It is important to mention that villages from each of the three categories in the rehabilitation process were studied. This included those which had been relocated, where *in situ* rehabilitation was supposed to take place and those where a strengthening and retrofitting programme was to be carried out.

Table 7.1   Questions for interviews with NGOs and CBOs

	NGOs and CBOs working in Gujarat and Marathwada, India	NGOs and CBOs in Kathmandu Valley, Nepal
References	Time and place of interview. How I got to know the respondent? In what capacity does he represent a particular NGO?	Time and place of interview. How I got to know the respondent? In what capacity does he represent a particular CBO?
Activities	What are the various activities in post-earthquake relief and rehabilitation?	What is the history of the concerned CBO? What are the various activities of the concerned CBO in the village? What are the challenges faced in carrying out these activities?
Stakeholders	What are various stakeholders involved in various activities? – low caste/artisans/women etc.	What are various stakeholders involved in various activities? – low caste/artisans/women etc.
Challenges	What were the main challenges encountered by the NGOs in undertaking rehabilitation activities?	What are the main issues/ problems confronting the village?

In Bungamati village in the Kathmandu Valley, random household discussions were conducted as part of the activity of the local VDC to update their database on the village. However, the selection of households for detailed discussions was carried out so that views of all sections of the community on the basis of caste, economic status, and geographical location were ascertained. Here also, standard questionnaires were not used. The language barrier was crossed through translators, who were employed from the village itself.

In Bungamati, the participation of local villagers was also sought in recording the transformations taking place in these villages and their day to day activities. Again, this was undertaken as one of the activities of Rotary Patan West; the local CBO, whose members became facilitators in this process. Some young members of the community were trained to make preliminary documentation of the vernacular built form, its design and construction, as well as condition, which was recorded by them through photographs.

Since in most cases I did not know exactly what kind of questions the respondent would be able to answer, I generally approached these with an open-ended format of questions or discussion points, which could be adapted as the conversation developed. This resulted in fascinating sets of information that had not been expected from a given respondent. Also, respondents were found to be more comfortable if questions were asked in a running conversation intercepted with comments and views that could sustain their interest. Mostly, I avoided taking

Table 7.2   Questions related to earthquake impact, recovery process and reconstructed shelters

Reference	Time and place for interview. How I got to know the informant?
Occupation	The kind of occupation, economic status.
Impact	Physical, social and economic impact of the earthquake.
Recovery	Self-initiatives for recovery and coping strategies. Which organizations/ agencies supported recovery after the earthquake, if at all? In what way? What is the level of satisfaction of the beneficiaries? What is the present status of victims?
Shelter	What kind of shelter is constructed after earthquake? – reconstructed, retrofitted or status quo. What is the level of involvement after the earthquake? What are various issues and problems encountered?

notes during the course of an interview as this could have made them conscious and thus affected the level of unbounded communication with me. However, interview notes were recorded not too long after the discussion.

It is important to mention here that these interviews were made not as an external observer posing questions to the informants but as discussions with them, undertaken as part of the activities of NGOs in which I volunteered to participate. Rather than presenting pre-defined questions to the potential respondents, I made a checklist for key points around which the discussions could centre. In that sense, these questions were rather addressed to myself and not the subjects of my research. Table 7.1 outlines the questions that I sought to get answered through interviews with various NGOs and CBOs in the three case study areas.

Various questions related to earthquake impact, recovery process and reconstructed shelters were posed to the affected people as outlined in Table 2.2.

Life stories give information about which experiences a person uses to make decisions, and how they explain the course of their life to themselves (Schütz and Luckmann 1967). Life histories of various informants in my research were also recorded while participating in the activities of various NGOs in all the three cases. Notable among these were the cases of the elderly, who narrated their experiences from past earthquakes. Furthermore, certain life histories of marginalized groups of people acquainted me with the main causes for their vulnerability and how they cope with various situations in their life. Some respondents could tell me about the transformations that have occurred in their village during their lifetime, which provided me with a very useful perspective on their perceptions of change and the resulting impact on a vulnerability condition. Such life stories were gathered through discussions with the informants, which would generally take place in an informal environment such as over a cup of tea in the public square or in the neighbourhood or house of the respondent. In most instances, the discussion would begin on a personal note and gradually would drift towards real life incidents experienced by the respondent that would have direct or indirect bearing on my research. Often I would steer the discussion as we moved along so that it did not go completely off track. Many times, certain respondents, especially those from the underprivileged sections of the society, would not feel comfortable to narrate their life experiences. In such cases, I would take the help of a local assistant from the same village, who would engage the respondent, while I just watched the discussions unfold.

It is worth mentioning here that in each of the case study areas I engaged a team of research assistants, who belonged to the local community. After basic training, these assistants gradually became very skilful in interviewing the local people. They would often accompany me to these interviews and discussions and wherever I sensed the hesitation of respondents to deal with me directly, I would happily get the local assistants to take over the discussion while I watched it as a mere spectator.

Conclusion

In this section, I wish to conclude with the challenges and limitations experienced by the researcher, who is engaged in participatory research aimed at examining the potential of local knowledge for disaster mitigation, by drawing upon the lessons learnt as a result of undertaking the research. Does the researcher only rediscover the knowledge, its current status and its link to disaster vulnerability, as a passive elite, or can he/she also be a generator of practical actions?

One of the basic assumptions of participatory action research has been that knowledge is a dialogue. Common people can consciously contribute to scientific knowledge in a process of mutual inquiry and learning, and scientists (researchers) can consciously expand the common peoples' knowledge base with new information and new ways of analysing their life situation. A natural consequence of such a process is that common people, non-specialists, participate in the analysis and planning and in the subsequent or simultaneous action. Action is part of knowledge formation while it contributes to the solution of the commonly identified problem. In this kind of research, knowledge formation is seen as an interactive process between practical knowledge and theoretical knowledge, where action regenerates knowledge (EADI 1996). In Participatory Action Research (PAR), we move on the border between theoretical knowledge, practical knowledge and practical action. The assumption is that in dealing with peoples' existential problems different knowledge systems have to interact. On what level and how they interact is a crucial question. Another crucial problem in this is that of communication: How do the different knowledge systems interact? Here I would like to review the limitations of participatory research in the light of my own work.

While I have a lot of faith in the potential of PAR, the essential pre-conditions for this to happen are rather difficult to achieve for a researcher who has limited time and resources at their disposal. These preconditions are linked to the level of education, empowerment and poverty alleviation, which are the larger issues of development that would enable the local community to directly participate in the research process.

Also on the part of the researcher, who is generally an outsider, there is a need to build not only a basic knowledge of local dynamics, but also a feeling of mutual trust and rapport with the local community, with whom they are entering into a seemingly unbounded dialogue, and this requires time and commitment. During the course of my research, I discovered a number of grass root non-governmental and community organizations in case areas, which are working closely with the community for a long time and have succeeding in winning their trust. However, their ability to be part of the participatory research process cannot always be guaranteed.

In such a situation, the best option for the researcher is to engage with these grass root organizations as a vehicle for undertaking participatory research with the local community. For this very reason, I used participatory methods for collecting the data by establishing a close relationship with these communities with the help of these civil society organizations, who have been working in these areas for a long time. Rather than directly participating with the local communities, I participated in the actions of these civil society organizations and used them as a bridge to gain the insights of the communities. However, I have not solely relied on their information, but rather made an attempt to cross-check it with other available sources.

As previously mentioned, the research took a very inductive approach in the way various situations have been investigated, without a predetermined narrow focus but thereafter establishing inter-linkages to the main research issues. However, the problem with inductive research is that one is never too sure. Therefore, the researcher cannot predict the path that their research will eventually take and, instead of the usual linear deterministic process, they would have to adopt lateral thinking tools, moving forward and then retracing the path to decide on the next step. This surely is much more challenging when the researcher is constrained by many factors such as time and resources.

Another issue that was encountered during this inductive participatory research was the difficulty in drawing a line between science and journalism. Many times, I encountered the danger of wandering into investigative journalism and losing track of the basic principles of truthfulness, reliability and validity in scientific research. Separation of researcher from the subject of their research is indeed a challenge in participatory research since continuous engagement with stakeholders makes it difficult for the researcher to view various perceptions/findings in an objective and rational manner, and they run the risk of getting carried away by the views and biases expressed with other participants in the research activity. The real challenge for the researcher is how to keep a distance and at the same time maintain a closeness that is necessary to effectively participate in the research activity. Being a total participant may make it difficult for the researcher to detach him or her self from the observed reality and in turn, values may influence them. They may force them to be partial in observing, collecting and analysing data.

Participatory research can assume different meanings depending on the nature of participation, which can be undertaken at various levels and to various degrees from mere involvement to a more closer engagement and, at best, empowerment of the research subjects. In one scenario, the researcher may gather empirical data through the participation of various stakeholders. Afterwards they would detach from the research setting and analyse this information through scientific research methods. The findings of the research can again be communicated by the researcher to the research subjects who have participated in gathering data. One may call this participation for the sake of gathering research findings. However, in the second scenario, which may be called participation in research, the researcher and his research subjects would participate not only in collecting the data but also in the scientific research process. This, as mentioned previously, necessitates many pre-requisites and is much more difficult to achieve. Above all, the researcher needs to earn the trust of the community or other stakeholders who participate in the research and should also have enough time at their disposal, which, as discussed before, may not be a realistic proposition in most cases.

While participating, a researcher acts like a practitioner who is as much engaged in finding information as in facilitating a dialogue that would lead to some proposals of direct benefit to the stakeholder(s) that are reached through consensus. As it is nearly impossible to adopt both the roles of a researcher and that of a practitioner at the same time, it is often necessary to link the two roles in various ways..

Last but not least, in order to do justice to those who participate in research activity, the final output should not be limited to a report that can decorate the library shelves. Research findings must be communicated through unbounded dialogue with the stakeholders, which include decision-makers, civil society organizations and above all, the local communities, especially those who have participated in the research process in one way or another. This can be achieved through various mediums and for various target groups through activities such as community level meetings, exhibitions and workshops.

It is important to keep in mind that post-disaster reconstruction provides an opportunity to reduce vulnerability to future disasters. Therefore, it is crucial that findings of participatory research in a post-disaster context are communicated to the decision makers, so disaster management policies and programs can be improved based on the insights provided by the research. Participatory research can indeed become the mouthpiece of various stakeholders, whose concerns ought to be addressed in any post-disaster programme.

References

Clifford, G. (1983), *Local Knowledge: Further Essays in Interpretive Anthropology* (New York: Basic Books).

European Association of Development Research and Training Institutes (EADI) (1996), *Participatory Action Research* (Bonn: EADI).

Jigyasu, R. (2002), *Reducing Disaster Vulnerability through Local Knowledge and Capacity* (Trondheim: Norwegian University of Science and Technology).

Naess, A. (1995), *Deep Ecology for the 21st Century* in Sessions G. (ed.) (Boston: Shambhala).

Nooraddin, H. (1996), *Al-Fina, a Study of in between Spaces along Streets as an Urban Design Concept of Islamic Cities of the Middle East with a Case Study in Cairo* (Trondheim: Norwegian University of Science and Technology).

Pelto, P.J. (1970), *Anthropological Research: The Structure of Enquiry* (New York: Harper & Row).

Pike, K.L. (1954), *Language in Relation to a Unified Theory of the Structure of Human Behaviour* (Glendale, California: Summer Institute of Linguistics).

Taylor, A. (1981), Assessment of Victim Needs, in Davis (ed.), *Disasters and the Small Dwelling* (Pergamon: Oxford) pp. 134–137.

UNDRO (1982a), *Disaster Prevention and Mitigation: A Compendium of Current Knowledge, Vol. 8* (New York: United Nations).

Chapter 8
Conclusion to Part I

Alpaslan Özerdem and Richard Bowd

Introduction

The previous five chapters in Part I focused on the development and post-disaster contexts for participatory research methods. However, as is often the case, it was a major challenge to identify certain contexts as purely that of development, while others as post-disaster or post-conflict because there are many overlaps between such environments, and many contexts often have various elements of disaster, conflict or development in one way or another. For example, Jones' research took place in the context of Rwanda which is a typical post-conflict environment but as the chapter explored the way participatory methods were used on the assessment of poverty baselines in preparation for the Rwandan Poverty Reduction Strategy Paper (PRSP), this chapter was presented as an example of development context. Similarly, the development context presented by Burns and Catley explored the use of participatory methods in a participatory impact assessment of a post-drought recovery and famine mitigation project in Zimbabwe. Although the programme itself was a post-disaster initiative, its characteristics were deemed to represent more of a development context. On the other hand, it was easier to label Mdee's chapter as development and those by Kanti and Dutt, and Jigyasu as post-disaster, though they had certain overlapping elements too. Nevertheless, apart from those contextual overlaps the five chapters actually represented completely different uses of participatory research methods, and the following section will provide a brief summary of the main strengths and weaknesses of participatory methods in development and post-disaster environments.

Strengths and Weaknesses of Participatory Research Methods

The main strength of the participatory approach for Mdee's research in Tanzania was the way it provided different opportunities for dealing with the challenge of insider and outsider perspectives. By structuring an active partnership with local community researchers as community mediators and representatives, she managed to analyse collective village life effectively in relation to the operation and impacts of a community-managed water project. Without such an insight from her local researchers the researcher would have faced a number of difficulties in her introduction to the community, gaining their trust and being able to appreciate many significant societal nuances. The application of a wide range of research tools was another significant strength of this research. From life histories and diary keeping to observation and institutional mapping, this myriad of techniques resulted in the gathering of rich and insightful information on the topic. For example, to understand the extent of individual participation in collective activities, life history proved to be highly beneficial to gather detailed information on types of agency used by individuals in shaping their lives. Meanwhile, the wealth-ranking exercise was critical to see how wealth shaped individual agency and collective action.

The Participatory Impact Assessment (PIA) experience in the context of the Gokwe Integrated Recovery Action Project also considered the role of community as critical for the successful application of the research process. Burns and Catley asserted that through the assumption of 'acknowledging that aid recipients are capable of identifying their own indicators of change' their approach was important for the realization of the local ownership, control and capacity building principles. With an objective of effective impact assessment, the community involvement in the process would help avoid an over emphasis of 'anecdote, ad hoc interview, and staff or consultant opinion'. Through a systematic use of participatory tools, Burns and Catley generated both qualitative and quantitative data, demonstrating project impact. Their work was also critical to show that 'a numerical value can be assigned to an impact indicator allowing it to be easily measured' which is 'flexible, and can be adapted to different projects, contexts and indicators. It is also accessible to practitioners, and with a minimum amount of training, it can be carried out by NGO staff with little or no technical oversight'. In other words, the participatory research approach in the application of an impact assessment proved to be highly productive in the generation of reliable data and information.

In Jones' research in Rwanda, which presented a practical guide for the participatory researcher, the main strength was not only achieving an economic assessment, but also that the research provided a more innovative tool for the definition of poverty. Through a careful use of Participatory Rural Appraisal (PRA) techniques, his research identified what poverty meant from the perspective of those people who were most affected by it. For example, to establish nuances in relation to poverty and wealth, the participation of the community allowed the research to understand that although both men and women agreed on the primary wealth differential variables as 'shelter – type/construction, number of goats and the number of meals eaten a day' there were also 'gender variations and emphasis on increasing means of production', which were possible to identify only through the use of participatory research methods.

In another impact assessment study, Kanti Paul and Dutt's focus was the post-disaster environment of Cyclone Sidr in Bangladesh. By examining the prevalent conditions under which participatory research methods were used, the analysis of their research process showed that as well as a development context the post-disaster environment would also be suitable for the use of such methods. Through the involvement of cyclone survivors the participatory research strategy managed to bring a critical insight on post-disaster challenges faced and how communities coped with them through their own preparedness and mitigation mechanisms. The composition of the research team was particularly significant for the successful application of this participatory research process but, more importantly, the 'willingness to freely interact with participants' was identified as a primary factor in its positive outcome, which indicates the importance of considering participatory methods not only as tools but also processes.

In the second post-disaster case study example, Jigyasu explored the potential role of local knowledge, resources and strengths of rural communities in India and Nepal for formulating long term planning and mitigation measures to reduce their disaster vulnerability, especially to earthquakes. The research process suggested why the use of participatory methods was particularly important for the following reasons. First, it was essential for the incorporation of local knowledge in the planning and implementation of disaster mitigation and preparedness, as often 'the bearers of knowledge may not be aware of its full potential'. Second, through such participatory methods it showed that it was possible to incorporate the 'views and perceptions of all the stakeholders including the local community'. Third, such a strategy presented a great level of flexibility as 'the fieldwork was conducted in an inductive way' and there was room for incorporating new dimensions to the research as it progressed in the field. Finally, rather than trying to establish a truth of the reality, by the use of a wide range of participatory methods the research managed 'to understand diverse perspectives of various government, non-government and individual stakeholders'.

Overall, it can be summarized that all five chapters in this section considered participatory research methods as highly effective tools for their data gathering processes. They agreed that by the application of such methods they had a much deeper and more nuanced understanding of their target communities, and the methods used could be applied in various ways, depending on the requirements and characteristics of the caseload and objectives of the research. By bringing an emphasis on gender, poverty and social status dimensions into the analysis in a more considered way, the participatory methods proved to be highly complementary to more conventional techniques and they served a great purpose for the triangulation of findings. The chapters also identified the way those participatory methods can be re-formulated for the purposes of such undertakings as impact assessments and evaluations. The possibility of being able to quantify certain social indicators showed that the application of participatory methods presents a number of opportunities that can be explored further by academics and practitioners. The overall research environment and its impacts on the research outputs did not show much variation between development and post-disaster contexts. Both environments had a similar set of challenges such as difficulties with transportation and access to populations or ensuring the willingness of communities to take part in the research process. Also, neither of the environments posed any particular risk for the well being of the researcher and researched due to security conditions. Apart from obtaining the usual permissions for research from a number of authorities, they did not have any major problems with the freedom of conducting research, though this was more of an issue in post-disaster environments.

In addition to these strengths, the chapters in Part I also identified a number of challenges in the application of participatory research methods in development and post-disaster environments. Before presenting a summary of those weaknesses, it is important to note that all of the case studies considered them as challenges rather than weaknesses, which is an important issue to explore in detail. There seem to be a number of reasons for this. First, as the case study chapters treated participatory research methods as more like processes than tools they placed much more emphasis on the contextual problems for their implementation such as those related to logistics and limited time constraints. Second, all of the chapters recognized the flexibility of adapting a menu of their participatory methods according to the changing circumstances of their research environments, therefore the variability of the design and application has reduced the chances of a wide range of biases being part of research findings. Finally, the case studies indicated the importance of the interaction between the researcher and the researched, and although some inherent challenges with participatory methods were identified, which will be explained next, those shortcomings were not considered as structural weaknesses of participatory research methods.

The main challenge with participatory research methods in Mdee's work in Tanzania was the way she could not overcome the power dilemma with the insider versus outsider perspectives as effectively as she initially planned. Although such techniques as visual timelines were particularly productive to understand socio-economic characteristics of local communities, if they were applied in a short period of time then there were questions over whether they could 'capture fully the different voices of the community – considering in particular the dominant discourses and potentially biases of such voices'. In other words, even for the researcher to test her own possible biases due to the conceptualization of the research question and selection of methods there needs to be sufficient time for the proper application of such participatory techniques. It is also important to note that participatory research methods should not be packaged as a solution for all possible research challenges. Mdee argued that 'tools are just tools, and that in this sense participation, and with it PRA' should not be 'commercialized' as there are some inevitable challenges with ensuring an absolute equality between the researcher and research team, transferability of all related concepts, and education and skill limitations of local researchers that would be almost impossible to avoid.

Jones also encountered similar challenges with the power relationship between himself and research participants. First of all, being considered a *mzungu* was identified as a major obstacle for him to establish productive relationships because of the way he was considered as an outsider white man. Furthermore, he recognized the possibility that some of those responses he received were exaggerated because of the community expectations from a *mzungu* to resolve their problems. Second, the respondents were reluctant to talk about their wealth in front of their peers as this could have caused jealousy between neighbours and friends, and perhaps this should be considered as a critical weakness for participatory methods, because it is directly related to how the research strategy aims to gather and extrapolate information. Third, although the research tried to find a better balance between the involvement of community members and key informants through the application of participatory research methods, the participation of the latter group was unavoidable in order to undertake such a research. Therefore, it is important to be realistic about the possibility of how much such a research can avoid key informants and their influences on the research process. Finally, Jones' research acknowledged another important fact with the usefulness of participatory research methods to recognize small wealth differences between different communities as 'there were very few real differences in perceptions and characteristics of wealth, and therefore the corresponding relationships to the physical differences of shelter and goat ownership'. However, this would not mean that non-participatory methods would have been more effective for such a challenge. It was possibly necessary to adopt more innovative techniques to measure such small differences.

The primary weaknesses experienced in the PIA research experience were outlined by Burns and Catley as follows: the possibility of peer bias which was a result of household interviews being conducted in groups of nine people; biases related to the expectations of project participants for further funding; the possible influence of group consensus phenomenon in group discussions; the objectivity of the research team due to the involvement of the implementing NGO in the research process; and finally, not being able to use more innovative techniques due to time limitations and reservations of the implementing agency for the fear of offending project beneficiaries. From this brief summary it can be clearly seen that the weaknesses experienced in this case study was largely due to the way they had to be implemented for a number of contextual, logistical and prudential reasons. It would be hard to qualify any of them as a weakness solely related to the concept of participatory research, and the group consensus factor is possibly the strongest weakness of participatory methods that seems to be emerging from this particular experience. Nevertheless, it was concluded that 'the strengths of the approach and methods used outweigh the weaknesses'. Also, in an ironic way the limitations of participatory research methods were considered as 'what give them the flexibility and advantage over more conventional approaches'.

The challenges experienced in the post-disaster case studies were also quite similar to those encountered in development environments, but differently from them there was an emergence of some specific characteristics too. First of all, the research process in the aftermath of a disaster is likely to encounter a socio-political environment where communities would have some real needs and also wish-lists of what they would like to have as part of relief and reconstruction programmes. Often as a consequence of ill-prepared and implemented disaster response programmes and the habit of making generous pledges for assistance after such catastrophes, local communities tend to expect a much higher level of assistance than the international community is prepared or able to provide. The arrival of foreign researchers is often welcomed as this is perceived as a possibility of needs being assessed and assistance provided in return. It is also important to note that as well as academic studies there would also be many needs assessments undertaken by a myriad of national and international agencies. The practice of not sharing assessment findings due to inter-agency funding politics often means that similar questions are asked by different relief organizations repeatedly. This is likely to have a number of consequences on the quality and effectiveness of research findings in disaster-affected areas.

First of all, as the chapters by Kanti and Dutt, and Jigyasu also indicated, with raised expectations the respondents are likely to give answers in which needs are exaggerated or emphasized in certain dimensions at the expense of others. For example, they are likely to place more importance on tangible and easily accessible goods rather than more structural problems. Kanti and Dutt tried to explain their identity as researchers as much as possible, but this did not prevent some community members from still hoping to gain direct assistance from the research process. Nevertheless, the application of different participatory methods was an effective response to this problem, as they managed to triangulate their findings and recognize the influence of raised expectations in their findings. The second possible risk was the way communities knew how to answer certain questions with the hope that this would increase their chances of receiving assistance, as they were asked similar questions by implementing agencies a number of times before, which resulted in some relief and rehabilitation programmes. Finally, when the research is undertaken after a considerable period of time after the occurrence of that disaster, one is likely to experience a certain level of reluctance to participate, as it is often the case that disaster-affected communities are often disappointed with those promises that were never realized, which tends to create some antipathy towards researchers.

Another significant challenge in a post-disaster environment is likely to do with the limited time that key actors would have to participate in the process, as they would be busy with addressing relief and rehabilitation needs of disaster-affected people. Similarly, when people are displaced from their homes and livelihoods, the expectation of them being part of a participatory research process may not be very realistic. This particular challenge is particularly the case if the research takes place in an emergency period, but unless there is a very good justification for conducting research in such an environment it would be difficult to satisfy the related ethical concerns and it would be advisable to avoid such undertakings. However, for practitioners to assess post-disaster impacts and needs such assessments would be an absolute requirement for the planning of response strategies, therefore the considerations related to whether or not such studies should be undertaken and how it should be done would vary according to the objectives of that research.

Overall, the case studies in this section showed that there are some possible weaknesses with the application of participatory research methods, but it would be an over-generalization to consider them as inherent weaknesses of those methods. Most of those challenges were experienced because of the contextual realities of such development and post-disaster environments. Some of them could have been addressed but at the same time it is necessary to note that regardless of whether research methods are participatory or not, those challenges would continue to pose a major risk for the effective implementation of the process. It is also important to recognize that the language bias due to translations did not appear to be a major issue in any of the case studies. Although the transferability of concepts was identified as an issue, the language bias did not really emerge as a critical weakness due to a number of reasons. Conducting research in such environments as Tanzania, Zimbabwe and India obviously made this less of an issue, as the official language in those countries is English, but the structure of research teams was also an important reason for it. In Tanzania, working with local researchers addressed this challenge for Mdee, while Kanti and Dutt were working in Bangladesh where they could use their mother tongue and also worked with a team of local researchers to deal with local dialects. Nevertheless, the main lesson to draw from these experiences is the importance of language issues for undertaking participatory research methods effectively. It can easily turn into a major weakness if it is not considered and dealt with carefully, as effective participation would require good communication, which will be further unpacked in the final conclusion chapter.

PART II
Participatory Research Methods in Post-conflict Reconstruction

Chapter 9

Introduction to Part II: Participatory Research Methods in Post-conflict Reconstruction

Richard Bowd and Alpaslan Özerdem

Conducting social research of any nature inherently entails difficulties that must be overcome whether they are problems of access, sampling, ethics, analysis or others. However, in a Post-Conflict Environment (PCE) such challenges faced by researchers are often magnified and further obstacles unique to a PCE must also be addressed. The research challenge faced by researchers in a PCE can therefore be more complex than in other environments and will subsequently require an enhanced or expanded set of methodological techniques to meet this challenge. This is the case regardless of the purpose of the research; academic researchers will face the same challenges as those researching for policy objectives or development programme design due to the environment in which they are functioning.

Essentially the challenges faced by researchers operating in a PCE fall into three themes: a respondent element; a researcher element; and an effectiveness element. All three elements are interlinked and interplay with each other, however, for the sake of simplicity and cohesion of argument it makes sense to look at the issues faced by researchers in a PCE through these three lenses. The respondent element includes challenges presented in one way or another by the respondent. Perhaps the most familiar and problematic of these is the issue of access. Generally it can be expected that social researchers from all disciplines face this issue. However its prevalence and complexity in a PCE is arguably greater, particularly if the nature of the research is sensitive. Officials or community members themselves may put in place restrictions on access and it is therefore often sagacious to identify individuals in positions of power or respect in order to gain access to not only the physical setting but also acceptance by the local population which is key for the quality of data collected. Official access may be dependent on the nature of the research and the agenda of those providing access (Lee 1995). Emotional access, that is, the ability of the researcher to gain social acceptance within the community, may be more difficult to achieve. Emotional access is crucial to the attainment of rich data that the respondents themselves hold (Bowd 2008). PCEs are characterized by a lack of trust, which may severely limit the ability of a researcher to gain the required data due to intense suspicion of the nature of the research and the outsider status of the researcher (Hermann 2001 and Smyth 2005). The gaining of emotional access is an arduous process made ever more difficult by the intensity and duration of the conflict and may be strongly influenced by decisions made by the researchers regarding the way in which they interact with officials and community members (Lee 1995 and Druckman 2005). Identifying and engaging a gatekeeper is key to enabling access as this can open doors otherwise closed to an outsider.

Arguably the most significant issue within the respondent element is the invasiveness of research in a PCE, particularly in cases where the research centres on sensitive issue and when participatory research methods are used as such techniques tend to be more invasive by their nature. Qualitative research methods investigating sensitive issues in a PCE seek to uncover aspects of individual's lives and societal trends and patterns that may have been suppressed and may cause distress to the respondent during the process of recall. This is particularly the case when researching psychosocial or societal issues. A significant role of a researcher operating in such a setting is therefore to acknowledge and respect the need for sensitivity throughout the research process. Indeed, as Smyth notes:

> conducting research in a manner that uses people as objects without due regard for to their subjectivity, needs and the impact of research on their situation is ethically questionable. This becomes particularly apparent is psychological terms, since respondents may be at a stage of denial in relation to the horrors that have happened to them (Smyth 2001: 5).

Such sensitivity is so crucial as the issues that arise throughout the research process can have important ramifications for present life as noted by Roberts, 'the recollection of past events is inextricably connected with people's current life and its place in the group and wider community' (Roberts 2002: 104). The need for sensitivity in the research process indicates the importance of both time and trust. When investigating sensitive phenomena in a PCE researchers must allow for an adequate amount of time in order to effectively address the issues and maintain sensitivity. Central to this is the establishment of a relationship of trust between researcher and respondent (Hermansson et al. 2003). Essentially, researchers operating in a PCE need to make an explicit commitment to the principle of do no harm and put in place measures that mitigate any undesirable effects of the research process.

The second element posing a challenge for researchers in a PCE is the researcher element, which includes challenges presented in one way or another by the researcher. Researchers operating in a PCE face the paradox of needing to develop close enough ties with those they study but at the same time retaining some distance, 'some social and intellectual distance' (Hammersley and Atkinson 1983: 102). However, research in PCEs, particularly of a sensitive nature, presents much greater problems for researchers. One such problem researchers may face is feelings of sympathy or empathy for those who we perceive to have committed immoral acts. When researching sensitive issues:

typically, fieldworkers put themselves in these positions so that they can understand the phenomenon well enough to stop it. But developing cognitive empathy (understanding why people think, feel, and as they do) can generate feelings of sympathy in the researcher. These feelings make the researcher uncomfortable (Kleinman and Copp 1993: 38).

This can have the effect of creating a dual problem in that researchers are more able to recognize the social or structural elements that result in immoral acts but also there is the issue of how to act with respondents and to what extent one engages in behaviour they believe to be immoral.

A further, and arguably more significant, emotional issue faced by researchers is that of the collection of sensitive data and the way in which it affects us. As Chaitin states:

> carrying out qualitative research in conflict-ridden contexts, in which people have experienced much social trauma in their lives is a difficult task…they are rich in detail, emotionally touching, and, at times, emotionally difficult. I do not always hear things that I would like to hear, and at times, I wished I had not asked the question (Chaitin 2003: 1146/1151).

In this sense we can see that sensitive research may affect not only the respondent, as commonly acknowledged, but also the researcher. Field research can be a highly isolated endeavour and it is somewhat natural for those in such circumstances to engage more rigorously in their work. Engaging at an intense level brings the researcher into close proximity to the traumas experienced by the respondents and this can be increasingly difficult for the researcher to cope with emotionally. When researchers are absorbed in copious amounts of research data the demands and challenges placed on them can be great. In addition to this, the nature of interviews can be highly charged emotionally (Johnson and Clarke 2003). Although it may be difficult, some degree of detachment needs to take place in order to be able to maintain the frame of mind conducive to effective research.

The third challenge grouping faced by researchers in a PCE is the effectiveness element, which incorporates challenges associated with effectively attaining rich data. Essentially this element is constructed from a combination of the respondent and researcher elements. The level of access researchers have in a PCE can be critical to the richness of data they are able to collect. Both official and emotional access is required in order to generate rich data that will enable a more comprehensive understanding of the phenomena being investigated. Without both forms of access, particularly emotional access, it is extremely difficult to engage in such a way with a respondent that is conducive to the attaining of rich data. Associated with the matter of emotional access is the question of researcher sensitivity, which as previously stated is significantly important in a PCE. If a researcher in a PCE demonstrates the required level of sensitivity, and that level will differ between each respondent and context, towards his or her respondents the likelihood that a deeper level of emotional access will be forthcoming is greater. Subsequently, with an increased level of emotional access, it is possible to argue that the richness of the data collected will also be greater. Conversely, if the researcher does not display a sufficient level of sensitivity emotional access is less likely to be forthcoming and consequently, a lower quality of data can be expected. The issue of sensitivity in a PCE therefore can be seen to have two prongs. The first is a moral and ethical obligation to do no harm and to make the research experience as painless as possible for the respondent, the second being the efficacious effects of sensitivity in terms of the richness of data collected.

The effectiveness element of research in a PCE will also be dependent on the role of the researcher. If a researcher operating in a PCE can strike the right balance between developing close enough ties to access rich data and retaining a level of professional distance then they will be in a position from which effective research can be conducted. Central to a researcher's ability to be able to strike such a balance is the way in which the researcher manages the collection of sensitive data. A researcher needs to be able to engage with highly sensitive data hearing, and perhaps seeing, disturbing things whilst reacting in a sensitive but somewhat detached manner. As previously stated, it is crucial to be sensitive during the research process however; if a researcher is to be able to cope with the outcomes of the research process they need to retain some degree of distance and detachment. The better a researcher can deal with sensitive data, the better position they are in to be able to access such data. Researchers operating in a PCE are required to draw on a portfolio of investigative skills that allay any fears of the respondent and generate an atmosphere that is conducive to the research process. If the researcher is unable to do this they will experience enormous difficulties in accessing sensitive data in such an environment (Sieber 1993).

The next part of this publication considers the way in which participatory research techniques may overcome some of the problems associated with conducting research in a PCE whilst also reflecting on the problems that such techniques may have that are specific to the PCE. Bowd's chapter on understanding social capital and reconciliation in Rwanda draws on participatory research conducted in Rwanda to provide an appreciation as to how such research methods contribute to our understanding of social capital and reconciliation in war-torn communities. Specifically, the chapter takes into account how the accomplishment of valuable research into social capital and reconciliation in the developing world can be problematic due to difficulty in identifying indicators and the intangible nature of the subject before considering the ways in which participatory research facilitates an environment in which those who are engaging in these processes lead the research agenda and thus enables a deeper comprehension of the issues. Beginning by situating the research subject and context, the chapter moves on to explore the particular participatory techniques used and provides a justification for their use. The chapter then details the application of these techniques in the context of Rwanda before engaging in a consideration of associated ethical issues and addressing relevant questions of analysing participatory data conducted in post-genocide Rwanda. The chapter concludes with a deliberation of the strengths and weakness of the use of participatory techniques in research of this nature.

In Chapter 10, Podder, utilizing experience of field research in Liberia, presents insights into the use of participatory methods to map reintegration outcomes for former child soldiers. By focusing on children a particular value of this chapter is the detailed consideration of the use of participatory research techniques to generate data from a complex source, which further augments our understanding of these methodologies. The chapter begins with a contextualization of the case background and situates Disarmament, Demobilization and Reintegration (DDR) within this context. It then progresses to establish the methodology used with attention to the practical aspects of the research and its possible limitations. Specific focus is then given to the issue of researching with children in a post-conflict context and the ethical considerations that may arise from such research. The chapter concludes with an appreciation of the weaknesses of participatory research methods, but highlights their applicability in child-based research in the post-conflict environment.

Chapter 11 engages with a very specific aspect of participatory research techniques; that of trust-building. The premise of the chapter is that in order to overcome methodological and ethical questions that may be apparent in the post-conflict environment, it is necessary for researchers to build trust with their research subjects. Drawing on participatory research conducted in Sierra Leone, Asiedu advocates the use of the traditional mechanism of door knocking to generate such trust and augment the research process. In order to do this, the chapter first highlights methodological inadequacies of conventional research approaches arguing for a greater focus on participatory methods. The chapter then discusses participatory techniques in the context of post-conflict environments to reveal the difficulties faced by researchers in this context, particularly that of low level of trust making it difficult for researchers to gain access – especially emotional access – to some respondents. Finally, the chapter introduces door knocking as a technique that provides a useful entry tool through which to address the question of a lack of access in post-conflict environments.

Examining the use of participatory methods when researching families of the disappeared in Nepal, Robins builds up the argument that through participatory research methods a deeper understanding of the effects of the conflict on communities, families and individuals, as well as the impact of disappearance, can be made. Crucially, he links this increased understanding to the potential for the development of interventions that extend beyond the currently favoured prescriptive approaches. The chapter begins by setting the scene in terms of Nepal's conflict and the issue of the disappeared. The next section of the chapter introduces a key development in participatory research: that of participatory research design. It is here that much of the value of this chapter lies as Robins develops new thinking on what participatory research methodologies are attempting to achieve. The chapter then details the participatory methods utilized in the research, including an appreciation of the implementation process, before then examining the response of participants to the research process. The chapter then concludes by acknowledging the limitations of the methodology and reflecting on the process as a whole.

In Chapter 14 Holt is concerned with a feminist approach to participatory research with Arab-Muslim women that enables the development of a more egalitarian relationship between researcher and researched. Based on research with Palestinian refugee women and Shi'i women in Lebanon it seeks to shed light on the gendered element of conflict and to show how women in both communities experience war and have a role in post-conflict reconstruction in terms of peace-making and peace-building. The chapter begins with a consideration of the theoretical approaches that inform this research and offers important clarifications as to why such approaches are necessary when developing a research framework to examine the effects of conflict and post-conflict reconstruction on women. Moving beyond the theoretical aspects of research design, the chapter then identifies three key issues that affect the way such research is designed and conducted: those of language and interpretation, the outsider status of the observer and oral history. Discussion of these issues offers important insights into how field research can be affected by the context. The final part of the chapter addresses the conducting of the research given the previously identified constraints. The chapter then offers the conclusion that women are not only victims, both in the research process and in the conflict and post-conflict reconstruction.

Next Connolly utilizes his experience of being a team leader in the mid-term evaluation of the National Solidarity Programme (NSP) in Afghanistan. The NSP study provides profound insight because it was grounded in participatory research principles though nation-wide and multi-level in scope. In order to unlock the insight from the NSP study and to examine the use of participatory research methods in relation to the three overlapping domains of meeting the aims and objectives of a mid-term evaluation, gathering valid evidence and managing the expectations of both research participants and programme stakeholders, the author employs his experience of leading the evaluation in Balkh province as the primary case study combined with comparisons to the research in the mid-term evaluation's other nine sampled provinces. The chapter begins by explaining important aspects of the NSP's background, context and methodological design: all issues that affect the conducting of this unique case of participatory research. The remainder of the chapter is then structured around the three overlapping domains identified above and demonstrates the influence of participatory methods in each of these domains. Insight from this then forms an analysis of the impact of participatory methods for a mid-term evaluation. It then offers the conclusion that participatory research methods are effective through focusing on their ability to manage the inevitable tensions between the three mid-term evaluation domains. Nevertheless, it also identifies reasons why such methods can fail to develop the capacities of research participants and programme stakeholders and explores ways to overcome specific challenges in the post-war context.

The final chapter of this part of the publication offers a very practical dimension to the use of participatory research techniques in a post-conflict environment through an exploration of the ways in which participatory research techniques can be taught as part of conventional postgraduate research method courses and the identification of how such techniques can be utilized in study visits individually or as a group by MA and PhD students. Starting an investigation from a set of ethical concerns in using such techniques by students under or without supervision in disaster and conflict affected areas, Ozerdem then questions how such methodologies can be taught, tested and practised in an ethical, effective and efficient way in the preparation of future researchers. The merit of this chapter lies in its practical recommendations surrounding methodologies for the teaching of participatory research techniques which build on the more research application forced issues of earlier chapters.

Chapter 10

Understanding Social Capital and Reconciliation in Rwanda through Participatory Methods

Richard Bowd

Introduction

This chapter draws on research conducted in Rwanda to provide an appreciation of how participatory research methods contribute to our understanding of social capital and reconciliation in war-torn communities. Accomplishing valuable research into social capital and reconciliation in the developing world can be problematic due to difficulty in identifying indicators and the intangible nature of the subject. Additionally, issues of access, both official and emotional (Bowd 2008), experienced in all forms of research are felt all the more when exploring such sensitive topics, particularly within a post-conflict setting. However, understanding the specific causes behind a given conflict is crucial to the effective reconstruction of the post-conflict environment. So too, is an appreciation of said environment, that is, the impacts of the conflict on the society in question. Indeed, it is only through an accurate comprehension of the challenges and threats that the reconciliation process faces, that any durable societal restoration can take place.

Participatory research facilitates an environment in which those who are engaging in the reconciliation process lead the research agenda and thus their increased sense of agency allows a stronger degree of ownership. The change in power balance (Gueye 1999) enables the establishment of an arena that is conducive to a deeper comprehension of the issues surrounding the conflict. Additionally, by being able to observe the ways in which respondents interact during the exercises, further information regarding the process of reconciliation and social capital restoration can be garnered.

Research Outline and Context

The research experience that formed the following insights and opinions was doctoral field research examining the social reintegration of former combatants in Rwanda. The central aim of the study was to examine how the successful social reintegration of former combatants can promote reconciliation in a Post-Conflict

Environment (PCE) through the renewal and strengthening of social capital. It is often posited that this group can be critical to the achieving of sustainable peace due to the potential security threat they represent (Colletta et al. 1996; Kingma 1997; Dercin and Ayalew 1998; Mokalobe 1999; Özerdem 2002). Additionally, it is also recognized that the reintegration of former combatants has the potential to contribute in a positive way to conflict transformation and peacebuilding (Nubler 1997; Kingma 2002; Ginifer 2003). However, despite the acknowledgment that the reintegration of ex-combatants can make positive contributions to the peacebuilding process, little is known as to how this may materialized. Indeed, as Gomes Porto et al. (2007: 147) state:

> Recognizing this important point (that in the immediate post-war setting, societies may seldom have the ability to effect sustainable reconciliation) points us in the direction of long term reintegration as a critical component of processes of social reconciliation – and the need therefore to conduct deeper research into the underlying and subtle process by which identities affect and are affected by the reintegration process.

Given our inchoate understandings of both reconciliation and the positive contributions to peacebuilding of ex-combatant reintegration, in theory and practice, this study sought to investigate the relationship between the two, utilizing the concept of social capital, in order to develop our understanding of both individual concepts of reconciliation and social reintegration and the way in which they may interact.

Critically, this research set out to investigate the main parameters related to the research: reconciliation, Disarmament, Demobilization and Reintegration (DDR), and social capital in the context of post-genocidal Rwanda. Specifically then, it sought to establish the impact genocidal conflicts have on social capital, in particular bonding, bridging and vertical social capital, and the implications this may have for reconciliation. It was anticipated that an understanding of the ways in which such conflicts impact on social capital will facilitate a more comprehensive consideration of how DDR programmes may promote the rebuilding of social capital and the ways in which such programmes may contribute to enhanced reconciliation. In turn, such an understanding may augment our understanding as to how DDR policy can best be designed and implemented in order to achieve effective reconciliation.

Rwanda presents itself as an ideal case study in which it was possible to examine all the concepts relevant to this research. The conflict in Rwanda culminated in 1994 with a genocide which left an estimated 800,000 dead, 130,000 detainees in the national prison system, 2 million Rwandan refugees, 700,000 returning Rwandan expatriates and 650,000 alleged participants in the genocide (Marks 2001). As a consequence of such devastation, the social fabric of Rwandan society was decimated; social capital was all but destroyed and reconciliation seemed impossible. The nature of the conflict and genocide in Rwanda affected all the major forms of social capital: bonding, bridging and vertical, which has had subsequent effects on the reconciliation process. This, in conjunction with the amount of time that has past since 1994, made it the only genocidal[1] case that would be suitable. The amount of time that had passed is an important factor to take into account as the three concepts of social reintegration, social capital and reconciliation all take time to re-establish. Therefore, it was necessary to take this into consideration when deciding on the case study. Rwanda had also undergone two DDR programmes since 1997 with the first phase designed and implemented by the United Nations Development Programme (UNDP) between 1997 and 2001 and the second phase from 2001 to 2008, which was designed by the Multi-country Demobilization and Reintegration Program (MDRP) and Rwanda Demobilization and Reintegration Commission (RDRC) and implemented by the RDRC. The process had been ongoing until recently due to the return of Hutu militias from the DRC who were involved in the conflict or recruited after the conflict to engage in ongoing paramilitary activity since 1994.

A total of five sites were selected from which to collect data for the research. The first site was that of the capital city, Kigali. It was necessary to conduct some of the research in Kigali due to the fact that the RDRC and MDRP, as well as other organizations that fell into category three of the sample (officials), are situated in Kigali. Whilst based in Kigali, I also conducted some research with former combatants and civilians. In the rural areas four sites were selected, one from each of the provinces: in the Northern Province a village near Busogo, in the Eastern Province a village near Ngenda, in the Southern Province a village near Ruramba and in the Western Province a village near Nyundo. The two main factors that directed site selection in the rural areas were the presence of former combatants and access. Prior to undertaking phase two of the research I obtained from the RDRC details of former combatant settlement patterns and identified a number of potential sites that contained enough former combatants from all three groups.[2] Ex-Rwanda Defence Force (RDF) combatants were much more numerous and so could essentially be found in most locations, however, those from Forces Armees Rwandaises (FAR) and the Armed Groups (AGs) were situated mostly in the north and northwest of the country, therefore it was not expected that I

---

1   This research was concerned with genocide as it is possible to strongly argue the case that the social fabric of a society that has experienced genocide is damaged to a far greater extent than other forms of violent civil conflict, unless that genocide is entirely successful. Therefore, the challenge faced by such societies in the post-conflict reconstruction effort after a genocide is more complex and, as such, appropriate measures need to be put in place.

2   The ex-FAR are those who demobilised at the end of the genocide in 1994 and did not enter any other armed force. The AGs are those who joined any armed group in the DRC after fleeing Rwanda. The RDF is the reformed RPA and includes original RPA, those from FAR who wished to join after 1994 and AGs who wish to join after their repatriation to Rwanda.

would find equal numbers in each site. Additionally, the number of ex-FAR and AGs to be interviewed was lower than ex-RDF due to the fact they represent a smaller proportion of all ex-combatants who entered the DDR programme. Having identified potential sites I then went on site visits to ascertain those most suitable for this research. In doing this I met with the District Reintegration Officer (DRO) of the area to conduct an interview and discuss potential sites. The DRO then took me to sites we had decided upon and we met with the sector executive secretary to discuss the research and to assess the suitability of the particular site.

The four sites decided upon fulfilled the two main criteria of presence of former combatants and the granting of access. They also enabled a degree of comparison thus enabling a more comprehensive understanding of the situation in Rwanda. Two of the four sites, North and West, were located on one of the major tarmac roads with good transport and communication links. The other two, East and South, were located away from a major road artery, requiring a minimum of one hour's travel on unmade roads by motorbike or *Matatu*.[3]

Research Methods

The research was conducted using a combination of qualitative research methods including ethnographic methods, life histories, elite interviews and Participatory Rural Appraisal (PRA) in order to best determine the ways in which the successful social reintegration of former combatants may promote enhanced social capital in a post-genocidal conflict environment and to identify the implications of such a promotion for reconciliation. The fieldwork research took place over two phases, the first being a period of three months in Rwanda, October–December 2006, during which semi-structured interviews were conducted with policy designers and implementers concerned with the Rwanda Demobilization and Reintegration Programme (RDRP), government officials and non-governmental organizations (NGOs) representatives, and the conducting life history analysis of a sample of former combatants and civilians based in Kigali. The life history analysis involved interviews of on average 45–120 minutes in order for the process to yield the most beneficial results. The data was transcribed then coded and analysed, allowing me to identify the areas most important to the reintegration process and restoration of social capital. During the first phase I also identified a number of potential sites for the ethnographical study in the second phase of fieldwork.

The second phase involved a three-month period, again in Rwanda, between April and June 2007. For the first period of this phase, approximately two weeks, I addressed issues arising from the first phase of the research and put in place logistical arrangements pertinent to the ethnographical study. The second period of this phase, approximately two months, included four ethnographical studies of approximately one week in each of the chosen sites during which PRA exercises

---

3   A Matatu is a shared taxi.

were conducted. The final period of around two weeks enabled me to finalize and conclude my fieldwork research and tie up any loose ends.

The specific PRA techniques I used were landscape mapping, institutional diagramming and analysis, social network mapping, and social capital indicators. Landscape mapping is invariably used as a tool to derive similar information that one would achieve from an aerial map (Rocheleau and Ross 1995). Essentially, it involves constructing a physical map of the community, which may include farming plots, water provision, schools, or whatever the mapping group decide is relevant. In terms of this study the use of landscape mapping did not result in concrete data used in the analysis; however this was not the intention in using such a technique. The primary motive of using landscape mapping was to introduce me to the community and engender their trust and this proved a useful method through which to do so. It also enabled me to observe the ways in which community members interacted with each other during the mapping process, which was useful for understanding community dynamics.

Institutional diagramming and analysis enables the researcher to 'understand the roles of local organizations and the perceptions that people have about them' as 'it clarifies which institutions are the most important, which have the respect and confidence and women and men, and who participates in and is represented by which ones'[4] (Slocum et al. 1995: 127). This is a particularly useful technique for better understanding how vertical social capital is embedded within society and how such vertical social capital may contribute to the development of bridging social capital. It is also a particularly useful technique, as not only does it contribute to an indigenous measure of social capital, but also provides an understanding of the local institutions which inform further ethnographic study.

Social network mapping facilitates the identification of the complex economic, social and cultural relationships that exist within a community and how they are manifest within that community (Weller-Molongua and Knapp 1995: 186). In particular it examines the way in which exchange takes place within the community focusing on the types of exchange and the direction of exchange, which provides indications of social inclusion and exclusion. This is significant as it enables a deeper understanding of social capital and how, and between whom, it is constructed. It also helps to determine how ex-combatants have undergone reintegration and the degree of reconciliation prevalent in the community.

The final PRA technique used was social capital indicators. This is a technique developed by the author, which facilitates a comprehensive understanding of social capital through the identification of proxies and proxy variables for social capital. These proxies are then discussed with community members who identify particular community events, formal and informal networks and associations, among others, that contribute to social capital in the community. This technique is particularly useful in deciphering ways in which social capital formulation occurs

---

4   Adapted by editors from Thomas-Slayter et al. 1993.

within the context of a developing country and thus builds on our understanding of the measurement of social capital.

The Application of Participatory Techniques

As previously noted, the key participatory research techniques used in this study were life history interviews and PRA. Life history interviews were conducted with a total of 72 respondents; 50 former combatants and 22 civilians. The purpose of using life history interviews was to develop insight into how individuals feel about the conflict and their role in the conflict in relation to their own lives. Individuals perceptions of conflict and their role in it feeds into their personality, and how they subjectively construct their own identities, but equally into how an individuals reality may add to our understanding of a given issue at a societal level, thus enabling us to construct policy more effectively which is important when examining concepts such as DDR, social capital and reconciliation.

Life histories, as Bell writes, provide 'culturally shared images and conventions to present and interpret experience, as well as to draw connections between individual and society' (2004: 49). Similarly, Goodson makes the claim that life histories 'have the potential to make a far-reaching contribution to the problem of understanding the links between "personal troubles" and "public issues"' (1983, cited in Cohen and Manion 1994: 59). This, I argue, augments the development of a comprehensive understanding of how the individual experience throughout the conflict and the reintegration process influences social capital and the implications this has for reconciliation. A life history approach also enables the gathering of richer data from respondents than could be achieved through structured or semi-structured interviews, due to the highly personal, subjective and sensitive nature of conflict and reintegration. It is for these reasons that life histories were employed as a primary data collection and analysis tool.

The types of life histories taken were retrospective, as the respondents reconstruct the past events in their life using present feelings and interpretations. The mode of presentation adopted in this research was a combination of thematically-edited and interpreted and edited, with more emphasis on the thematically-edited mode (Hitchcock and Hughes 1995).[5] Themes were identified throughout the course of the life history and then became the guiding principles for the interpretation and editing process. This was due to the interpretivist tradition directing the methodological choices taken in this research, which aims to construct theories

---

5   Hitchcock and Hughes (1995) present an analysis of the three possible different types of modes of presentation of a life history: naturalistic, in which the life history is told as a life story largely in the words of the participant; thematically-edited, in which the informants words are preserved intact but presented by the researcher in a series of themes, topics or headings; and interpreted and edited, in which the researchers has sifted though the data and edited and interpreted accordingly.

via the understanding and interpretation of the phenomenon under investigation, in this case, the social reintegration of ex-combatants.

The life history data for this research was collected during one life history interview per interviewee with each lasting from 5–120 minutes. All interviews were audio recorded with permission of the interviewee[6] and notes were taken during the interviews. Although initially I planned to carry out three life history interviews with each interviewee as I hoped this would engender trust between the interviewee and myself, as well as providing me with an opportunity to focus the latter interviews on pertinent issues and unanswered questions, this proved difficult to do. First, to conduct three interviews with each interviewee required a significant time commitment on their behalf and this was something I could, understandably, not gain. Second, due to time constraints of my own I would have been forced to sacrifice breadth in favour of depth to some degree. In order to maintain interviewee commitment and to strike a balance between breadth and depth I chose to opt for a single round of interviews. However, through using PRA techniques prior to starting the life history analysis, I was able to introduce both myself and my research to the community prior to interviews thus gaining a degree of trust that was built upon in the interview process which was critical to the gaining of emotional access given the nature of the study. Additionally, this enabled me to attract suitable interviewees who would commit to the time necessary for such interviews to take place as those who volunteered to be interviewed were generally interested in the work and were willing to be interviewed further.

It was intended that 12 ex-combatants and eight civilians would be interviewed in each site thus providing a total of 100 interviews with a representative number of men and women among the civilians and female ex-combatants, child soldiers and disabled veterans. This, however, was not possible to achieve primarily due to the understandable unwillingness of some to give up a significant amount of their day for unpaid work and to those who committed to being interviewed but did not turn up at the arranged time. Those included in the sample for these two groups were selected through negotiation with a gatekeeper. In Kigali ex-combatants were identified and called for interview by the DRO in one of the districts and civilians were identified through my translator and through UN Habitat who took me on a field visit to one of their housing projects. In the communities my first port of call was the Executive Secretary in charge of the sector in order to introduce myself and notify them of my presence, the research I was conducting and the support I had from the RDRC for this. We would then meet with the President of the Demobs[7] to discuss the research and what I was looking for in terms of sample composition and an interview venue. We then arranged a time to meet a number of

---

6 Excluding two interviewees who would not give their permission for audio recording. Instead I took detailed notes of these interviews.

7 The President of the Demobs is an ex-combatant who is elected by other ex-combatants to represent them in the area in which they reside.

ex-combatants to brief them on the research and allocate interview times for those who were willing to be interviewed.

Civilians for the PRA exercises and interview were identified by the Executive Secretary or one of their subordinates. PRA is a particularly effective research technique as it empowers those being researched and challenges the dominance and power of the researcher thus giving more prominence to the voices of the researched (Gueye 1999). One of the primary reasons for using this technique was to be able to obtain a reasonably fast comprehension of the situation in the community prior to the use of other participatory methods whilst building the trust necessary for effective research. PCEs are characterized by a lack of trust and this may severely limit the ability of a researcher to gain the required data due to intense suspicion of the nature of the research and the outsider status of the researcher. In order to gain access it is often sagacious for a researcher to approach individuals in a position of power or respect as this not only enables initial access to the physical setting but also gains acceptance from the local population which is key to the quality of data collected. PRA techniques, conducted as the first research technique with community members, provided me with an opportunity to get to know those in the community to some extent before I engaged in a life history analysis, as well as enabling me to assess the overall dynamic in the community which, although somewhat superficial, provided me with a foundation from which I could build the bulk of my research. This period proved to be particularly important for the rest of the research process.

The PRA techniques were conducted in three of the four[8] community sites over two days prior to interviewing. Sessions were open to all members of the community. However, as the composition of these sessions was constructed by local leaders this would suggest that not all civilians had an equal chance of attending. Whilst such methods of sampling, both for PRA and life history analysis, are not ideal and issues of sample bias may have arisen as a result it was, nevertheless, the only way I could conduct the research. First, the existence of gatekeepers is a very real issue for social research of almost any nature and in Rwanda this proved to be an even bigger issue. Although I had obtained permission by the Chairman of the RDRC to conduct this research I had to also obtain permission from local leaders as they essentially controlled my access to the ex-combatants and the population as a whole. Second, there existed no sample frameworks for either the ex-combatant sample group or the community member group; therefore my ability to use probability sampling was restricted. Third, because there were a number of sub-groups within each sample group, each needed to be chosen based on their representing a certain type or group that is conceptually important (Miller 2000). In order to effectively achieve this, the use of selective sampling took precedence over that of probability sampling and as noted this was carried out through the identification of key gatekeepers in each research site.

---

8   In the Western Province I could not get people to attend the PRA sessions as it meant giving up a significant amount of their time which they would not agree to.

The time during the PRA techniques served as an introduction period to the community, as well as providing me with vital data concerning the physical and social constitution of the community and community dynamics. The first PRA technique to be conducted in each location was landscape mapping. This began with a briefing regarding the nature of the research and how the PRA techniques would be performed. All participants were given a chance to pull out of the exercise at any time. The use of landscape mapping proved to be an ideal entry-point technique in that it provided me with an excellent tool to engage the community members in the practice of PRA without risking the collection of valuable data. The development of a geographical map of the area, whilst interesting, was not of primary importance to the results of this study. It did provide me with an interesting overview of the village but, more pertinently, it did two things: first, it allowed me to build up a rapport with the community members which was of significant importance when conducting the other three PRA techniques and the life history interviews; second, it eased the participants into the PRA process giving them an understanding of, and confidence in, what they were doing which was crucial to gaining rich data in the subsequent PRA techniques. During this easing-in process, community members began to find their voice and would express themselves more. This enabled me to observe patterns of social capital and reconciliation within the participants themselves which would inform my analysis. This will be discussed further.

One of the more significant PRA techniques used was institutional diagramming and analysis as it enables an understanding of the levels of social capital in the community, particularly vertical social capital, and how they interact. The carrying out of this technique revealed a lot in terms of the maps derived but also in the mapping process. When deciding what institutions to include, whether they were internal or external and of small, medium or large importance to the community, as well as the criteria by which such importance could be measured, the discussion at times became somewhat heated. Whilst in most cases it would be important for the researcher to manage this situation and ensure everyone had their say, I did not do this. The specific reason for this was that the way in which people communicate and interact provides an indication of social capital and reconciliation. If certain groups are excluded from the activity it demonstrates a weakness in community networks that may suggest reconciliation is not occurring at a level previously thought or advocated. As the purpose of this research was to ascertain levels of social capital and reconciliation, observing the tacit relations between participants was important.

The undertaking of social network mapping was also of significant consequence to the understanding of social capital and reconciliation. Being able to comprehend complex social interactions is crucial to an accurate appreciation of how social capital is generated, restored and strengthened within and between communities, as well as what implications this has for the reconciliation process. Similarly with the institutional diagramming and analysis, debate arose between participants as to the directions and strengths of exchange within the community and this informed

Table 10.1   Rwanda social capital indicators

Proxy	Variable
Bonding and Bridging Social Capital	
Community Events	Increased feeling of solidarity Improved communication Promoted civic mindedness
Informal Networks	Informal exchange of information Informal exchange of resources Factors that shape exchange
Trust and Social Cohesion	Channels and mechanisms for exchange of information Existence and nature of associations and reason for creation Intermarriage and extended family relations Intercommunity relations and conflict resolution mechanisms Types, nature and organization of exchange and interdependence Nature and organization of assistance, mutual aid and cooperation Collective responsibility
Associations	Structure, rules and roles of associations Function: nurture, self-help, solidarity and cooperation
Vertical Social Capital (Synergy)	
Village Leadership	Types of leadership Roles in political, social, Religious and welfare activities How they shape networks within and between communities
External Agencies	Community links to Govt, NGOs and private sector

Source: Adapted from Colletta and Cullen 2000.

my analysis of social networks. Although specific issues were contested during the mapping process, on the whole concurrence was reached. Whilst this may suggest a level of exclusion, much of this was based around traditional categories of hierarchy such as men speaking over women and older participants dominating over younger ones. This in itself is important to realize as social networks in rural Africa remain very much defined by these customary structures and this does not necessary reflect low levels of social capital or reconciliation. Being able to allow the discussion to flow is an important skill a researcher needs to develop when attempting to achieve a truer understanding of current social dynamics.

The final PRA technique used was one developed by the author using previous work conducted by Colletta and Cullen (2000). Indicators of social capital developed by Colletta and Cullen for case study analysis in Cambodia, Guatemala, Rwanda, and Somalia were adjusted in light of the findings of the first phase of field study to reflect the changing nature of social capital. Specifically, these indicators sought to identify the key factors that constitute social capita in Rwanda. Table 10.1 contains the indicators used.

Community members were engaged in a discussion in which they identified proxies that contributed to the given variables in the table. This was, conceptually, the most difficult of the PRA techniques utilized. However, the debate that materialized through the brainstorming session gave raise to a number of valuable contributions to the understanding of how social capital is formed in Rwanda and identifying community-based mechanisms that facilitate reconciliation. Indeed, whereas when applying the previous techniques participants had, at times, been somewhat discordant in their discussion, community members now worked together to puzzle through the exercise. Moreover, in retrospect it appeared that the longer the participants worked together, the greater the agreement reached. This may have been a result of research fatigue but equally it raises questions regarding the contribution proximity and familiarity can have on reconciliation. Observation of participants interactions throughout the PRA exercises indicated that the longer they worked together over a two day period, and the more familiar they became with each other, the more in agreement their answers became and the congenial their association became.

Being Ethical in the Application of Participatory Techniques

Issues of ethics are of particular importance for two main reasons in this research. First, PRA and life history research, by their very nature, are invasive. They seek to uncover aspects of one's life that may have been suppressed for some time and may cause the respondent distress to recall and talk about. The issues that arise in a life history interview and throughout ethnography can also have ramifications for present life as noted by Roberts 'the recollection of past events is inextricably connected with people's current life and its place in the group and wider community' (2002: 104). Second, any research of a psychosocial nature in a PCE such as Rwanda will also give rise to a situation in which the content of the interviews may be disturbing for the respondent, and indeed for the interviewer. There is, therefore, a need for sensitivity throughout the research process. Indeed, as Smyth notes:

> conducting research in a manner that uses people as objects without due regard for their subjectivity, needs and the impact of research on their situation is ethically questionable. This becomes particularly apparent in psychological terms, since respondents may be at a stage of denial in relation to the horrors that have happened to them (2001: 5).

The combination of life history research and PRA in a PCE presents a potentially volatile situation in which ethical considerations must be a significant priority in the planning of the research and must permeate throughout the research period.

The issue of informed consent is one that is continuously of great importance when considering ethics in social science research. In life history research the dynamics of power regarding informed consent can be very different from other research methods. On one hand the respondent holds a great deal of power in that they control the degree and depth of information given to the researcher. This not only places them in a more comfortable position, but also ensures the researcher behaves in such a way so as to gain access to the information they require. On the other hand, the use of deception regarding the purpose of the research can swing the pendulum of power back to the researcher. In either case, informed consent needs to be acquired through the briefing and debriefing of each respondent prior to and concluding each session. Respondents were asked if they understood what the research was about and what was to be asked of them and were informed they were free to withdraw at any time.

Anonymity is another ethical factor taken into consideration when designing this research and was guaranteed to each respondent. The guarantee of anonymity is necessary for three main reasons: first, it is more difficult to attain a sample of informants if they believe statements attributed to them may be made public knowledge. Second, the quality of the material collected is better if the respondent trusts the researcher. The guarantee of anonymity is a good foundation on which to build a relationship of trust between researcher and respondent. As Hermansson et al. state 'interviews about painful experiences require adequate time and a relationship of trust' (2003: 144). Third, and most importantly, to protect respondents from any danger the information they provide may place them in.

The reasons identified for the need for anonymity are indicative of the need to be sensitive throughout the interviews. Crucial to the collection of life histories is sensitiveness, empathy and non-possessive warmth on the part of the interviewer (Plummer 1983). Without these attributes not only will the interview fail to yield the rich data required for a study of this nature but, more importantly, may result in distress and trauma for the respondent. Although sensitivity is critical to life history research, the very nature of the unstructured/semi-structured interview enhances such sensitivity. By allowing the respondent to recall events throughout their life over a period of time and in a relationship of trust the interviewee need only divulge information they feel comfortable with. If the researcher lessens the degree of direction they place on the interview the informant feels more at ease and is more likely to provide richer data.

Analysing Data Generated Through Participatory Techniques

In terms of analysis, this research was guided by the interpretivist tradition in that it aimed to construct theory via the understanding and interpretation of the phenomenon under investigation. Due to this, the analysis of the data collected in this study followed the realist approach in which 'the key point is that of constantly evaluating the developing concepts in light of concrete data – hence "grounding" the theory in data' (Miller 2000: 114).

The first phase of the research enabled me to identify areas that required particular attention, both in terms of interview technique and issues addressed, and as such provided me with a period of reflexive time in which I could further develop the methodology in order to be most productive in the second phase. In the first phase the life history interviews followed a loose form, thus allowing the participant to provide their account through monologue as much as possible within the constraints of the study. This, in turn, enabled me to identify pragmatic categories throughout the account, which would provide the foundations for analysis.

A strict following of the realist approach would involve the development of these categories through several readings of the transcripts after all interviews were conducted. The method employed in this research differed, however, in that the initial coding of the transcripts taken from the first phase, and the subsequent identification of the categories embedded within the data, was then followed by a second period of reading and coding from the second fieldwork phase. This revealed issues that required further exploration in the second phase and enabled the development of a frame with which to guide these interviews. The transcripts of interviews from the second phase were then read and coded using the previously identified categories, and any others identified. In this way, although positively contributing to data in their own right, the interviews conducted in phase one acted as a pilot study through which it was possible to refine the methodology for the second phase.

Finally, transcripts from the first and second phase for all interviewees were analysed and coded for a second time in light of the findings from each separate analysis. This, I believe, enabled the facilitation of the coordinated codification of the identified categories. Essentially, this process provided a skeleton, via the first phase, on which to affix the flesh of the second phase.

As with any methodology, qualitative or quantitative, issues of validity, reliability and generalization are of significant importance in the generation, analysis and presentation of data. These issues are particularly pertinent to life history research as the credibility of such methodology is often brought into question by the positivist, deductive school (Cohen and Manion 1994 and Plummer 1983). Questions of validity are 'concerned with assessing whether what actually is being measured corresponds to some external reality' (Scott and Alwin 1998: 123). In order to address these issues Plummer (1983) identified the following checks:

1. The subject of the life history may present an auto critique of it, having read the entire product.
2. A comparison may be made with similar written sources by way of identifying points of major divergence or similarity.
3. A comparison may be made with official records by way of imposing accuracy checks on the life history.
4. A comparison may be made by interviewing other respondents.

This research directly followed as many of the recommendations Plummer has made as much as possible. Numerous interviews were recorded enabling comparison interviewees. Available official records and written documents were also examined. This was done to ensure claims of validity are justified. In terms of Internal Validity it can be claimed that although the research meet with problems in the field, it was designed and executed in such a way as to enable causal conclusions. Similarly, External Validity can be claimed, as it is possible for the results of this research, at least in part, to be generalized to a macro level within the conceptual boundaries of this research. Finally, Construct Validity has been achieved when we take into account the theoretical framework at the beginning of this chapter and the way in which the methodology serves to operationalize such a framework.

Conclusion: Strengths and Challenges of Participatory Methods

The conducting of this research, as to be expected, threw up some challenges and obstacles that perhaps had not been expected and as such, necessary changes were made throughout. By conducting two phases of fieldwork it was possible to identify changes and adjustments that needed to be made and incorporate them into the second phase. However, such changes were relatively small and the basic structure of the research methodology remained unchanged. The adaptability necessary within this research is, however, important and it is throughout the research process that such skills are developed. By being reflexive and triangulating research methods within this study it was possible to mitigate against the biases that are a feature of most social research. This is particularly important as it is only through being reflexive that one can design methodology as robustly as possible and adapt it when necessary.

In the face of such challenges, the value of thorough preparation before one enters the field cannot be understated. Although one cannot be 100 per cent knowledgeable of the environment in any given place at any given time and a great deal of flexibility is required in order for researchers to be able to effectively adapt to the environment, it is through detailed preparation that such flexibility can be maximized. By preparing one's field trip as thoroughly as possible, with the awareness of what is being planned, in particular timetabling and lists of desired interviews, which will almost certainly not occur in the way planned, researchers are able to be flexible in their approach: a must for the effective and beneficial use of participatory methods.

Included in the preparation of fieldwork is the choosing of the methodological techniques that will result in the richest data. In terms of assessing the success of ex-combatant social reintegration, social capital restoration and the reconciliation process, life history interviews have proved to be very useful. By investigating individuals' life trajectories one can identify the events and issues most meaningful to them through their experiences; indeed, it is the respondents themselves rather than the researcher who identifies these issues. By triangulating the life histories of a number of respondents within the same group it is possible to gain a more detailed understanding of issues such as social capital and reconciliation. Additionally, by comparing the perspective of different respondents it is possible to gain a more nuanced understanding of the same issue. When researching social dynamics, life history interviews demonstrate a particularly beneficial approach to these issues.

A further way in which such issues can be examined with greater clarity is through the use of PRA techniques which, when used in conjunction with other methods, enable further triangulation and comparison through offering an additional perspective from the same respondents. Through their participatory nature, PRA techniques enable the creation of an environment in which contestation of perspective is encouraged and the debates that arise through the mapping of a village, for example, provide great insights into the power relations and social relationships within that village. By observing the playing out of these relationships in a cooperative endeavour one is privy to social dynamics that perhaps may not be forthcoming in individual interviews. Such techniques are therefore useful when time is short. In addition to the above benefits of PRA techniques, if used before any other technique they can facilitate the building of a relationship between the researcher and the researched through the relaxed nature of the process and the familiarization of the research topic.

Bibliography

Bell, S.E. (2004), 'Intensive Performances of Mothering: A Sociological Perspective', *Qualitative Research* 4(1), 45–75.

Bowd, R. (2008), 'From Combatant to Civilian: The Social Reintegration of ex-combatants and the Implications for Social Capital and Reconciliation', Unpublished PhD Thesis, PRDU, University of York.

Cohen, L. and Manion, L. (1994), *Research Methods in Education 4th Ed.* (New York: Routledge).

Colletta, N.J., Kostner, M. and Weidehofer, I. (1996), *Case Studies in War-to-Peace Transition: The Demobilization and Reintegration of Ex-Combatants in Ethiopia, Namibia, and Uganda* (Washington D.C: The World Bank).

Colletta, N.J. and Cullen, M.L. (2000), *Violent Conflict and the Transformation of Social Capital: Lessons from Cambodia, Rwanda, Guatemala, and Somalia* (Washington D.C: The International Bank for Reconstruction, The World Bank).

Dercon, S. and Ayalew, D. (1998), 'Where Have All The Soldiers Gone?: Demobilization and Reintegration in Ethiopia', *World Development* 26(9), 1661–75.

Giele, J.Z. and Elder, G.H. Jr. (eds) (1998), *Methods of Life Course Research: Qualitative and Quantitative Approaches* (Thousand Oaks, CA: Sage Publications).

Gifiner, J. (2003), 'Reintegration of Ex-combatants', in Malan, M. et al. (eds), *Sierra Leone: Building the Road to Recovery*, ISS Monograph Series 80, March 2003.

Gomes Porto, J., Parsons, E. and Alden, C. (2007), *From Soldiers to Citizens: The Social, Economic and Political Reintegration of UNITA Ex-Combatants* (Aldershot: Ashgate Publishing).

Goodson, I. (1983), 'The Use of Life Histories in the Study of Teaching', in Hammersley, M. (ed.), *The Ethnography of Schooling* (Driffield: Nafferton Books).

Gueye, B. (1999), 'Wither Participation? Experience from Francophone West Africa', *Drylands Programme Issue Paper 87, International Institute for Environment and Development, London.*

Hammersley, M. (ed.) (1983), *The Ethnography of Schooling* (Driffield: Nafferton Books).

Hermansson, A-C., Timpka, T. and Nyce, J.M. (2003), 'Exploration of the Life Histories and Future of War-Wounded Salvadoran and Iranian Kurd Quota Refugees in Sweden: A Qualitative Approach', *International Journal of Social Welfare* 2003(12), 142–53.

Kingma, K. (1997), 'Demobilization of Combatants after Civil Wars in Africa and their Reintegration into Civilian Life', *Policy Sciences* 30, 151–65.

Kumar, K. (ed.) (1993), *Rapid Appraisal Methods* (Washington D.C: The World Bank).

Marks, K. (2001), 'The Rwanda Tribunal: Justice Delayed', *International Crisis Group, Africa Report* 30, 7 June 2001.

Miller, R. (2000), *Researching Life Stories and Family Histories* (London: SAGE Publications).

Mokalobe, M. (1999), 'Demobilization and Re-Integration of Ex-combatants in South Africa', *A Defence and Development Project Publication. Group for Environmental Monitoring.*

Nubler, I. (1997), 'Human Resources Development and Utilization in Demobilization and Reintegration Programmes', *Paper 7, Bonn International Centre for Conversion: Bonn.*

Özerdem, A. (2002), 'Disarmament, Demobilization and Reintegration of Former Combatants in Afghanistan: Lessons Learned from a Cross-cultural Perspective', *Third World Quarterly* 23(5), 961–75.

Plummer, J. (1983), *Documents of Life: An Introduction to the Problems and Literature of a Humanistic Method* (London: George Allen & Unwin).

Roberts, B. (2002), *Biographical Research* (Buckingham: Open University Press).

Rocheleau, D.E. and Ross, L. (1995), 'Landscape/Lifescape Mapping', in Slocum, R., Wichhart, L., Rocheleau, D.E. and Thomas-Slayter, B. (eds), *Power, Process and Participation: Tools for Change* (London: ITDG Publishing).

Scott, J. and Alwin, D. (1998), *Retrospective Versus Prospective Measurement of Life Histories in Longitudinal Research*, in Giele, J.Z. and Elder, G.H. Jr. (eds), *Methods of Life Course Research: Qualitative and Quantitative Approaches* (Thousand Oaks, CA: Sage Publications).

Slocum, R., Wichhart, L., Rocheleau, D.E. and Thomas-Slayter, B. (eds) (1995), *Power, Process and Participation: Tools for Change* (London: ITDG Publishing).

Smyth, M. (2001), 'Introduction', in Smyth, M. and Robinson, G. (eds) (2001), *Researching Violently Divided Societies: Ethical and Methodological Issues* (Tokyo: United Nations University Press).

Smyth, M. and Robinson, G. (eds) (2001), *Researching Violently Divided Societies: Ethical and Methodological Issues* (Tokyo: United Nations University Press).

Thomas-Slayter, B., Barbara, P. and Ford, R. (1993), 'Participatory Rural Appraisal: A Study from Kenya', in Kumar, K. (ed.) (1993), *Rapid Appraisal Methods*, (Washington D.C: The World Bank), pp. 176–211.

Weller-Molongua, C. and Knapp, J. (1995), 'Social Network Mapping', in Slocum, R., Wichhart, L., Rocheleau, D.E. and Thomas-Slayter, B. (eds) (1995), *Power, Process and Participation: Tools for Change* (London: ITDG Publishing).

Chapter 11

Door Knocking in Sierra Leone: A Necessity in Post-conflict Research

Victor Asiedu

Introduction

Research in post-conflict environments has been gradually shifting from the conventional[1] to participatory methods such as rapid rural appraisal (RRA) or participatory rural appraisal (PRA). Such participatory methods are used mostly in rural areas where illiteracy often poses a major problem in obtaining the required information through structured questionnaires. Additionally, they are used to ensure that the researched become part and parcel of the whole research process. Whilst the use of participatory methods continues to grow, there is the need to question whether they, as stand-alone methods, provide the required information to obtain research validity in post-conflict environments where lack of trust poses major issues of concern. The critical insights developed within this chapter emerged from a technique used in Sierra Leone known as door knocking to gain the trust and confidence of communities before and during the research process.

Sierra Leone, a West African country rich in natural resources was plunged into political turmoil in the early 1990s when the Revolutionary United Front (RUF) led by Foday Sankoh invaded the country from Liberia. The political upheavals led the UN to intervene, and as part of the mandate, established a disarmament, demobilization and reintegration (DDR) programme as part of its peace-building process. DDR of ex-combatants is considered by many international policy makers to be one of the most vital elements in peace-building which stabilizes a post-conflict situation; reduces the likelihood of renewed violence; facilitates a society's transition from conflict to normalcy and development; and strengthens confidence between former factions and enhancing the momentum toward stability (UN Security Council 2000). Colleta et al. (1996) argue that a successful DDR programme is the key to an effective transition from war to peace.

DDR of ex-combatants, though a vital element in peace-building, has been criticized by some academics and practitioners alike that it focuses more on ex-combatants rather than communities and this can hinder efforts towards achieving

---

1 Conventional research method is where the researcher leads the process through structured questionnaires or interviews without participatory approach from the researched.

sustainable peace-building (see Galama and van Tongereen 2002; Özerdem 2009). Some of the criticisms raised are that ex-combatants are given preferential treatment over other groups such as disabled, aged, females and child soldiers, and this can create a feeling of resentment among people within communities (Galama and van Tongereen 2002: 220). DDR programmes are tailor-made for ex-combatants, and such individually oriented programmes can impede social reintegration (UNDP 2006). A community coming out of war is so devastated in its infrastructure and has few opportunities to generate income to be focused more on individual combatants instead of communities. Thus, to achieve sustainable peace-building, more research is emerging to suggest that everyone affected by the conflict needs to be assisted, not just the former fighters (Kingma 2002; Özerdem 2009). Özerdem (2009) points out that DDR programmes as part of the entire peace-building process need to be explored further to achieve a more sustainable peace-building. The research, from which the critical insights emerged for this chapter, explored how community-based reintegration could contribute more effectively to sustainable peace-building. It aimed at identifying and exploring critical factors for planning and implementation of community-based reintegration. It examined programmes implemented by non-governmental organizations (NGOs) with some level of community participation; and programmes planned and implemented by communities in order to identify the critical factors. The research hypothesized that if post-conflict communities involved themselves actively in the planning and implementation of reintegration programmes, it would contribute to a more sustainable peace-building. This research was conducted in some districts of all the four regions in Sierra Leone such as Bo, Port Loko, Kenema and the Western Areas (Greater Freetown and Western Rural) for a period of three months. These districts were selected specifically due to the large number of ex-combatants who settled in such communities with the assumption that community reintegration programmes in such areas would comprise of both ex-combatants and non-combatants.

This chapter first highlights methodological inadequacies of the conventional research approach such as lack of participation, and argues that many alternatives to this approach focus on participatory methods such as PRA. Next, PRA is discussed in the context of post-conflict environments to reveal the difficulties faced by researchers in this context, including the way in which conflict leads to animosity among citizens and creates an environment of distrust which makes it difficult for researchers to gain access, especially emotional access, to some respondents. Finally, the chapter introduces door knocking as a technique that provides a useful entry tool through which to address the question of a lack of access in post-conflict environments. Its application, benefits and challenges are also discussed within the context of the research conducted in Sierra Leone. The conclusion highlights door knocking as a useful research tool which enables trust building through familiarization, makes possible the gathering of valuable information by gaining both physical and emotional access to respondents, facilitates repeated interviews to enable cross checking of information, and ultimately enhances research validity.

Problems Associated with Conventional Research Methods

Over the last two decades, a growing awareness of the methodological inadequacies of conventional research approaches in post-conflict environments has stimulated the development of a variety of alternatives (Chambers and Mayoux 2005; Slocum and Thomas-Slayter 1995; Cornwall et al. 1993). These conventional research methods can be considered top-down with less participation from locals because research design and information gathering tools are regarded as that of the researcher (Preece 2006). Moreover, research projects that have involved communities have sometimes failed to effectively address issues of gender, age, and status due to limited community involvement which results in researchers including some groups to the exclusion of others. Lack of participation has therefore become an ethical consideration in research practice, necessitating the involvement of communities in information gathering for research and analysis (Chambers and Mayoux 2005). The importance of involving communities in research has made many alternatives to the conventional approaches to focus more on participatory methods such as PRA.

PRA, originally developed for use in rural areas, has evolved into a methodology that is used in a variety of situations including urban communities and this gives it a new term of Participatory Appraisal (Preece 2006: 202). In parallel with the persistence of traditional participatory methods, PRA is being used in various contexts, and according to Chambers (2007: 11) 'more and more practitioners/ facilitators have become creative pluralists, borrowing, improvising and inventing, PRA methods to suit particular contexts, sectors and needs'. This means that PRA is gradually shifting from its original principles of learning from rural people through face-to-face participatory approaches in different contexts. The question is how appropriately are these methods being applied in the new contexts?

PRA and the Post-conflict Environment

Although PRA has become a popular research method in post-conflict environments, there is the need to raise questions about its feasibility. Unlike other local communities, post-conflict environments are associated with a lack of trust and cooperation, emotional stress and trauma, grieving over the loss of loved ones, and abject poverty. In post-conflict research, an investigation sometimes enquires into an individual's personal life history or discusses very sensitive and emotional issues such as death or abuse. Hence, obtaining access to such people's information could be difficult, if not impossible, due to lack of trust.

Lack of trust may also limit a researchers' ability to gain emotional access[2] and therefore the required data from respondents. According to Bowd (2008), gaining

---

2 Emotional access refers to the ability of the researcher to gain social acceptance within the community and gain access to the rich data that respondents themselves hold.

emotional access is a difficult process sometimes due to the intense suspicion of the nature of the research and the researcher's status of an outsider.[3] Lack of trust restricts access to respondents and this eventually leads to under-representation[4] and poor quality information, both of which are methodological problems. It is important to note that the issue of trust is not new in social research and authors such as Lincoln and Guba (1985) have underscored the importance of maintaining a trusting relationship with gatekeepers and respondents in order to facilitate the research process. However, trust has not been addressed as a primary issue in social research whereas in post-conflict environments where respondents can hold back some information due to lack of trust it represents a cornerstone of effective research.

The lack of trust in post-conflict environments prompts questions related to the viability of using PRA methods, as stand-alone methods, to obtain the necessary information. Have they been borrowed inappropriately for post-conflict environments as suggested by Chambers (2007) above, and if so, are researchers obtaining the needed information? For example, how can a female ex-combatant who suffered sexual abuse in a conflict situation be willing to narrate her ordeal to a researcher she has known only for a day or less when that society or community abhors women with multiple partners? Also, how can an ex-combatant who sees foreigners as people who oppose their cause of action genuinely participate in some PRA methods and provide authentic information needed for a research? It is difficult for ex-combatants to provide information about themselves to researchers who are considered outsiders to jeopardize their position in the community (Jacobsen and Landau 2003).

Based on lack of trust in post-conflict environments which can hinder the process of obtaining information from some respondents, this chapter introduces a door knocking technique as a process that can facilitate the building of trust and thus addresses some methodological issues in participatory research process in post-conflict environments. It enables the researcher to gain access to respondents without the respondents holding back information as a result of lack of trust in post-conflict environment. Its use originates from marriage ceremonies in some African countries in which it is utilized to announce a suitor's intention of marriage so that they can familiarize themselves with their girl friend's parents in order to plan a formal marriage ceremony.

Door Knocking: a Useful Entry Tool

Door knocking as a concept has different meanings in different spheres of life such as politics, religion, aid and marriage. In politics, the term door knocking is used

---

3   An outsider is a foreigner or stranger who is not considered as part of a community. Such people are denied access to very sensitive information in a community.

4   Under-representation means insufficiently or inadequately represented.

to get supporters to do what is expected of them such as registration of voters to enable them cast their votes. In a House of Commons deliberation in the UK, on Friday 12 February 1993, Mr Stern, an MP, in canvassing for political parties to be active, stated that the Labour Party should carry out door knocking at all times and ask its supporters to register so that they can cast their votes and win the elections (House of Commons Debate 1993). In religion, door knocking is used to reach out to unbelievers and convert them. For example, in Switzerland, members of an evangelical church used door knocking to reach out to more people and preach to them about the Word of God. Door knocking turned out to be effective and people listened to the Word of God (Revival News 2006: 4). With humanitarian aid, door knocking is used to approach people for assistance. In Colorado, a Mexican couple who were deported from the US after living there for 16 years with their families knocked on the Casa's[5] door looking for work and a way to rebuild their lives (The Casa de los Amigos 2007: 5). However, door knocking as an entry tool in post-conflict research is analogous to that of marriage rites.

Door knocking is a ceremony where a man's family knocks at the intended fiancée's parent's house with a simple message that their son has seen a beautiful woman in their household and wants to seek her hand in marriage. The man's family present drinks or cola nuts as custom demands. Anarfi (2003: 32) termed such items as the knocking fee which establishes the man's intention of marrying the lady; the knocking fee serves as an indication of the seriousness of the suitor's intentions. The parents of the girl ask their daughter whether the drinks should be accepted. If the girl agrees, the items are accepted to signify her approval of the proposed marriage. After accepting the knocking fees both families can then meet to discuss the formal marriage ceremony. This requires some form of planning where the extended family[6] members will be invited to witness the ceremony. This means that marriage ceremony is not a one day process, but takes a number of months to several years (Ampofo 1997). Door knocking is however the initial ceremony that brings both the man and the girl's family members together in any marriage process.

From the different usages of the term door knocking, its utility is identified in certain key words: approachability, familiarization, trust and assistance. For instance, door knocking enable suitors to familiarize themselves with their partner's parents so that they can discuss other issues further and plan the marriage ceremony. Without such familiarization, suitors are considered aliens to the girl's family and therefore cannot discuss any marriage plans. It is only when a man has been introduced to the parents of his fiancée at a door knocking ceremony as discussed above that he can engage in discussions concerning marriage ceremony. This enables the family members to know the would-be husband of their kin. Considering the above, I argue that door knocking is a useful concept that captures

---

5   Casa de los Amigos (a non-profit organization) is a Centre for Peace and International Understanding in Mexico City.

6   Extended family comprise of parents, uncles, aunts, cousins and grandparents.

and conveys the need for familiarization in post-conflict environment to build trust and cooperation so that researchers can gain the information they need through the discussion with respondents in a manner that reduces the need for respondents to withhold some information. Like the marriage ceremonies, the researcher becomes part and parcel of the community and this gives them the chance to study the community in detail to know more and obtain the information needed.

The Application of Door Knocking

Door knocking was applied in Sierra Leone to gain access to respondents in communities. I used the first week to familiarize myself with the people in various communities I researched. Having door knocking in mind as a useful ceremony to gain access, I used a bottle of local gin to knock at the chief's palace. Following customary procedure, I used the linguist to announce my presence and mission to the chiefs and their elders. As a sign of respect I first called on the chiefs who are the head of the communities. During these meetings I informed the chiefs of my purpose and the importance of my research to the communities. After a short deliberation with their elders, the chiefs used their authority to grant me permission and asked their subjects to give me the necessary assistance for the research. The door knocking at the chiefs' palaces was very necessary in the sense that in certain places I visited, people wanted to know whether I have been officially introduced to the chief as a form of assurance that my mission was not covert, but of importance to the communities. Likewise, to avoid any doubt of my presence because outsiders are easily recognized in small post-conflict communities and their presence creates suspicion. I must say that the support I received from the chiefs was not one off because they assisted me in diverse ways throughout my stay in the communities.

Apart from formally presenting myself to the chiefs, I also presented small gifts such as books, children's toys, candy, and torch lights as tokens to facilitate the gaining of informal access to locals in the communities. I gave out these gifts as tokens of friendship to gain familiarity with the locals prior to conducting interviews, which meant that not all who received these tokens were interviewed. I could not even recognize some of them when we met for the second time but they were able to make me out and we had a chat. Also, some of these tokens were given at the end of interview sessions to show an appreciation of the time spent with respondents.

Additionally, I participated in social functions to create an enabling environment for discussions which provided me with much information, and also an opportunity to set out dates to meet for formal interviews. These social gatherings include community works, sports and games, funeral ceremonies, religious activities and having drinks together in order to identify various groups in the community such as the elites, ex-combatants (male, female, disabled and children), internal displaced persons (IDPs), and refugees. These community gatherings were places where people met and discussed issues pertaining to their communities. For example, during community works, the conditions of other community projects were made known to the locals, and also some local announcements were made. Newcomers were introduced to their neighbours at such events. During one of such community works I met an ex-combatant who became my friend and helped me greatly during my interview process later on acting as a gatekeeper.

It is important to note that prior to going to Sierra Leone as a researcher, I had worked in the country as a peacekeeper for over eight months; so returning to Sierra Leone as a researcher not only facilitated my familiarization process but made some locals to recognize and considered me as one of them – an insider. As an insider, it was assumed that I understood their predicament, hence people were very friendly and more approachable. It would not be out of place for one to argue that my acceptance into these communities was as a result of my previous encounter with some of the communities and not necessarily as a result of the door knocking process. Whilst this could be the case, it is important to note that I applied door knocking as a research technique to new communities as well as those familiar to me through my previous work. This indicates that familiarization enables access to communities whether they are communities with which one has previous work experience or new ones.

Door Knocking: Can You Do Without it in a Post-conflict Environment?

Having received this form of cooperation and friendliness from the locals, I contemplate how the situation may have been if I had not sufficiently familiarized myself both with and to the communities I conducted my research. How would they have responded to me? Would they have given me the same form of assistance or something short of that? In Sierra Leone, I realized that people living in these communities did come into contact with researchers every now and then, and an ex-combatant remarked that 'researchers who were more friendly and down to earth were able to get access to respondents better than those who approached them formally'.[7] On the contrary some locals were fed up completely with researchers, and deemed research processes as a waste of time, much more so with academic research which did not yield immediate benefits to them. This research fatigue in post-conflict environments can lead to respondents holding back information from researchers because of the perceived waste of time without any direct economic gain.

The use of door knocking addresses some methodological issues in Sierra Leone. First, door knocking facilitates access both physical and emotional to individuals and communities. On physical access to individuals, it was realized that despite the number of researchers who visit some of these war torn countries,

---

7 Author's conversation with an ex-combatant in Kenema on 2 November, 2008.

there are some people who have never reached out to researchers despite the wealth of information they possess. In Sierra Leone a respondent remarked that:

> since the end of the war, I have seen researcher come and go, but I have never spoken to any of them. They are a nuisance to me and my family because of the way they engage people's time without any reward. You are the first person I have spoken to at length concerning this war and this is because you have been with us through thick and thin. I wish other researchers will do the same.[8]

The above statement points to the fact that despite the number of researchers who visit war torn countries, some people have never reached out to researchers despite the wealth of information they possess. Despite the fact that lack of reward was mentioned, one cannot overlook the issue of trust in the statement.

Apart from individual access, getting access to communities is based on taking part in community activities such as watching football matches, participating in community activities, and attending religious services. This and other community activities helped me in organizing people for PRA techniques which formed part of my research methods. Taking an active part in community activities is a useful method because it enhances familiarization and enables information to be obtained.

Also, in post-conflict environment, getting emotional access is considered very important. People with low self-confidence and trust normally avoid researchers. The lack of self-confidence results from issues such as abuse, grief, loss of possessions, and unemployment. Even in ordinary life, one needs to get close to other people in order to know their past experience. During the door knocking process, I observed that such people find it difficult to talk about past experiences. As a peacekeeper, I realized that most female combatants for instance did not want to talk about what they went through during the war. Some female ex-combatants did not participate in the DDR process because of the stigma attached to being an ex-combatant. At a religious ceremony, I met a female ex-combatant who failed to participate in a DDR process due to the stigma attached. She shared her story with me based on a degree of familiarization and the fact that we shared the same faith. Meanwhile prior to meeting her, obtaining such information from a female ex-combatant had been very difficult. It can be argued that researchers need to use every opportunity to gain trust of respondents through door knocking.

Second, through door knocking, I chose my fixers[9] within the communities. I realized how difficult it was to get access to female respondents during the door knocking process due to some cultural and religious practices in the local communities. To break this barrier, female fixers were chosen to assist me in

---

8   Author's interview with a male ex-combatant in Kenema, Sierra Leone on 1 August, 2008.

9   Fixers are people who help researchers to get access to communities. They introduce them to gatekeepers and also help them to find their way around in the research area.

reaching female respondents who otherwise would have been difficult to access. In most of our interview rounds my fixers targeted females and involved them in conversation to establish good relations. It is noted that women understand each other much better because they have similar issues which are often ignored by men.

Also, I used my fixers as translators and had no doubt whatsoever that they were being deceptive in their translation because of the trust we had established. However, one cannot dispute the fact that inaccuracies sometimes do occur in translation due to a lack of exact words in some local languages: in an attempt to substitute some of these words with similar ones, one could change the whole meaning of a sentence. I checked these inaccuracies by asking the same question differently to confirm whether the same answers were given. I argue that door knocking enables researchers to choose competent and trustworthy fixers or translators to assist them obtain the information they need for their research.

Third, door knocking serves as a useful tool for snowballing in post-conflict environments. This is important because in snowballing a researcher can be biased unknowingly towards a particular group in a community when respondents lead the researcher to members within their own groups. The exclusion of other groups through snowballing runs a high risk of producing a biased sample (Jacobson and Landau 2003). In one of the communities I researched, the issue of exclusion of some groups became evident through familiarization. My first gatekeeper, who is a local councillor, gave me contact details of his confidants, better known as *kabal* in local parlance. I did not know that there was a power struggle over the management of the local community centre. The councillor who is a member of the ruling party wanted to constitute a new management committee to manage the community centre, and this was opposed by the members of the committee who were elected by the community. Through door knocking I was informed about that impasse and managed to meet the management committee for their side of the story. If I had not familiarized myself well with the community, I would have left without even knowing that I possess a biased data. The door knocking process enables me to identify various gatekeepers within communities who introduced me to their colleagues without much difficulty. The issue of focussing on some groups instead of all was avoided because I was able to identify various groups during the door knocking process in the communities. It can therefore be argued that door knocking is a useful process of getting access to various entry points to reduce research biases

Fourth, door knocking facilitates construct validity. In many qualitative research works, various variables are used to investigate issues. The question, however, is whether researchers frame questions to the understanding of respondents; and if they do, whether responses are a true reflection of what is being asked. In situations where researchers are unable to construct appropriate questions and respondents' answers fail to give accurate indication of what is being explored, research biases could result. Through door knocking, I realized the need to explain certain key concepts such as community participation, social capital, community capacity, and community capability to respondents to ensure they understood these variables and that their answers to the questions reflected this understanding. This was done through a pilot project where interviews were randomly conducted to ascertain the level of respondents' understanding. It is very easy for researchers to assume that respondents understand terms used in framing questions, but through familiarization it is possible to establish whether or not there is a need to explain these terms further. Even in situations where researchers explain these terms to respondents, the issue of trust will help the respondents to speak out regarding any misunderstanding that may arise. The importance of addressing such misunderstanding at the initial stages of the research is paramount for the collection of valid data and ultimately enhances research validity.

Door Knocking and Ethical Considerations

The issue of trust also plays an important role of informed consent. Door knocking enables researchers to inform locals about the nature and purpose of their research well in advance. During this process, I had the opportunity to negotiate and convince those who were not very comfortable of participating in the research process to do so. The trust that was derived from the door knocking process enabled respondents to give their consent to participate in the research process. In post-conflict research where respondents sometimes narrate life histories, consent is very necessary in the sense that any attempt to overlook that is tantamount to invading their privacy. During one of my interviews a gentleman who was narrating what happened to him after he had been captured by the enemy and taken as prisoner of war broke down in tears. I informed him of his right to discontinue, but he remarked that 'you are my brother so I don't mind telling you my past experience. How can I continue to keep all this information? Though I feel very bad telling people, it takes some of the stress away'.[10] These remarks indicate that however difficult it is for such people to open up to researchers, through familiarization and trust building their consent could be gained.

Additionally, building of trust encourages a large number of people who are undecided to take a firm decision to participate in research projects. In most of the communities, familiarization with the youth through community projects and social gathering enabled me to convince them to take part in some PRA techniques. I was able to mobilize people who were undecided to be part of these projects. One youth leader who wanted to travel to another village on some errands cancelled his trip so that he could be part of a PRA group. It is argued that a large number of respondents could enrich data collection.

Confidentiality is also based on trust. Without trust, it is difficult gaining personal information from respondents. The issue of promising anonymity alone

---

10 Author's interview with a male ex-combatant in Kenema, Sierra Leone on 1 August, 2008.

is not enough for respondents to provide the researchers with their personal information. Trust gives respondents assurance that their personal and confidential information will not be made public. Gaining such trust is not a one day process. It requires a period of familiarization through playing of games, going out, eating and sometimes drinking together. As a practitioner, I made friends with some ex-combatants who could confide in me. The trust was built over a period of time, and thereafter I obtained more information from them. The question, however, is how can researchers get enough time to familiarize themselves with respondents. Here, the issue is not to provide a time frame for researchers, but for them to be aware that guaranteeing anonymity alone is not enough for respondents to provide all the information they hold.

During the door knocking process in Kenema and Bo districts, I made it clear to respondents that their identity will be anonymous. Also I assured them that under no circumstance would my report point exactly to someone which could compromise the issue of confidentiality. Conversely, I encouraged those who wanted their names to be published. It is important to note that not all respondents wanted to be anonymous in post-conflict research. This is because not all information deals exclusively on personal issues. But in situations where confidentiality is required, researchers need to build a healthy relationship to gain trust of respondents in order to obtain the information they need. It is noted that confidentiality alone will not encourage respondents to provide every bit of information about them but, trust. Thus confidentiality and trust must go together to enable researchers gain much information from respondents.

Challenges of Door Knocking

Challenges of door knocking can be discussed under the categories of subjectivity, research ethics, and time. First, door knocking ensures that, to a degree, I became integrated into the communities' way of life. This could cause researchers to be subjective in their way of thinking and to reflect the community's perspective rather than being objective and independent in their analyses. In post-conflict environments where people cannot afford basic necessities such as food and water, researchers can be integrated into such communities by offering them some assistance. The gift giving nature of door knocking for instance can influence responses of respondents to reflect the views of the researcher and compromise the research findings. These gifts may seem insignificant to the researcher, but to people living in post-conflict communities, they will be considered as essential. At one point in time, I realized that I was getting more positive answers from familiar respondents than unfamiliar ones. This may indicate a desire on the part of these familiar respondents to satisfy what they thought I required rather than being critical in their responses so I kept comparing answers from both familiar and unfamiliar respondents to reduce subjectivity and research biases. I therefore argue that through constant self assessment and adjustment, and critically reflecting on the aims and objectives of the research, researchers can reduce subjectivity.

Also, door knocking could raise ethical concerns. It could be argued, particularly in western societies that giving presents to respondents is a form of bribery and therefore unethical; but how can we explain the time spent with respondents without given them any token? Many locals in post-conflict environments spend time with researchers who visit them to conduct research. The question is, are researchers exploiting these vulnerable individuals in such areas considering the fact that many researchers rely on their research to earn a living, promotion or qualifications? Can we say it is ethical to exploit these people who rely on foreign aid for their basic needs due to the effect of conflict? In many traditional African communities, visitors are customarily required to present tokens to their hosts because it is assumed that they have come from cities with all the fancy items. Apart from that, tokens are offered to show an appreciation or to return a favour, and in this regard, for the time spent with respondents. It does not mean researchers are enticing respondents with gifts to persuade them to provide information which they are looking for. Like door knocking in marriages, these tokens serve as an indication of the seriousness of researchers' to discuss issues with respondents and fix a date for formal interviews.

Another challenge associated with door knocking is the length of time it took to get emotional access to females: locals, IDPs, refugees, or ex-combatants. This difficulty could be attributed to culture, where women in Sierra Leone normally take backstage in activities unlike men who are always at the forefront and therefore easily approached, and religion, where the majority of the population are predominantly Muslims, and in the Muslim tradition visitors are welcomed by men. These traditions have influence on Christian families as well because I encountered the same welcome process. Many of my door-knockings first introduced me to men before having opportunity to speak to women. Apart from the cultural and religious factors, I realized that being a male researcher also contributed to this barrier. Female researchers, for instance, might have had easy access to women. I therefore argue that in order not to be biased, men researchers need to go the extra mile in their door knocking process to get emotional access to women.

Conclusion

Despite the shortcomings of familiarization, the need to establish a level of trust between researchers and researched in a post-conflict environment needs to be stressed. Door knocking facilitates the collection of data through building of trust between the researcher and the researched. In Sierra Leone, I used door knocking to familiarize myself with, and gain access to, individuals and communities. Through door knocking, I was able to familiarize myself with some ex-combatants and females who were difficult to be reached due to lack of trust; and also broke the barrier of the misconception that researchers are outsiders. Such familiarization facilitated my research process and enabled me to obtain the necessary information for my research

Additionally, door knocking enables researchers to choose competent fixers and translators; and also help in identifying various groups in communities to reduce biases in research. In certain communities, my research would have focused on some groups, but for door knocking I managed to identify different groups. Moreover, door knocking helps researchers to conduct repeated interviews or other PRA methods to cross-check information obtained from respondents; thus it provides rich data and enhances validity in research. Besides, door knocking enables researchers to identify misunderstandings that could be associated with certain key terms prior to the commencement of the application of the research methods. In Sierra Leone, the initial explanation regarding certain key words such as community-capacity, community-capability, community-located and community-based during my familiarization process contributed to the understanding of my research project by the communities.

Moreover, the importance of using local culture – door knocking – in addressing local problems cannot be overemphasized. It builds on local knowledge and it is understood by the indigenous people. In Sierra Leone giving out and receiving gifts is part and parcel of community way of life. It is a form of showing an appreciation but not bribery as some people would interpret it. Also, knocking at people's doors is the main process of reaching people within communities. In rural communities where mobile phones, telephones and internet are rarely used, the first approach to any family is to knock at the door at sunset when they are back from work. This however might not be convenient to other parts of the world where people work both day and night and use modern equipment such as mobile phones. It is therefore imperative for researchers to use an approach that is suitable to their area of study.

Furthermore, door knocking can be substituted to suit cultures in other post-conflict areas. Many local areas have cultures which can be used by researchers to familiarize themselves and gain the trust of the locals. I used door knocking in Sierra Leone due to the importance it plays in people's lives. In other communities, different forms of door knocking could be used to get close to the researched. I conclude by stressing the fact that in post-conflict environment the issue of trust should be the key word that needs to be remembered in all research situations.

References

Adams, J. (1998), 'The Wrongs of Reciprocity: Fieldwork Among Chilean Working-class Women', *Journal of Contemporary Ethnography* 27(2), 219–41.

Ampofo, A.A. (1997), 'Cost and Rewards – Exchange in Relationships, Experiences of Some Ghanaian Women', in Rosander, Eva Evers (ed.) *Transforming Female Identities, Women's Organizational Forms in West Africa* (Stockholm: Gatab).

Anarfi, J.K. (2003), 'To Change or Not to Change: Obstacles and Resistance to Sexual Behavioural Change Among the Youth in Ghana in the Era of AIDS', *Research Review* 19(1), 27–45.

Arnstein, S. (1969), 'A Ladder of Citizen Participation', *American Institute of Planners Journal*, July, 216–24.

Bar-On, A.A. and Prinsen, G. (1999), 'Planning, Communities and Empowerment: An Introduction to Participatory Rural Appraisal', *International Social Work* 42(3), 277–94.

Botterill, L. and Fisher, M. (2002), 'Magical Thinking: The Rise of the Community Participation Model', A refereed paper presented to the Jubilee conference of the Australasian Political Studies Association, Canberra, Australian National University, October 2002.

Bowd, R. (2008), 'From Combatant to Civilian: The Social Reintegration of ex-Combatants in Rwanda and the Implications for Social Capital and Reconciliation', Unpublished PhD Thesis, University of York.

Boyd, G. (2000), 'Village Appraisal – Is this a Case of Elegant Power?' http://www.caledonia.org.uk/appraisal.htm, accessed 15 August, 2008.

Chambers, R. (1997), *Whose Reality Counts? Putting the First Last* (London: Intermediate Technology Publications).

Chambers, R. (2007), 'From PRA to PLA and Pluralism: Practice and Theory', IDS Working Paper 286 http://www.ids.ac.uk/ids/bookshop/wp/wp286.pdf, accessed 15 August 2008.

Chambers, R. and Mayoux, L. (2005), 'Reversing the paradigm: quantification and participatory methods', Paper presented at EDIAIS Conference, University of Manchester.

Christoplos, I. (1995), 'Representation, poverty and PRA in the Mekong Delta' Research Report No. 6. Linköping, Sweden: EPOS Environmental Policy and Society, Linköping University.

Colletta, N.J., Kostner, M. and Wiederhofer, I. (1996), *Case Studies in War-to-Peace Transition: The Demobilization and Reintegration of Ex-Combatants in Ethiopia, Namibia, and Uganda* (Washington D.C: The World Bank).

Cornwall, A., Guijt, I. and Welbourn, A. (1993), 'Acknowledging Process: Challenges for Agricultural Research and Extension Methodology', Institute of Development Studies, Discussion Paper 333.

Galama, A. and van Tongeren, P. (eds) (2002), *Towards Better Peacebuilding Practice: On Lessons Learned, Evaluation Practices and Aid and Conflict* (Utrecht: European Centre for Conflict Prevention).

Gilchrist, A. (2004), *A Well-connected Community: A Networking Approach to Community Development* (Bristol: Policy Press).

Guijt, I. and Shah, K.M. (1998), 'Wake Up to Power, Conflict and Process' in *The Myth of Community: Gender Issues in Participatory Development* (London: IT Publication).

House of Commons Debate (1993), 12 February 1993 http://www.publications. parliament.uk/pa/cm199293/cmhansrd/1993-02-12/Debate-1.html, accessed, 15 August 2008.

Jacobson, K. and Landau, L.B. (2003), *The Dual Imperative in Refugee Research: Some Methodological and Ethical Considerations in Social Science Research on Forced Migration Disasters* (Oxford: Blackwell).

Kingma, K. (2002), 'Demobilization, Reintegration and Peacebuilding in Africa', in Newman, E. and Schnabel, A. (eds), *Recovering from Civil Conflict: Reconciliation, Peace and Development* (London: Frank Cass), pp. 181–201.

Kapoor, I. (2002), 'The Devil's in the Theory: A Critical Assessment of Robert Chambers' Work on Participatory Development', http://www.jstor.org. stable/3993578 accessed 19 August 2008.

Lincoln, Y. and Guba, E.G. (1985), *Naturalistic Inquiry* (Newbury Park, CA: Sage).

Marwell, G. and Oliver, P. (1993), *The Critical Mass in Collection Action: A Micro-Social Theory* (Cambridge: Cambridge University Press).

OECD (2001), The DAC Guidelines, Helping Prevent Violent Conflict http:// www.oecd.org/dataoecd/15/54/1886146.pdf accessed 21 August 2008.

Omari, P.T. (1960), 'Changing Attitudes of Students in West African Society Towards Marriage and Family Relationships', *The British Journal of Sociology* 11(3), 197–210.

Özerdem, A. (2009), *Post-war Recovery, Disarmament, Demobilization and Reintegration* (London: I.B. Tauris).

Padgett, D.K. (1998), *Qualitative Methods in Social Work Research: Challenges and Rewards* (Thousand Oaks, CA: Sage).

Preece, J. (2006), 'Participatory Rural Appraisal: Lessons for Countries in the North?' *International Journal of Action Research* 2(2), 198–221.

Putnam, D.R. (2000), *Bowling Alone, The Collapse and Revival of American Community* (New York: Simon & Schuster).

Slocum, R. and Thomas-Slayter, B. (1995), 'Participation, Empowerment and Sustainable Development', in Slocum et al. (eds), *Power, Process and Participation – Tools for Change* (London: Intermediate Technology Publications).

Revival News (2006), The Revival Fellowship Holland http://www. revivalfellowship.nl/reports/2006/eu_feb_2006.pdf accessed 19 August 2008.

The Casa de los Amigos (2007), 'La Voz de la Casa' http://www.casadelosamigos. org/documents/la%20voz%20de%20la%20casa/English%20spring07.pdf accessed 20 August 2008.

The World Bank (1996), 'The World Bank Participation Sourcebook', http://www. worldbank.org/wbi/sourcebook/sba104.htm accessed 11 August 2008.

The World Bank (1995), *The Participation Sourcebook* (Washington DC: World Bank).

The World Bank (1994), Agriculture Technology and Services Division (AGRTN), Agriculture Technology Notes, No. 6. Washington, D.C.

UNDP (2006) Practice Note on Disarmament, Demobilization and Reintegration of Ex-combatants, 2nd Quarterly Report (April – June), UNDP – MINUSTAH.

Chapter 12

Mapping Child Soldiers' Reintegration Outcomes in Liberia: A Participatory Approach

Sukanya Podder

Introduction

Traditional theoretical constructs of children as objects mediated by protective victimhood paradigms have today given way to a more nuanced understanding of children's participation, role and agency in disparate contexts of war, terror and global politics (James and Prout 1990; Rosen 2005; Watson 2007; Brocklehurst 2007). This shift creates the necessary intellectual space for reorienting the ethics and methods for researching children's experiences in conflict contexts and post-war reconstruction. At present studies on former combatant experiences use a mixed basket of methods, some invoking survey questionnaire formats for quantitatively significant samples (Humphreys and Weinstein 2004; Taylor, Samii, and Mvukiyehe 2006; Pugel 2006; Boas and Hartloy 2008) while a large body of work is qualitative (Utas 2005; Peters 2006; Jennings 2007). These range from ethnographic participant-observation including interviews, focused group discussions and more participation, to more proactive action research approaches. At the same time, research on children's involvement in armed conflict is both incipient and evolving, and hence the best possible methodological strategies for understanding child soldiering experiences and reintegration outcomes in particular continues to be understudied. Drawing on recent field research in Monrovia, Liberia, this paper situates the methodological puzzle in mapping reintegration outcomes for former child soldiers in contexts like Liberia where the distinction between civilian and combatant is ambiguous and overlapping at best. This poses challenges of its own and the role of participatory techniques through insider perspectives in reintegration programmes offers a qualitatively different vantage point for understanding the policy and execution of disarmament, demobilization and reintegration (DDR) programmes and its impact on youth.

The chapter begins by delineating the case background and explains DDR in Liberia in its operational and practical aspects. The second section sets out the methodological strategy, research design, possible limitations, biases and the actual process of field research. The third part focuses on important ethical dilemmas that complicate research with child soldiers, rendering the use of a flexible, fluid and inclusive research design necessary. The conclusion reiterates that data collection in post-conflict contexts like Liberia must be adaptive; while insider perspectives into DDR programming provide a valuable triangulation tool and enhance validity by including policy perspectives to balance former combatant and elite level renditions, they are not foolproof. Biases, and the dangers of fabrication and concealment remain and hence all narratives and self-reports need to be represented carefully and cross-checked with more authentic sources of information about reintegration programmes and profile of beneficiaries.

Background

Youth participation in civil conflicts in West Africa has been interpreted as a crisis of youth, a product of limited educational and social access, making youth easy recruits (Richards 1996; Abdullah et al. 1997). Both Sierra Leone and Liberia have been sites for large scale UN mandated DDR programmes, which provide the context for analysing recent reintegration praxis for former child soldiers, given the large number of children and youth who participated in these conflicts. Also, many combatants who demobilized as adults began their participation as young people and underwent specific personal and conflict related experiences, transformations. Another point here is that protracted and recurrent conflicts in Liberia has not only robbed an entire generation of youth of education and professional development opportunities, but also weakened the control of traditional elders and erstwhile stringent social norms on youth. This has important implications for post-conflict social dynamics and is intrinsically related to the question of youth empowerment in the region.

In Liberia, the initiation of a protracted civil conflict can be traced to 1989, when Charles Taylor, a rebel leader, advanced to topple President Samuel K. Doe's regime on Christmas Eve, 1989. Fourteen years of conflict was interspersed with truncated truce attempts prominently in 1997 when a DDR process was launched. A failed DDR and the installation of warlord Taylor as President breathed new life into the conflict. During 1999–2003 the Liberians United for Reconciliation and Democracy (LURD) and the Movement for Democracy in Liberia (MODEL) insurrections provided fresh poles of resistance to Taylor's hegemonic rule (Brabazon 2003; Levitt 2005; Pugel 2006) and finally brought the conflict to a close. The second DDR programme in Liberia formally began in December 2003 following the Accra Accords (2003).[1] The DD components came to a formal end in November 2004 (Jennings 2007: 209) and the reintegration phase is towards its last stages in 2009.

Problems with DDR programmes range from cheating, exclusion, lack of access, to spiraling enrolment and inflated caseloads. Some of these problems were part and parcel of DDR in Liberia. The entire process has been donor driven

---

1   UN Security Council Resolution 1509 provided the legal framework for the deployment of peacekeeping operations in Liberia.

with D and D undertaken by the United Nations Mission in Liberia (UNMIL) and the RR by the United Nations Development Programme (UNDP). In terms of costs, the D and D phases had a budget of US $12.4 million, while US $72 million was allocated to the R and R phases under the Trust Fund for disarmament, demobilization, rehabilitation and reintegration (DDRR).[2] Responsibility for reintegration was transferred to the National Center for the Dissemination of Disability Research (NCDDRR) from the UNDP in April 2007 although UNDP programmes were completed only in October 2007. The reintegration phase has been extended by presidential decree and is slated to be completed by the end of 2009 with the focus now on training 23,000 ex-combatants part of a residual caseload list prepared by the NCDDR. This final phase is being funded with an additional 20 million dollars from the Norwegian government.[3] With respect to child soldiers, the United Nations Children's Fund (UNICEF) is the designated lead agency. Nevertheless a host of other international and local non-governmental organizations (NGOs) have been engaged in reintegrating former child soldiers into society.

According to UNMIL (2006) an estimated 11,780 children, 9,042 boys and 2,738 girls, went through a system of demobilization, interim care, family tracing, and reunification following the 2003 peace agreement. This was my target group, however given that five years had elapsed since the Accra agreement, the majority of those who demobilized as child soldiers are now adults, hence there was an attempt on my part to focus on youth in their early 20s inorder to grasp the dynamics of reintegration outcomes in Liberia. The next section sets forth the research methodology, choice of techniques and some of the practical challenges encountered in mapping of reintegration outcomes for former child soldiers in contexts like Liberia.

Research Methodology

Contemporary narratives on child soldiering appear to be polarized between capabilities/agency and the incapacity/vulnerability dichotomy. Even terminologies such as child soldier have come to connote a specific discursive content and pejorative

---

2   The Trust Fund for DDRR was responsible for funding the reintegration phase implemented by the UNDP until October 2007. The Trust Fund included contributions from European Commission (22.2 million) US (19.9 million) Sweden/AIDS (6.8 million) UNMIL (devolution) 6.4 million, UK DFID (5.4 million), Denmark (3.5 million) Ireland (1.2 million) Norway (1.2 million) Switzerland (0.8 million) CPR-Small Arms Reduction (0.6 million) Iceland (0.01 million) with total contribution of 68 million dollars. Other initiatives were funded by the European Commission and USAID, and implemented by agencies like UNICEF (www.pangea.org).

3   Interview with Programme Manager, IOM, Liberia Mr Ferdinand Paredes (3 December 2008) and Ms Muriel Nelson NCDDR Programme Coordinator for Residual RR Caseload (7 December, 2008); Interview with Ms Joan Bao In Programme Manager UNDP (10 December, 2008) Monrovia and Mr Philip Assale, Programme Manager, UNDP Monrovia and Lofa (14 December, 2008).

connotation which needs to be balanced with more nuanced and contextualized perspectives. No longer can children be approached from a simplistic protectionist and vulnerability lens, preliminary fieldwork with child soldiers in Mindanao and present ethnographic evidence from West Africa (Shepler 2002; Hoffman 2005; Richards 2005; Utas 2005; Peters 2007; Stovel 2007; Jennings 2007; Boas and Hatloy 2008) support the agency elements of children's decision to participate in armed factions.

Flowing from there, the ontological position that informs this research is constructivist – interpretist in lineage and belief. The social world gains meaning from the interpretations and interactions of social actors, and in this research, operational concepts of childhood, child, and soldier are all contingent on contextual and cultural particularities. Any study which seeks to understand experiences, motivations and intentions that inform choices of participating in armed groups, decisions to leave or return to home communities, or settle away from one's roots, involves distinct stages and processes of individual decision-making choices independent of external and structural conditions. This fluidity inherent in reintegration dynamics demands a deeper understanding of operational lapses and possible shortcomings which ethnographic methods can offer.

In this research, three main ethnographic tools were used – elite interviews, life histories, and participant observation as part of an international agency programme on reintegration of ex-combatants. Denov and Maclure suggest that 'by illuminating identities that are often shaped in childhood and adolescence, life histories can provide listeners and readers with insights into the course of human development and the workings of the human mind' (2007: 246) and this was true in my own experience of researching former child soldiers. However, ethnographic research transmutes between insider/outsider perspectives which involves important issues of neutrality, and ethics (Wessels 1998: 638). As Labaree points out 'a common assumption made about participant observation is that being an insider offers a distinct advantage in terms of accessing and understanding the culture' (2002: 97). However, these advantages as I found out are not absolute, ethical and methodological dilemmas associated with entering the field, positioning and disclosure, shared relationships and disengagement which need to be privileged in the research design (Labaree 2002: 97–8; Groves 2006: 103–4).

During this field probe, two main groups were targets for my research. The first were policy makers and implementers of DDR, for which elite interviews were conducted. The second were the ex-combatants part of the DDR programme. In Liberia, there is great diversity with respect to the ex-combatant caseload, which subsumes different groups of beneficiaries, spread across variant age groups, with involvement spanning over different time periods, diverse levels and forms of participation. My sample population for interviews was constructed on the basis of non-probability sampling involving quota and snowballing techniques, for identifying key elites and ex-combatants who had received some form of reintegration support under the DDR programme.

Possible sources of bias in this research include methodological, respondent biases, and problems flowing from insider/outsider dichotomy (Hermann 2001) given that the likelihood of exaggeration or fabrication in self-reports and in key informant interviews always remain. The main tool for correcting these is through a test–re-test method, which is triangulation by using different methods, or in-method variation, diverse sources, theories or frameworks of analysis. With respect to methodological triangulation, there can be within-method and between-method choices (Denzin 1978; King, Keohane and Verba 1995; Stern and Druckman 2000; George and Bennett 2004; Berg 2007). However, triangulation in this research as was restricted to the use of multiple data-gathering techniques.

Data Collection Process: Insider Perspectives, Life Histories and Participant Observation

The following discussion delineates the steps involved in the data collection process. Although 20 policy level interviews were conducted to incorporate governmental and elite perspectives on post-conflict reconstruction and ex-combatant reintegration, this section focuses only on the more participatory aspects of the research, namely data collection through life history analysis of beneficiaries within the International Organization for Migration (IOM) project on waste management and participant observation of beneficiaries as well as trainers in the programme.

Insider Perspective

My attachment to the IOM, which was executing a German government funded initiative for reintegration of ex-combatants, provided opportunity for gaining an insider perspective on reintegration programme planning and implementation dynamics. With its focus on waste management training the IOM programme was perhaps one of the more innovative schemes compared with more conventional training options namely, tailoring, auto-mechanics, or carpentry and veered on the agricultural option which was underemphasized at the beginning of R and R in Liberia (see Pugel 2007). Working with a modest caseload of 200 ex-combatants, the IOM worked with four targeted communities in Monrovia, Soniwen, Clara Town, West Point and Old Road, to process and produce non-chemical fertilizer through composting. The fertilizer produced after two months of composting was shared with the communities for their agricultural production activities. Trainees were also involved in the production of wooden and metal bins for composting as part of their practical training that were also distributed to the communities (IOM 2008: 1–2).

A significant volume of literature over the years has dealt with the insider–outsider debate in qualitative research (see Labaree 2002). Merton (1972) defines the insider–outsider position as

....an epistemological principle centered on the issue of access. The issue of access can take two forms. It is either a monopolistic access, in which the researcher possesses exclusive knowledge of the community and its members, or the researcher has privileged access, in which he or she has a claim to the hidden knowledge of the group that an outsider must otherwise acquire at greater risk (cited in Labaree 2002: 99).

However, for me, working with the IOM trainers helped resolve issues of access and provided entry into the life and experiences of ex-combatants. These trainers had gained trust of the beneficiaries over an eight month period of daily interaction, and in working with them, it was possible for me as an outsider to be accepted easily and to establish an ethical research relationship, which helped in conducting interviews for life histories.

Participatory Research Design

As a way of grasping the experiences and challenges faced by the former combatants in the programme, many of whom began their participation as child soldiers, and of the intervening agency, a participatory research design was developed as an evaluation tool for reintegration programming success at a macro level and for mapping micro level impact on beneficiaries in what proved to be a fluid and flexible learning process for me and my IOM colleagues.

In terms of designing the research, semi-structured interviews I felt could provide an insight into the workings of the inner mind, given that most of the beneficiaries had a limited time in which they could be engaged, most were on placement and learning composting in weekly schedules. Also, given low levels of educational attainment among my research participants, there was need to avoid analytical or technical exercises with them. The process of engaging them in free conversational mode, where they could add or illustrate by providing insights proved to be more productive instead. As a result most of the in-depth interviews veered towards being narrative and open ended story-telling, to allow a free and participatory research process. However this was interspersed with some structured questions on age, affiliation, status and mobility during the different phases of the conflict to keep a tab on timelines and experiences prior to and post-demobilization.

The most important issue for this research was defining the unit of analysis (Ames 2006) and here I focused on the specific rebel group to which former child soldiers were affiliated as an appropriate unit of analysis. I conducted 26 in-depth interviews. Disaggregated across factions, 11 of my informants were former LURD, eight were ex-National Patriotic Front of Liberia (NPFL)/Taylor militia/GoL, four were ex-MODEL, one ex-United Liberation Movement of Liberia for Democracy (ULIMO), two were ex-Armed Forces of Liberia (AFL) and one ex-Liberian Peace Council (LPC). There were some cases of overlap, for example one former AFL cadre had later joined LURD in late phases of the conflict, and another had changed affiliation from the United Liberation Movement of Liberia for Democracy (ULIMO) to the LURD, while a third had shifted from the Taylor militia to the LURD.

Most of my interviewees were men, partly due to the relatively lower enrolment levels of women in the Liberian DDR programme, and only two women ex-combatants were interviewed. A typical person-to-person interview lasted 60–75 minutes. Recording of interviews was allowed in some instances, however the presence of a tape recorder often created hesitation, hence after a few recordings, it was felt a free conversation in an isolated room with the help of my research assistant (Jestina Sannoh, one of the IOM staff and a trained nurse) would be more productive and this turned out to be true, with greater frankness being apparent in the non-recorded interviews. The participants were observed at their placement sites like the Monrovia Municipal Council (MCC) and interviewed in the IOM office in the capital.

During these interviews, questions were often used as probes, to help learn about what age the respondent had joined an armed group, which armed group and how the process of recruitment took place. Details on family and ethnic background, educational attainment, marital status, current and past employment and issues of demobilization, resettlement as well as exposure to violence and displacement during the different phases of the conflict were taken note of. There was complete freedom on the part of participants to interrupt, elaborate or add their own experiences to the context of the recent civil war in Liberia and nuance on the contextual particularities of participation, motivations, demobilization and post-war experiences, current livelihood and future expectations. Liberian English, though at times difficult, did not need translation and hand written notes were taken by us both. As I transcribed these notes later, inputs from my IOM colleagues, often helped in cultural interpretation and contextualization of Liberian life which was gradually pieced together through the life stories. One of the key objectives of participatory research lies in empowering the respondent and viewing them as agents in the process. In my experience, although the research did not incorporate mapping, drawings, or timelines as explicit participatory methods, this free flowing process of sharing ex-combatant experiences greatly enabled the respondents to feel they had legitimate grievances which made them fighters, as well as a sense of achievement for traversing difficulties and surviving in war-torn Liberia. This made many of the younger respondents and women, reflect on their current situation more objectively.

In terms of findings, most informants enrolled in the DDR programme at IOM said they appreciated the training, and felt such an opportunity was necessary for sustainable peace. Some responded with confidence that they did not wish to rejoin fighting, but seemed ambivalent on the issue of crime and post-war ex-combatant networks. This was clearly an area of discomfort with a high incidence of robberies in Monrovia in the past few years; in fact there was a major jail break during my stay there. Most had ambiguous plans about the future, but some wanted to become doctors and engineers and leave Liberia to secure a better education. In terms of post-war outcomes, most respondents had attended school, some were enterprising enough to finish schooling beyond the three year DDR support, either with family support or by selling scratch cards, or 'small small business' (Jennings 2007: 206) on a wheelbarrow. These snapshots into their daily lives – the difficulties of existence, like commuting from afar, to secure training and reliance on reintegration support payments to bring up their children added to my understanding of Liberian life. Most aspired for a more stable and permanent livelihood but remained uncertain as to how this can be achieved as revealed in excerpts from their life stories below.

Life Histories

During the war, an overarching compulsion for physical survival informed the decision to join armed groups and militias roaming the countryside for many. Looting and capturing villages for food and kidnapping civilians for manpower became a mainstay of survival. Girls in particular, who had been abducted or forcibly taken by rebels with the LURD, MODEL, or by Taylor militia men, found protection and stability in a single commander who offered a way out for them from forced and multiple sexual encounters. However by their own admission, these were short lived alliances that provided temporary solace and now when the war is over, children born out of such relationships live with these girls and have been taken in by their extended families, yet with limited support under the DDR programme most felt obligated towards family and kin, or felt trapped and ill-treated by them.

For instance, one of my respondents, now a woman of 27 years, revealed her immense courage in navigating her way to safety after being abducted by the Taylor militia men, and her life with another three girlfriends who were kept by these young men for sexual gratification. However, when real fighting broke out on the streets of Monrovia, the girls were abandoned on Broad Street and they avoided being recaptured by LURD members by concealing the password left for them by the Taylor militia men. She recounted that at a time when the LURD rebels were looking for men and women associated with the Taylor militia to kill and capture '...I managed to escape, and went back to my ma...she was very happy to see me alive'. This small story of deception and using the men to survive in war-torn Monrovia till the point of abandonment was evidence of tactical agency (see Utas 2006).

Another story of pure opportunism was narrated by an eighteen year old boy, whose brother was with the MODEL. He revealed how '...very young boys, feeling good and strong...' (i.e., empowered through the possession of a gun) were lured by the opportunity to '...ride around town in jeeps to loot...' and wreak havoc on shops and storehouses.

In the same vein, a young man of 23 years revealed without much fear, that he had recently invested US$25 to buy a demobilization ID in June 2008. 'I bought me a ID card...my family want me to learn, do something...' The idea was to access some form of reintegration training, and thus he found his way into the IOM programme. These excerpts suggest that both recruitment and reintegration experiences in Liberia have been problematized by macro level issues of economic underdevelopment, widespread political instability and continuing infrastructural and institutional lapses. A key issue in participatory research is trust, which has to be gained over time and is at best a fluid and variable issue, and is far from absolute, yet constant interaction with the beneficiaries and IOM staff over four weeks resulted in familiarity, which put my respondents at ease and resulted in a fruitful data collection exercise.

Participant Observation

I also incorporated principles of participant observer role during my time spent with the IOM staff and beneficiaries. Keen observation of behaviour, mannerisms, communication and body language in intra-group and inter-group interactions revealed important insights. There seemed to be some degree of distrust between the beneficiaries although one would ordinarily expect camaraderie in a group of ex-combatants, one particular incident illustrates this point. After speaking informally to one of the older beneficiaries, a former AFL cadre, and taking note of his demobilization card which he wanted me to see, it so happened that a smaller boy also part of the programme, came into to speak to me in my cubicle. While we spoke, there was a major commotion outside in the office space, and later it was revealed that the older man had lost his demobilization card. As events unfolded he was convinced that the smaller boy had taken it from him when they were briefly together in my cubicle. But to all our relief, in an hour's time the ID was located in one of his smaller jacket pockets, where he had not checked. This was a definite eye opener about how an older government soldier would look upon a younger, relatively inexperienced man who had spent at most six months with LURD, considering him a thief and less of a conventional soldier something he mentioned to me in his interview as well.

During weekends I would spend time at the workshop where reintegration kits were made. I could observe that some beneficiaries had become friendly with the trainers and they would hang out together and spend time assembling kits and exchange ideas of how to find more permanent employment. This showed a cooperative environment with the beneficiaries willing to learn outside of classroom schedules. Yet, the awarding of certificates at the Monrovia Municipal Hall in front of all-important officials from the NCDDR, the UNMIL and the German government was a contrasting, but insightful experience. Many of the awardees from the recently concluded batch of trainees were missing and seemed disinterested at the prospect of graduating from the training while some later explained difficulties in transportation others simply seemed to view the event as unrelated to their broader life challenges and were now on the lookout for new reintegration support programmes where they could enroll in the interim. These revelations were relevant for me, and helped me grasp the dynamics of reintegration both at a micro-level, and institutional level better. However conduct of this research confronted me with important ethical concerns centred on issues of gender, age, race and reflexivity which will be discussed in the following section.

Ethical Concerns in Researching Child Soldiers

There has been considerable academic debate over the ethical implications and potential harm of conducting social research, for both the researcher and research subjects (Hammersley and Atkinson 1995). Research is not a neutral exercise, and especially in post-conflict contexts like Liberia there remains considerable potential to infringe on the privacy, wellbeing and security of research subjects. Questioning young soldiers about separation, loss, rejection, death, violence and torture may revive past memories, and fears (Boyden 2000). Hence, several ethical concerns were central to the conduct of this research with former child soldiers and in mapping their reintegration experiences and outcomes. The first issue was that of acquiring access in an ethical and safe manner. In Liberia, where the ex-combatant label is often invoked as a privileged symbol, finding a group of ex-combatants who had experienced the war and who could offer valuable insights was a considerable challenge. This hurdle was negotiated during the field probe, by focusing attention on certified DDR participants, although in the course of the research process loopholes and cheating was evident as some of the beneficiaries had bought demobilization cards for as little as 25 dollars and gained entry in the waste management training.

The researcher's entry into the field and initial reception is intrinsically related to issues of cultural contextualization of his or her social identity, for instance marital status, age, physical appearance, racial, ethnic, class and national difference. For me as a single female researcher, there were issues of being perceived as available and some of the ex-patriot and local NGO people I interviewed and met would often engage in conversations which sought to probe my emotional availability, while others made blatant overtures and even went on to propose marriage. This was expected beforehand and I found ways of talking myself out of such uncomfortable situations and avoided being alone in interviews, and had my research assistant as company in most meetings. With the younger boys, and women in the IOM programme, being a woman proved to be an advantage, because they felt comfortable in sharing issues about their sexual experiences, regrets and hopes, with the older male respondents however this was at once a disadvantage. There was a tendency on their part to bottle up on these issues and most admitted to having witnessed incidents of sexual violence, but these did not elaborate on their own role.

A study about child soldiers or children more generally can be complicated by the unequal power relation that exists between children and adults (Alderson 1995; Mayall cited in Christensen and James 2006). This is compounded by physical differences which were relevant during the research process. On the issue of power differences, Wolf (1996: 2) suggests that these stem from several sources, such as differences in personalities of the researcher and the researched, contours of the research relationship which is established, and also in the post-field work dissemination of results. In my case affiliation to a western university and the IOM did project a certain degree of power and status associated with disparities in economic and educational background. But my personal effort involved being extremely honest, approachable and frank in my interactions. This resulted in interviews often serving as a conduit for transmission of grievances laced with an incipient hope that more interventions would be designed to address the limitations of present reintegration initiatives.

On the issue of race, colour and nationality, as an Indian Hindu woman, I did not feel a complete foreigner in the sense of the black/white racial dichotomy, besides having grown up in a multi-ethnic, multi-religious setting, I could identify with these cleavages in Liberia's social fabric. My previous exposure to pockets of rural and underdeveloped India also made Liberian underdevelopment somewhat familiar. Nevertheless my status as a foreign researcher was viewed as one of privilege by the locals and some of my respondents often asked whether I could help them study in the UK or give them money to buy books for school.

Another ethical concern was posed by the conflict between classical renditions on research with children which advocate data collection through adult care givers, and more recent studies which argue that children's understanding, interpretation and coping mechanisms are often different from that of adults (Morrow and Richards 1996: 98) and need to be leveraged in findings. In my experience, given the harsh and difficult circumstances that entail child soldiering, often informants who are below eighteen, though technically children are sufficiently mature and well-versed in daily survival skills. Hence they are far from children in the classic sense and quite capable of deciding for themselves. Besides, the process would have been far more complicated to mediate through their families who were often based in more rural counties.

Other ethical concerns included managing expectations, accountability and honesty in the research process and the question of rewards (Boyden 2000). These were addressed by honest submissions about the academic nature of the research, and reliance on small tokens of appreciation like pens, key chains, biscuits or a cold drink during the interview in order to make participants feel rewarded for their participation. In principle, I made an attempt to avoid making false promises of help with resources requested by some of my respondents, since it was impractical and would have raised their expectations. To ensure accountability, and willingness, informed consent was sought at all stages and any questions of a distressing nature could be refused a response if the informant felt uncomfortable or unwilling to talk on the issue. Efforts were made to strictly adhere to the requirements of confidentiality and secrecy in the interviews since there was a common acceptance of the fact that revelations of past deeds could have ramifications for the well-being of informants especially at a time when hearings under the Truth and Reconciliation Commission were ongoing.

These ethical challenges made it preferable to opt for ethnographic methods to gain insider perspectives into DDR programme implementation together with a participatory research design for interviews. This kept the research process in tune with the participants' selected lens for relating narratives about their recruitment, participation and time spent with an armed group, other war related memories and post-demobilization opportunities. Hence the research process was deliberately flexible and sought to give informants control over the research process. It offered transparency and minimized intrusion into their private lives outside the consent of participants.

Conclusions

My experience of field work in Liberia suggests that ethnographic and participatory methods are complementary in the context of children and armed conflict research. The use of participant observation and life histories, were a valuable source of information in mapping reintegration outcomes. Despite this, narratives and self-reports always carry the possibility of bias, concealment, or exaggeration and hence attempts must be made to cross-check information collected with more general authentic sources of information about reintegration programmes and profile of beneficiaries. Here insider perspectives into DDR programming gained through my close interaction with trainers and beneficiaries in the IOM programme, together with elite interviews with programme managers and government officials provided a valuable triangulation tool, enhancing validity by including policy perspectives to balance former combatant and insider views.

The research tools I selected provided a comprehensive understanding into the mindset, and underlying strategy of various stakeholders who have planned and implemented reintegration programmes in Liberia. At the other end of the spectrum, expectations and hopes of beneficiaries were also revealed in my conversations with them and their actual purpose of availing training in many cases seemed unrelated to the project itself. For most the monthly stipend helped them survive difficult economic circumstances and limited opportunities, several cases of cheating through manipulation or illegal purchase of demobilization cards and the recycling of the same ex-combatants in several of the reintegration programmes was also evident.

My research also suggests that mapping of reintegration experiences is largely contingent on the selected loci of analysis. The ex-combatant lable has had dual consequences both positive as well as negative, for former combatants and child soldiers. On the one hand, it has made it easier for this group to be identified, particularly those who have enrolled in the various reintegration programmes under formal DDR support, on the other hand, many former combatants who were not part of the formal DDR and are now without a demobilization ID have found themselves neglected and feel bitter due to this exclusion from benefits.

Data collected during the field probe gained from an inclusive, free and flexible and participatory research framework. At the same time, several ethical issues made the topic of child soldier reintegration a sensitive caseload to research in post-conflict contexts. Identifying the right informants is a major challenge in most contexts and is complicated further with child soldiers because with time they become adults and hence their life stores are reflective of childhood experiences laced with current adult life challenges. Transparency and inclusiveness in the research process though attempted in all stages does not guarantee reliability of data collected. Despite efforts to triangulate and talk to programme managers, elites and conduct focus groups with various child protection officers, the danger of fabrication in self-reports remain. Hence information collected in the form of life histories has to be accepted with some reservations. It is related closely to issues of trust and honesty, credibility of gatekeepers who provide access. One of the lessons drawn from this research is that the experience of child soldiering is a fluid continuum, hence the task of mapping reintegration outcomes needs to be flexible, and must transcend strict categories of participant observation.

Acknowledgements

This field probe benefited from the support and encouragement of several people, especially my family, Dr Alp Özerdem, my supervisor, Shri Upjit Singh Sachdeva of the Jeety Trading Corporation and all staff, beneficiaries at IOM, Monrovia.

References

Alderson, P. (1995), *Listening to Children: Children, Ethics and Social Research* (London: Barnardo's).
Ames, B. (2007), Methodological Problems in the Study of Child soldiers [online] Available at se1.isn.ch/serviceengine/FileContent?serviceID=47&fileid=0E93A C49-D6C4-1246-1020-7B28748FFED5&lng=en accessed 12 March 2009.
Bangura, Y. and Ibrahim, A. (1997), 'Lumpen Youth Culture and Political Violence: Sierra Leoneans Debate the RUF and the Civil War', *African Development* 22(3/4), 171–216.
Berg, B.L. (2007), *Qualitative Research Methods for the Social Sciences*, 6th edn, (Boston: Pearson Education International).
Bøås, M. and Anne, H. (2008), '"Getting In, Getting Out": Militia Membership and Prospects for Reintegration in Liberia', *Journal of Modern Africa Studies* 46(1), 33–55.
Boyden, J. (2000), 'Conducting Research With War-affected and Displaced Children: Ethics and Methods', *Cultural Survival Quarterly* 24, 70–73.

Brabazon, J. (2003), 'Liberia: Liberians United for Reconciliation and Democracy (LURD). Armed Non-State Actors Project', Briefing Paper No. 1 (The Royal Institute of International Affairs: Africa Program).

Brocklehurst, H. (2006), *Who's Afraid of Children?: Children, Conflict and International Relations* (Aldershot: Ashgate Publishing).

Caesar, R. (2007), 'The DDRR Process in Liberia', in Center for International Peace Operations (ZIF) and Kofi Annan International Peacekeeping Training Centre (KAIPTC) *Post-Conflict Peacebuilding in Liberia – Much Remains to Be Done*, Report of the Third ZIF/KAIPTC Seminar, November 1–3, 2007, Accra/Ghana, pp. 31–9.

Christensen, P. and James, A. (2000), *Research with Children: Perspectives and Practices* (London: Falmer Press).

Denov, M. and Maclure, R. (2007), 'Turnings and Epiphanies: Militarisation, Life Histories, and the Making and Unmaking of Two Child Soldiers in Sierra Leone', *Journal of Youth Studies* 10(2), May, 243–61.

Denzin N.K. (1978), 'The Logic of Naturalistic Inquiry', in Denzin N.K. (ed.) *Sociological Methods: A Sourcebook* (New York: McGraw-Hill), pp. 1–29.

Druckman D. and Stern, P. (1997), 'Evaluating Peacekeeping Mission', *Mershon International Studies Review* 41, 151–65.

Gary, K., Keohane, R.O. and Sidney, V. (1994), *Designing Social Inquiry: Scientific Inference in Qualitative Research* (Princeton, NJ: Princeton University Press).

George, A. and Bennett, A. (2004), *Case Studies and Theory Development in the Social Sciences* (Cambridge: MIT Press).

Groves P. (2006), 'Insider, Outsider, or Exotic Other? Identity, Performance, Reflexivity, and Post-critical Ethnography' [Online] Available at coe.csusb.edu/ Murillo/documents/InsiderOutsiderorExotic-Groves.doc accessed 15 February 2009.

Hammersley, M. and Atkinson, P. (1995), *Ethnography: Principles in Practice* (New York: Routledge).

Humphreys, M. and Weinstein, J. (2005), 'Disentangling the Determinants of Successful Disarmament, Demobilization, and Reintegration', [Online] Available at http://weber.ucsd.edu/~kgledits/igcc/dscwtv/hw_igcc2005.pdf.

IOM (2008) *Quick Impact Project on Reintegration of Ex-combatants through a Local Environment Initiative*, First Quarterly Narrative Report, October.

James, A. and Prout A. (1990), *Constructing and Reconstructing Childhood: Contemporary Issues in the Study of Childhood* (London: Falmer Press).

Jennings, K.M. (2007), 'The Struggle to Satisfy: DDR through the Eyes of Ex-combatants in Liberia', *International Peacekeeping* 14(2), 204–18.

Jennings, K.M. (2008a), 'Unclear Ends, Unclear Means: Reintegration in Postwar Societies: The Case of Liberia', *Global Governance* 14, 327–45.

Jennings, K.M. (2008b), *Seeing DDR From Below: Challenges and Dilemmas Raised by the Experiences of Ex-combatants in Liberia* (Oslo: Fafo).

Jennings, K.M. (2008c), 'Securitizing the Economy of Reintegration in Liberia', in Pugh, M. Cooper, N. and Turner, M. (eds.) *Whose Peace?: Critical Perspectives on the Political Economy of Peacebuilding* (London: Palgrave), pp. 157–172.

Labaree, R. (2002), 'The Risk Of "Going Observationalist" Negotiating Hidden Dilemmas Of Being An Insider Participant Observer' *Qualitative Research* 2(1), 97–122.

Levitt, J.I. (2005), *The Evolution of Deadly Conflict in Liberia* (Durham: Carolina Academic Press).

'Liberia DDRR' [Online] Available at www.pangea.org/unescopau/img/programas/desarme/mapa/liberiai.pdf accessed 15 March 2009.

Merton, R. (1972), 'Insiders and Outsiders: A Chapter in the Sociology of Knowledge', *American Journal of Sociology* 78 (July), 9–47.

Morrow, V. and Richards, M. (1996), 'The Ethics of Social Research with Children: an Overview', *Children and Society* 10, 90–105.

O'Kane, C. and Thomas, N. (1998), 'The Ethics of Participatory Research with Children', *Children and Society* 12(5), 336–48.

Paes, W. (2005), Eyewitness: The Challenges of Disarmament, Demobilization and Reintegration in Liberia. *International Peacekeeping* 12(2), Summer, 253–61.

Peters, K. (2006), *Footpaths to Reintegration: Armed Conflict, Youth and the Rural Crisis in Sierra Leone.* PhD Thesis (Wageningen University).

Peters, K. (2007), Reintegration Support For Young Ex-combatants: A Right or a Privilege? *International Migration* 45(5), 35–59.

Pham, J.P. (2004), *Liberia: Portrait of a Failed State* (New York: Reed Press).

Pugel, J. (2006), 'What the Fighters Say: A Survey of Ex-combatants in Liberia'. Report prepared for the United Nations Development Programme, Liberia. Monrovia: UNDP Liberia at http://www.lr.undp.org/UNDPwhatFightersSayLiberia-2006.pdf (accessed 18 May 2008).

Pugel, J. (2007a), 'Deciphering the Dimensions of Reintegration in Post-conflict Liberia', in Marshall C. and Knight A. (eds) *Assessing DDR Processes in Africa* (Alberta: University of Alberta Press), pp. 157–72.

Pugel, J. (2007b), 'The DDRR Process in Liberia', in *Post-Conflict Peacebuilding in Liberia – Much Remains to Be Done* [Center for International Peace Operations (ZIF) and Kofi Annan International Peacekeeping Training Centre (KAIPTC), Report of the Third ZIF/KAIPTC Seminar, November 1–3, Accra/Ghana], pp. 40–46.

Pugel, J. (2008), 'Disaggregating the Causal Factors Unique to Child Soldiering: the Case of Liberia', in Gates, S. and Reich, S. (eds) *Child Soldiers: Children and Armed Conflict in the Age of Fractured States* (Ford Institute for Human Security: University of Pittsburgh Press).

Rosen, D.M. (2005), *Armies of the Young: Child Soldiers in War and Terrorism* (New Jersey: The Rutgers Series in Childhood Studies).

Rosen, D.M. (2007), 'Child Soldiers, International Humanitarian Law, and the Globalisation of Childhood', *American Anthropologist* June, 109(2), 296–306.

Richards, P. (1996), *Fighting for the Rain Forest: War, Youth and Resources in Sierra Leone* (London: James Currey).

Richards, P. (2005), 'To Fight or Farm? Agrarian Dimensions of the Mano River Conflicts (Liberia and Sierra Leone)', *African Affairs* 104/417, September, 571–90.

Shepler, S. (2005), 'The Rites of the Child: Global Discourses of Youth and Reintegrating Child Soldiers in Sierra Leone', *Journal of Human Rights* 4, 197–211.

Stovel, L. (2008), 'There's No Bad Bush to Throw Away a Bad Child: "Tradition" – Inspired Reintegration in Post-war Sierra Leone', *The Journal of Modern African Studies* 46, 305–24.

Taylor, G., Samii, C. and Mvukiyehe, E. (2006), *Wartime and post-conflict experiences in Burundi: An individual level survey*, September 2006 [Online] Available at [www.columbia.edu/~cds81/burundisurvey/burundi/Taylor_ Samii_Mvukiyehe_Burundi_APSA06_061003b.pdf] accessed 13 March 2008.

Utas, M. (2003), *Sweet Battlefields: Youth and the Liberian Civil War* (Uppsala: Department of Cultural Anthropology and Ethnology, Uppsala University).

Utas, M. (2005a), 'Building a Future?: The Reintegration and Re-marginalisation of Youth in Liberia', in Paul, R. (ed.), *No Peace, No War* (Oxford: James Currey Ltd) pp. 137–54.

Utas, M. (2005b), 'Victimcy, Girlfriending, Soldiering: Tactic Agency in a Young Woman's Social Navigation of the Liberian War Zone', *Anthropological Quarterly* 78(2), 403–30.

Watson, A.M.S. (2006), 'Children and International Relations: A New Site of Knowledge?', *Review of International Studies* 32, 237–50.

Wessels, M.G. (1998), 'Review: Children, Armed Conflict and Peace', *Journal of Peace Research* 35(5), 635–46.

Wolf, D. (1996), 'Situating Feminist Dilemmas in Field Work', in Wolf D. (ed.), *Feminist Dilemmas in Field Work* (Colorado: Westview Press) pp. 1–55.

Chapter 13

A Participatory Approach to Ethnographic Research with Victims of Gross Human Rights Violations: Studying Families of the Disappeared in Post-conflict Nepal

Simon Robins

Introduction

Participatory research methods have increasingly become orthodox in empirical studies in both development and post-war recovery. In the development context in particular participatory approaches have been successful in not only learning about problems and needs from a grassroots viewpoint, but in developing solutions to address them. Whilst some of these approaches do not necessarily translate well into work with conflict victims, this volume demonstrates the success with which participatory methods are now being used in post-conflict environments.

Responses to gross violations of human rights have typically been motivated by a desire to either build peace following conflict or institute a legal response to crimes committed. As a result, in many post-conflict interventions both the individual and collective consequences of violations remain largely unexamined. To go beyond a prescriptive approach, studies are required that engage with those who have experienced violations, understanding the meaning that populations give to such events and the symbolic and social worlds people occupy (Pouligny et al. 2007). To root a response to gross violations in the experience of those most affected demands an empirical and an ethnographic approach to reach a holistic understanding of the transformations wrought by conflict. Such an approach necessitates empirical work of a highly interdisciplinary nature and an understanding of the role of the so-called primary institutions of the family and community that hold the key to recovery from such extreme events.

A participatory methodology is presented that allows such a comprehensive approach to the global impact of conflict on a population or particular subset of a population. This methodology allows the researcher to work with the conflict affected to understand their needs holistically, whether or not those needs are a direct consequence of their victimhood, and so inform interventions to address those needs. Here I will describe the application of this methodology with a set of victims of disappearance during Nepal's Maoist insurgency. Since a majority of those disappeared were men, the typical research subject was an indigenous rural woman from a peasant background of little formal education, disempowered both within her family and community and in the broader society, and potentially traumatized. A participatory approach to the research design and conceptualization, through a relationship with associations of families of the disappeared, offered a solution to the significant ethical and practical issues that arose. Giving victims agency over the research design and involving them beyond being merely generators of data increased their ownership of the research process. In addition to choosing and steering the research goals and methodologies, the community of victims was able to provide counselling and support to families around the research process.

Above all the aim is to allow the voices of victims to contribute to the debate about dealing with the past in post-conflict contexts. The methodology engages victims and their organizations in a way that identifies local resources, builds capacity and gives those organizations a concrete advocacy tool to increase their effectiveness. The approach has potential relevance in many post-conflict contexts, particularly in developing societies, where widespread poverty and unequal social relations sharpen many of the issues victims face.

Nepal's Conflict and the Disappeared

Nepal's Maoist insurgency was driven by a legacy of centuries of feudalism in a Hindu kingdom built on a codified framework of social and economic exclusion that marginalized indigenous people, lower castes and women. The vast majority of the nation's 25 million people live in rural areas, working in agriculture and living lives of desperate poverty. Within families and communities traditional culture relegates women to a subservient role, and women have been largely absent from decision making at all levels (e.g. ADB 1999; Majouria 1991; Geiser 2005).

In 1996, a small party from among Nepal's fractious Marxist left, the Communist Party of Nepal [Maoist] (CPN-M), declared a People's War against the newly democratic regime. The insurgency grew rapidly from its initial base in the hills of the impoverished Mid-west with the Maoists conducting military operations throughout the country. They propounded a politics that explicitly encompassed an end to exclusion on the basis of ethnicity, caste and gender and as a result a significant fraction of their cadres were drawn from these marginalized groups (Hangen 2007). Whilst disappearances had occurred from the start of the conflict, and even before it, the introduction of the Royal Nepal Army into the conflict in 2001 dramatically increased human rights violations of all kinds (INSEC 2007). Between 2000 and 2003 Nepal was responsible for a greater number of cases of disappearance reported to the UN's Working Group on Enforced Disappearances than any other state (Human Rights Watch 2003). Whilst disappearances[1] were also perpetrated by the Maoists, the vast majority were the responsibility of the forces of the state. Because of the ethnic profile of the insurgent forces, many of those disappeared belonged to indigenous minorities.

The conflict came to a dramatic end in April 2006, with a second People's Movement uniting the Maoists and the constitutional parties against a king who had again seized absolute power. As part of an ongoing peace process the monarchy has been abolished and, following elections to a constituent assembly, the Maoists are now the largest party in the legislature, and their leader Prime Minister. The conflict has left a legacy of some 15,000 dead (INSEC 2007), and more than 1,200 unaccounted for (ICRC 2008). Many of the agreements that formalized the peace process, including the Comprehensive Peace Accord and the interim constitution, committed both parties to the conflict to address the issue of disappearances in the short term. This included commitments to establish a Commission of Inquiry into Disappearances and a Truth and Reconciliation Commission. However, neither body has yet been established.

The disappeared are victims but so too are their families for whom the suffering of war continues. Whilst a minority of the disappeared are educated and urban with a significant number of students among those missing, most come from rural peasant backgrounds. As a result, most families of the disappeared are illiterate and poor. The disappeared are predominantly younger males with the result that families have been deprived of breadwinners and women of husbands, often with young children to support, further reducing economic security. Within communities, families of the disappeared are often stigmatized due to their association with the Maoists, and wives of the disappeared excluded due to their failure to behave according to their perceived status as widows. Families of those disappeared by the Maoists are very often displaced from their homes due to fear of the Maoists, and their problems compounded by a lack of access to land, property and community. Within families, the loss of a husband often reduces a woman's status, increasing vulnerability.

Families close to the CPN-M first established an association of families of the disappeared in Kathmandu during the conflict. This group, known as Sofad (Society for the Families of those Disappeared by the State) brought together families to campaign for the state to inform them of the whereabouts of relatives and to release them. Sofad also acted as a channel for economic support from the CPN-M to victim families. Soon after the end of the conflict family associations were established in other parts of the country, organized at the district level, often independent of any political party and trying to represent all victims, of both sides. Whilst all emphasize a campaigning agenda one of their most important roles has

---

1 According to the definitions of international human rights law only forces linked to a state can perpetrate enforced disappearance (UN Convention on Enforced Disappearance 2004); here, disappearance will be assumed to refer to cases perpetrated by both parties to the conflict in Nepal.

been to bring families with similar experiences together. In this way the family associations offered informal emotional and psychological support services to families of the disappeared.

The Research Concept: Participatory Research Design

In many contexts in transition from conflict there is a gap between the agenda of victims and that articulated by those working on their behalf. Whilst the victims' agenda includes demands for justice it also embraces needs around livelihood issues and social problems caused by victimization, which are rooted in the cultural context. In Nepal, the researcher worked during and after the conflict with families of the disappeared, and played a key role in catalyzing one of the earliest Associations of Families of the Disappeared. Since the end of the conflict victims, often from marginalized ethnic communities in rural areas, have become increasingly frustrated both at their inability to influence the transitional agenda and at being represented by elites from the capital remote from their own lives. This research aims to exploit the mutuality of the research agenda and the desire of victims for dissemination of their needs. This co-dependence allows a deep understanding of both the problems victims face, and their resources and strengths.

The research agenda is driven by the concept that victims best know their needs and how such needs should be articulated. As such, the research design and conceptualization process was executed in a participatory way with the family associations. The associations, together with individual families who are their members, determined the goals of the research process and the methodology. This was done over a period of about two months through a process of continuous interaction with two family associations, one in the capital and one in the rural Mid-west. The association leadership led the process but involved ordinary members of the association, both in their offices and through trips to field made by the researcher with association leaders. The researcher provided expertise and facilitated decision making through the presentation of options and discussion of possibilities. This was essentially an emancipatory approach (Oliver 1997) to participation, with the research driven by the researched. This is clearly a close relative of action research. 'Action research aims to contribute both to the practical concerns of people in an immediate problematic situation and to the goals of social science by joint collaboration within a mutually acceptable ethical framework' (Rapoport 1970, 499).

Participatory research design is an alternative to action research that can be used where, as in this case, the community being researched lacks the potential to implement a project autonomously. In addition to permitting group action that would otherwise be unachievable for the community being researched, participatory research design also empowers the community through close exposure to the implementation of the project of the research.

The aim of this participatory research design process was that the research would be rooted in an advocacy effort, would be ethnographic, and that the family would be the unit of analysis. The families' priority was for their needs to be communicated and advocacy can attempt to address this. The advocacy approach allows the addressing of many of the ethical challenges by ensuring that families both understand and are supportive of the research and can potentially benefit from it. The final research report, produced together with the associations, allows the dissemination of the results as a tool of advocacy. The family associations benefited from the expertise of the researcher whilst gaining a degree of ownership over the research results. The research must be ethnographic: many of the issues being investigated are both sensitive and culturally embedded, and only an ethnographic approach can offer the insights needed to understand the lives of victims and the impact their victimhood has had on them. The family is the unit of analysis: the nature of disappearance is such that it impacts families, rather than communities or individuals alone. In the Nepali context the family is the principle unit of social organization and is the most natural way to approach the issue. The range of victim families reflected the huge variety of Nepal's population, ethnically, by caste, geography and economic status. It was decided that whilst a qualitative methodology would be used, efforts would be made to ensure that the sampling would be such as to represent all victims to validate the advocacy component and as such, the sampling technique used was more typical of a quantitative approach.

The family associations participate in the research as a community of victims and following finalization of the research design were partners in the implementation of the study, with their leadership and members acting as gatekeepers and mediators with families. They briefed family members on the nature of the research and assisted in the building of trust between the researcher and the researched. Ethically, this engagement with family associations helped to address many issues (see below) and facilitated access to families, through the construction of an ethical relationship with research subjects.

Sampling

Different perceived needs exist in rural and urban, rich and poor families, and between families with significant contact with human rights agencies and those without. As such a sampling procedure was developed to reduce biases from preferential selection of certain types of victim. To achieve an unbiased sampling it was clear that families must be visited, rather than allowing some self-selection by research subjects through an invitation to a meeting.

The sampling frame used for the study is a list of persons missing[2] as a result of the conflict drawn up by an international agency, the International Committee of the Red Cross (ICRC), and published immediately prior to the start of data

---

2   The International Committee of the Red Cross (ICRC) use of the term 'missing' aims to include those disappeared by both parties to the conflict, as well as all others whose

collection (ICRC 2008). A selection of 10 districts from among Nepal's 75 was made that permitted the worst affected districts to be included, whilst also ensuring that a spread by region, geography: plains, hills and mountains; ethnicity and perpetrator: state and Maoist, was achieved. These 10 districts account for 43 per cent of those missing in Nepal. Within these districts a random selection was made, and these families visited and interviewed.

The concerned family associations selected focus group participants, independent of those interviewed in a family group. Whilst this does not yield a representative sample, it does allow peer groups to be created. These included: victims of the CPN-M or victims of the state from a particular district, wives of the disappeared from a particular ethnic group, etc.

The total number of families met for interview was 87, constituting 7.1 per cent of all victim families listed, with a further six per cent (74 individuals) who met in focus group discussions.

Research Methods

The research methods used in this investigation were chosen to optimize the utility of the data collected, and in particular to mix methods to increase the possibility of effective triangulation, given the various challenges to reliability and validity that may be present.

Semi-structured Interviews

For a study such as this, interviews are an ideal technique to allow families of the disappeared to tell their own stories and articulate their own needs. The interview is semi-structured, following a format prepared with family associations. A typical interview lasted around 90 minutes, beginning with a general discussion of family circumstances and an open question about priorities. Traditional hierarchies would often mean that a certain member of the family, typically the father or the eldest son, would be presented as the principal interviewee. Usually the entire family would be met as a group, with the result that all members of the family would have an opportunity to contribute to the discussion, much as in a focus group. This can be positive, not only for the support it offers during what might be an upsetting discussion, but also because it gives an insight into family dynamics. Since wives, particularly younger ones, were most likely to be impacted by social stigma where possible they were spoken to in private or with other wives of the disappeared, so as to best understand the social and family pressures to which they may be subject.

---

fate is unknown as a result of the conflict. In practice almost all of the missing in Nepal are those arrested by the parties to the conflict.

Focus Group Discussions

For individuals who may feel vulnerable a focus group can create an environment that is more secure for the expression of feelings, particularly where all members feel some solidarity. The most striking success of this technique was when wives of the disappeared were invited to discuss their problems, and chose issues in the family and community that have not previously been widely articulated by conflict victims in Nepal, and that were not heard in mixed or family groups. The different peer groups for which focus group discussions were held included wives of the disappeared from the Tharu ethnic group, family members from a single village where many disappeared, family members of a single incident of disappearance by the state, families from indigenous ethnicities as well as groups defined by the perpetrator of the disappearance such as state or Maoists.

Participant Observation

The traditional ethnographic method of participant observation was also used throughout the contact the researcher had with families of the disappeared. Given that the researcher met more than 160 families over a period of six months, as well as leaders of family associations repeatedly, there was an opportunity to collect a large volume of data. In particular, participant observation was an additional tool for triangulation, since it allowed the possibility to confirm or refute the verbal data gathered in interviews and focus groups discussions.

Implementation

Following the two-month participatory research design phase, data collection took place over a four-month period. The vast majority of families were visited in their homes, and some, in Kathmandu, at their work places. The researcher led all interviews and focus groups. A research assistant, whose role was to interpret both linguistically and culturally, accompanied the researcher in almost all interviews. Interviews were conducted in both Nepali and languages of some of the Nepal's minorities.[3] All focus groups contained or were accompanied by a member of the family association that had assisted in its organization, and a minority of interviews with families also included a family association representative.

The aim of the research, and in particular its advocacy goal, was explained to families, with the assistance of the family association members, and their consent sought for participation in and recording of the interview and focus groups,

---

3   Tharu and Maithili: Tharu is the language of the indigenous Tharu people who constitute the largest single indigenous group in the plains of Nepal; Maithili is one of the languages of the Madeshi community of the plains, people considered to be of recent Indian origin.

subject to the maintenance of the confidentiality of the participants. Consent to record was refused on two occasions, where notes were taken by hand. No family member declined to be interviewed. The recording of the interview or focus group discussion was later translated into English from the original language by a research assistant and transcribed for analysis. The texts emerging from the translation and transcription process were analysed together with the researcher's field notes of all interviews and focus groups, by the researcher himself. These texts were iteratively coded for analysis by both frequency of topic data and for selection of relevant text segments.

Response of Subjects to the Research and Ethical Issues

The response of families to the research was largely positive. A large number reported that the interview had allowed them to raise issues that troubled them, in an appropriate environment. One thread that ran through comments was gratitude that an outsider was taking an interest in their issues, and that this was the first time anyone had consulted them on their opinion of their needs and the action they sought. The advocacy approach was readily understood by almost all interviewees, who saw the researcher as a conduit for the transmission of their needs and problems to the authorities. 'Through you our voice reaches the Government and the work starts as soon as possible' (Wife of man disappeared from Kathmandu). The fact that the researcher offered a route to the authorities, who are perceived to be able to address their needs, was seen as empowering by victims owing to the remoteness and inaccessibility of the Kathmandu Government to many.

The data collection of this research involved interviews and group discussions with members of families of the disappeared. In most cases the individuals and families concerned were poor, of low formal educational attainment, often women and very often from socially marginalized ethnic or caste groups. They are also people who have survived the traumatizing effect of conflict, live in an environment that may still be highly divided and are being questioned about the issue of a disappeared relative that is potentially traumatizing. Such research subjects are highly vulnerable in many ways, and there are significant ethical issues to be addressed. The ethical approach is driven by the principle of *non-maleficence*, do no harm, (Beauchamp and Childress 2008), but beyond this, aims to achieve reciprocity with participants that promotes agency and builds capacity, through an ethical relationship between the researcher and the researched.

Security and Access

Security issues arise largely from an ignorance of local circumstances and thus could be understood through the family associations who were aware not only of local conditions, but knew the individual families concerned. Since most families were victims of the state, and the state remained largely absent in rural areas, there were few such issues. When dealing with victims of the Maoists however there remained potential issues, and in some cases families were met away from their homes for their security.

Access to victims is not just a matter of physical access, but also 'emotional access' (Bowd 2008), to ensure that research subjects feel able to talk. The volume and quality of data collected was a direct result of the victims talking freely and openly about their experiences and problems. This was most in evidence when the environment of the discussion lent itself to frankness. For example, women would only mention problems within their families when absent from them, for example:

> The relationship with my relatives and in-laws has been ruined. They see me as someone else's daughter, so I am an outsider and relations continue to get worse. They see the other sons [of the family] bringing money home and they see my children and me as just a financial drain: money is important to them. […] Sometimes I feel like leaving the house, but because of the love I have for my children, I cannot go (Wife of disappeared man, Dhading).

Discussions between family members were often the most revealing. An interview with the young wife of a missing man, in the presence of her father-in-law, had been unsuccessful; she was reluctant to say anything. Later, during a focus group, a loud argument erupted between them in which they discussed which of them would benefit from compensation since she had left the family home. Accessing such personal discussions demonstrates the trust with which the researcher was received; the participation of the family associations was essential in this.

Consent and Power Relations

Social science research demands that subjects understand the terms in which they participate in research and that they give informed consent to those terms. However, in developing states, relationships between a foreign researcher and the researched are likely to be asymmetric. To find what have been called 'routes to accountability' (Petesch et al. 2004), the consideration of ethics has to go beyond the terrain of confidentiality, consent, and risk/benefit considerations: in these cases, ethics is as much about being attentive to a collective morality that resonates in the context as to do with respect for the individual rights of the subject. As such, the best approach is one that prioritizes an understanding of the context and its local mores, and one in which local people, and the peers of those being researched wherever possible, provide the logic for the form of contact with subjects. In this research the main tool to promote this is the participation of the associations of families of the disappeared. Those leading family associations share culture and status, in almost all its forms, economic, ethnic, caste, and social with their members, but are often somewhat better educated. They are thus able to understand both the nature of the research and the demands made on the researched in a way that places them suitably to explain it to other families. The long-term relationship between the researcher and the family associations amounted to a prolonged process of negotiation of the obligations of the researcher, in analogy to the concept of iterative consent (Mackenzie et al. 2007).

Through the adoption of an advocacy approach, families could readily appreciate that the research could potentially offer them indirect benefit. Giving research subjects a stake in the research and its results, with a goal that could be understood by all, thus provided a route to accountability, in which the researcher is seen as a conduit for victim needs. 'Thank you very much for coming here and understanding our feelings. We just request you to give them [the authorities] pressure from our side' (Mother of disappeared man from Bardiya).

Social science research has traditionally adopted a very Northern primacy of the individual approach and considered the individual as the most appropriate unit of study. This focus has practical implications for researchers when seeking informed consent from individuals located in highly deferential communities (Nuffield Council 2002: 43). In this study these problems are reduced by the fact that the family is the unit of study, itself a more natural approach in a Nepali context. Whilst many families deferred to the researcher, families appeared content to see the researcher working for them from his perceived position of authority. There was, however, a significant number of families, notably those involved in the associations, where the researcher's long-term engagement with the research allowed a much more equitable relationship to develop, and where there was a perception that the researcher and families were working together towards a common goal. In turn, these families served as mediators with other families, able to explain concepts of the research in relevant terms that may otherwise be difficult for many families to grasp.

The concrete issues to be understood and consented to by all subjects included confidentiality and the anonymous transmission of statements. Recording was justified by the need to take the words of the families to the authorities, an accurate shorthand for the process of transcription and reporting, and was mostly well understood. Consent was then the result of a discussion within the family and involving the researcher. One potential problem with the family making the decision is the resulting dependence on traditional power relations within it: women, for example, will generally have less input to such decisions. This was an additional reason to ensure that interviews with women were made in groups of their peers, rather than family groups.

Psychological Issues

Interviewing those who have lived through conflict about their experiences is necessarily highly invasive. This is particularly true where, as in this study, the psychological impact of events is under explicit investigation. Whilst there is a literature on working with traumatized victims of conflict from a therapeutic viewpoint, there is little written on how researchers without an agenda to intervene therapeutically should proceed.

Some researchers 'believe that with skilful and sensitive interviewing, subjects actually benefit from talking openly about their experiences' (Bell 2001: 185), and there is some quantitative data to support this (Newman and Kaloupek 2004). Negative effects of trauma victims participating in research have also been found: there is a danger that having reopened the trauma, the researcher can cause emotional distress and then leave the subject in an environment that is unsympathetic (Bell 2001; Newman and Kaloupek 2004). However, most literature emphasizes the re-traumatization potential of public truth telling (e.g. Broneus 2008; Ilic 2004), particularly in judicial settings, a very different experience from this research. Re-traumatization is most likely to occur in those persons showing symptoms of post-traumatic stress disorder (PTSD) (Kammerer and Mazelis 2006). It is important to understand however that having a disappeared relative is not a pathology (Boss 2004), and that the vast majority of families live with no clinical symptoms of Post-traumatic Stress Disorder (PTSD), which may anyway not be a relevant approach outside a northern culture (Bracken et al. 1995).

Smyth (2001) draws attention to the timing of interventions with the traumatized: meeting subjects too soon after a traumatic experience may report early shock and denial, in contrast to the true impact of trauma. In this study the most recent violations have occurred at least two years previously, and on average five years earlier. Bell (2001) suggests that interviews should be made in the company of peers and that efforts should be made to provide support for subjects following interviews. In rural Nepal however no professional therapeutic service is available and peer support must be relied on. Efforts were therefore made to create the most supportive environment possible by making interviews either in a family context or in a group of peers. Individuals and families were met only after confirming with the family association that they were not considered to be vulnerable. In the case of three families, it was reported that family members had experienced extreme and disabling mental illness as a result of the disappearance. In all these cases the families themselves suggested that it was not appropriate to meet these individuals, suggesting that families had a good idea of which individuals could be negatively impacted by such discussion. The research protocols followed allowed the study to be implemented on the understanding that there was minimal risk[4] to those participating.

Many subjects became distressed during interviews, at which point the family was asked if they wanted to terminate the interview, but this offer was never accepted. On occasions when a wife or mother became distressed, a son or other family member took the role as the principle discussant, another advantage of the family based approach. The environment of discussion within a family or peer

---

4   *Minimal risk* is defined as the probability that harm or discomfort anticipated in the research is no greater than that ordinarily encountered in daily life (National Commission for the Protection of Human Subjects of Biomedical and Behavioral Research 1978).

group appeared to be both supportive and sustainable beyond the presence of the researcher. No interviewee was met where the upset caused by the interview lasted beyond the end of the interview, and no reports were received from the family associations of family members suffering any ill effects of interviews following the departure of the researcher. A handful of subjects made negative statements about the impact of the research:

> We had almost forgotten our pain; you came and reminded us of these things. The wound was healing and you scratched it again. We who have lost our husbands and our sons have been gradually forgetting the pain in our hearts, now you called us to gather and share these things. Why did you do this? (Focus group participant from Rolpa).

This prompted a discussion within the focus group about the nature of remembering the disappeared and the incidents that led to disappearance. Other members of the same group disagreed with the statement, saying that they did not seek to forget, and could not forget. 'I have lost my son, how can I forget him'. This goes to the heart of the nature of healing following such trauma, and the experience of the research very much confirmed the literature that suggests the most healing approach is indeed that of remembrance within a supportive environment. None of these statements challenged the minimal risk hypothesis. At the end of the interview or focus group all subjects were asked if they had any questions or comments on what had been said. This opportunity was not used by any subject, even those who had made negative comments, to mention a problem experienced during the research process.

Some of the symptoms described by respondents coincide with those of PTSD, including anxiety, nightmares, obsession and sleeping problems. However, another symptom of PTSD is difficulty in the verbalization of a traumatic experience, which was almost never seen in this study. Indeed, perhaps the greatest evidence in favour of interpreting the research experience as minimal risk for the vast majority of families was the enthusiasm with which interviewees talked: there was a determination to 'tell the story' of the disappearance and its impact. Whilst it is probable that some respondents had been impacted by the trauma of disappearance, there was no evidence of any harm being sustained by any interviewee, beyond the natural upset of discussing the disappearance. Hamber points out that 'the psychological healing process of testifying or telling one's story is not dependent upon the content of the story (as lawyers tend to assert) but rather on the environment and the process of the actual re-telling' (Hamber 1996). The modalities of the research resemble to such an extent the approaches to dealing with and addressing such trauma, in particular the disempowerment and disconnection[5] induced by trauma, that it can be said that the assumption of minimal risk is confirmed. This

5   Herman (1992, 135), writes that '[t]he core experiences of...trauma are disempowerment and disconnection from others'.

is further supported by the enthusiasm of respondents to talk, no adverse affects observed during interviews, and none being raised by the family associations in the weeks and months following the interviews.

Limitations of the Methodology

The greatest limitation to the generalization of this methodology is the need for mutuality between the research agenda and the goals of the community being researched. Equivalently, a participatory research design demands that the researcher yield some control of the research agenda, and indeed the research question, to the researched. Whilst this can be considered a violation of the positivist view of social research aims, it is a prerequisite of participatory research design and indeed of any emancipatory approach. Such an approach can only work where the research agenda seeks articulation or addressing of issues that the community prioritizes.

Whilst this methodology could well be used directly with a community, in this study much of the participatory contact was with the leaders of the associations, as well as with families directly. This demands that the group being researched has an organization or organizations that are truly representative: the power of the approach lies in the ceding of control to a group, rather than just to a small elite.

This methodology demands a significant investment of time by the researcher: the research described here took some six months, including two months for the participatory research design phase. Thus, this methodology is not appropriate for short term investigations or rapid assessments.

Conclusions and Reflections

This chapter has argued that the participatory research philosophy that has become routine in development work must be used in transitional contexts to fully understand the needs of populations emerging from conflict and so ensure that interventions and transitional processes are tailored to meet them. The participation of victims in particular in such recovery processes can best be ensured by both mobilizing those concerned to advocate for their own needs and ensuring that research engages with them. In many contexts victims come largely from those marginalized both within the state and within their own communities, and include the indigenous, the poor and women. With such populations traditional research presents significant challenges of access and ethics.

Here a participatory engagement with victims' associations has been presented that takes on board the participatory development approach and refigures it for an enhanced degree of participation, through a participatory research design. By ensuring that victims' groups are engaged in the research design as well as the implementation, a higher level of participation is ensured. This participatory engagement with family associations permitted a level of access and acceptance by the research subjects that would not have otherwise permitted the ethnographic approach that was sought. More than this it has served to build capacity within the victims' organizations. This engagement was predicated on the victims' own agenda and resulted in an advocacy approach that concretized the mutuality of interests of the researcher and the researched.

The methodology has resulted in insights into research approaches that can only emerge when the researched play a role in directing the research process. Here, the fact that it is the family as a unit that is impacted by disappearance, particularly in traditional cultures such as those of Nepal, determined the family as the unit of analysis in the study. This has further aided the addressing of some of the ethical dilemmas of studies with potentially vulnerable victims. Issues of consent and potential re-traumatization are lessened by conducting interviews in either a family group or in small peer groups, where support is available to those telling their stories and will continue to be available in the family or community once the interview is complete. Ensuring that the form and aims of the study are understood and that informed consent can be given was made easier both through the advocacy aim of the study and by the presence of well informed family association members who could mediate between the researcher and research subjects.

This study demonstrates the disservice that is done to victims by those who attempt to speak on their behalf, by generalizing or summarizing needs and by making presumptions about their needs, driven by limited understandings of both the experience of conflict and of the cultural basis of their lives.

References

ADB (1999), 'Women In Nepal, Country Briefing Paper, Asian Development Bank, Programs Department West, Division' (Manila: Asian Development Bank).

Beauchamp, T.L. and Childress J.F. (2008), *Principles of Biomedical Ethics* (New York: Oxford University Press).

Bell, P. (2001), 'The Ethics of Conducting Psychiatric Research in War-torn Contexts', in Smyth, M. and Robinson, G. (eds), *Researching Violently Divided Societies: Ethical and Methodological Issues* (London: Pluto Press).

Boss, P. (2004), 'Ambiguous Loss Research, Theory, and Practice: Reflections After 9/11', *Journal of Marriage and Family* 66(3), 551–66.

Bowd, R. (2008), 'From Combatant to Civilian: The Social Reintegration of ex-combatants and the Implications for Social Capital and Reconciliation', Unpublished PhD Thesis, PRDU, University of York.

Bracken, P., Giller, J. and Summerfield, D. (1995), 'Psychological Responses to War and Atrocity: The Limitations of Current Concepts', *Soc. Sci. Med.* 40(8), 1073–82.

Broneus, K. (2008), 'Truth-Telling as Talking Cure? Insecurity and Retraumatization in the Rwandan Gacaca Courts', *Security Dialogue* 39(1), 55–76.

Geiser, A. (2005), *Social Exclusion and Conflict Transformation in Nepal: Women, Dalit and Ethnic Groups* (Bern: Swisspeace).

Hamber, B. (1996), 'The Need for a Survivor-Centred Approach to the Truth and Reconciliation Commission', *Community Mediation Update*, 9 (January), 5–13.

Hamber, B. (2001), 'Does the Truth Heal: A Psychological Perspective on the Political Strategies for Dealing with the Legacy of Political Violence', in Biggar, N. (ed.) *Burying the Past: Making Peace and Doing Justice after Civil Conflict* (Washington: Georgetown University Press).

Hangen, S. (2007), *Creating a "New Nepal": The Ethnic Dimension*, Policy Studies No. 34 (Washington: East-West Center).

Herman, J.L. (1992), 'Complex PTSD: A Syndrome in Survivors of Prolonged and Repeated Trauma', *Journal of Traumatic Stress* 5(3), 377–91.

Human Rights Watch (2003), *Between a Rock and a Hard Place: Civilians Struggle to Survive in Nepal's Civil War* (Washington: Human Rights Watch).

ICRC (International Committee of the Red Cross) (2008), *Missing Persons in Nepal: The Right to Know* (Kathmandu: ICRC).

Ilic, Z. (2004), 'Psychological preparation of torture victims as witnesses toward the prevention of retraumatization', in Spiric, Z., Knezevic, G., Jovic, V. and Opacic, G. (eds), *Torture in War: Consequences and Rehabilitation of Victims: Yugoslav Experience* (Serbia: IAN Center for the Rehabilitation of Torture Victims).

INSEC (Informal Sector Service Centre) (2007), *Human Rights Yearbook 2007* (Kathmandu: INSEC).

Kammerer, N. and Mazelis, R. (2006), 'After the Crisis Initiative: Healing from Trauma after Disasters', presented at the *After the Crisis: Healing from Trauma after Disasters* Expert Panel Meeting, April 24–25, 2006, Bethesda, MD.

Mackenzie, C., McDowell, C. and Pittaway, E. (2007), 'Beyond "Do No Harm": The Challenge of Constructing Ethical Relationships in Refugee Research', *Journal of Refugee Studies* 20(2), 299–319.

Majouria, I. (1991), *Nepalese Women: A Vivid Account of the Status and Role of Nepalese Women in the Total Spectrum of Life, Religious, Social, Economic, Political and Legal* (Kathmandu: M. Devi).

National Commission for the Protection of Human Subjects of Biomedical and Behavioral Research (1978), 'The Belmont Report: Ethical Principles and Guidelines for the Protection Of Human Subjects Of Research', (DHEW Publication No. OS 78-0012) (Washington: Department of Health. Education, and Welfare).

Newman, E. and Kaloupek, D.G. (2004), 'The Risks and Benefits of Participating in Trauma-Focused Research Studies', *Journal of Traumatic Stress* 17(5), 383–94.

Nuffield Council on Bioethics (2003), *Pharmacogenetics: Ethical Issues* (London: Nuffield Council on Bioethics).

Oliver, M. (1997), 'Emancipatory Research: Realistic Goal or Impossible Dream?', in Barnes, G. and Mercer, G. *Doing Disability Research* (Leeds: The Disability Press).

Petesch, P., Smulovitz, C. and Walton, M. (2005), 'Evaluating Empowerment: A Framework with Cases from Latin America', in Narayan-Parker, D. (ed.), *Measuring Empowerment: Cross-disciplinary Perspectives* (Washington: World Bank Publications).

Pouligny, B., Chesterman, S. and Schnabel, A. (2007) *After Mass Crime: Rebuilding States and Communities* (Tokyo: UN University Press).

Rapoport, R.N. (1970), 'Three Dilemmas of Action Research', *Human Relations*, 23, 499–513.

Smyth, M. (2001), 'Introduction', in Smyth, M. and Robinson, G. (eds), *Researching Violently Divided Societies: Ethical and Methodological Issues* (London: Pluto Press).

UN Convention on Enforced Disappearance (2004), *UN International Convention on Protection of all Persons from Disappearance* <http://www2.ohchr.org/english/law/disappearance-convention.htm>, accessed 14 January 2009.

Chapter 14

Unexamined Lives: A Methodology of Women, Violence and War in Lebanon

Maria Holt

While women and girls share experiences with men and boys during armed conflict, the culture of violence and discrimination against women and girls that exists during peace times is often exacerbated during conflict and negatively affects women's ability to participate in peace processes and ultimately inhibits the attainment of lasting peace (UN 2002).

Introduction

In the late 1990s, I undertook a fieldwork-based research project into the effects of violent conflict on Palestinian refugee women and Shi'i Muslim women in Lebanon. My objectives were to find out whether women who lived through the violent conflict in Lebanon, and the aftermath of conflict, have been inhibited from full participation either in the conflict itself or in the ensuing processes of reconstruction and reconciliation by various forms of violence, both aimed at them directly and present in the general environment; and also, to explore how the efforts made by women themselves are making a positive contribution towards post-conflict resolution.

The components of my research were first, an exploration of Shi'i and Palestinian women's experiences of violence during the Lebanese conflict and in the aftermath of conflict; second, a more precise understanding of the treatment of women in Palestinian and Lebanese society in terms of Islamic positions on violence and female participation in conflict; third, an analysis of the development of national identity, its relationship with religious identity and how it is differently expressed by men and women in the two case studies; and, lastly, a discussion about the need for a new approach to thinking about conflict, one which will take into consideration the concerns and responses of women and also the possibility that violence may not be the normal or the only way of settling conflict. I am arguing that women are not only victims but play a full and varied part both in conflict and in post-conflict reconstruction. The fieldwork for the project was carried out with Palestinian refugee women and Shi'i Muslim women in Lebanon between 1998 and 2004. It raised challenging methodological questions about how best to conduct scholarly research in embattled environments and how to deal sensitively with women who have been traumatized, who may have suffered harm themselves or may have lost family members, who have seen their homes destroyed and have witnessed and lived through periods of intense violence.

Theoretical Approaches

One of the arguments I was keen to test was that behaviour during times of conflict diverges from traditional patterns and therefore, we need to create a new methodology to conceptualize violence, conflict and power dynamics. In order to understand better what happens to women during times of conflict, I combined three theoretical approaches. The first refers to feminist theories that equate male violence against women with power and men's need to control (Brownmiller 1975; Barry 1979; Dobash and Dobash 1998; El-Bushra 2000; Moser 2001). Male power is exercised not only in the home and national society but also in the ownership of communal memory. The voices of men are regarded as authoritative and thus history, by its nature, 'tends to exclude marginal groups such as women' (Sayigh 2007:137). In the case of Palestinian refugee and Shi'i women in Lebanon, evidence suggests that the threat or reality of violence, including the violence of social and traditional pressures, tends to act as a curb on behaviour. Both societies are relatively conservative and few women are willing to confront the prevailing culture as this might place them in a vulnerable position.

My second theoretical approach stems from a human rights perspective. Feminist activists and scholars have argued that 'human rights are not static and fixed but are determined by historical movements and struggles' (Bahar 2000: 267). To do justice to this position, I took into account the criteria that the women themselves believe to be applicable to their situation. In both case studies, women frequently referred to human rights as a standard of international behaviour; in both communities, organizations have been established to educate women about their human rights and their rights according to Islam. For many Palestinian and Shi'i Muslims in Lebanon, as my fieldwork revealed, Islam – as a religious tradition, a popular movement and a means of empowerment – is regarded as an important unifying factor and a source of values and comfort in the face of external oppression and, for these reasons, the third strand of my theoretical framework takes Islam as a key reference point. By considering the phenomenon of violence in terms of power relations, the specific environments of Islam, conflict and traditional male-female dynamics, set against a backdrop of human rights and entitlement, and by making use of relevant quantitative indicators to establish aspirations and progress, I was able to contextualize the raw data collected in the field in order to gain a picture of Palestinian and Shi'i women's position in Lebanon in the early 21st century.

Interactive Feminist Research: Considerations of Power and Powerlessness

Whereas there have been exciting recent developments in feminist methodology in the west, the field of Middle Eastern studies 'continues to marginalize women due to its lethargy in delving into more innovative scholarship that utilises creative approaches and explores new focuses' (Fleischmann 1996: 353). New methods are needed, therefore, to transform the task of gathering data from human respondents in Arab contexts into a more dynamic and egalitarian process. My fieldwork with Palestinian and Shi'i women in Lebanon was intended, as far as is feasible, to be interactive. It began by acknowledging traditional power relations and the imbalances caused thereby between the researcher and the objects of her research and then made a conscious effort to hand over as much of that power as possible to the participants. This meant that, rather than being a process imposed from outside, the research involved the participants, their needs and their priorities from an early stage. Such involvement is essential since an important component of my research was the active shaping by women of their lives and the ways in which they are seeking to make constructive contributions to post-conflict reconstruction.

The research also explored the notion of the research process as a potentially empowering experience for those taking part in it. By empowering I mean, on the one hand, the reality of female empowerment in Lebanese and Palestinian society, as indicated by rising participation in education, the work force and political life and, on the other hand, feelings that women have of being empowered, which may stem from personal attributes and a sense of effectiveness within the family or the community. Changes in legislation that benefit women also encourage feelings of empowerment. When I began this project my intention was to invite the women themselves to set the agenda. During preliminary visits to Lebanon I made contact with women's organizations within the two communities. These meetings were positive; they led to a degree of co-operation and I received valuable assistance both in identifying suitable participants for the project and articulating issues of concern. In this way women's real experiences, rather than my abstract outside agenda, were a principal controlling factor.

Power relations undoubtedly play a part in the scholarly process. In terms of her own project, the researcher is a powerful figure; she exercises greater control over what happens than her subjects who are not usually in a position to exert significant influence. This has traditionally been the way of carrying out fieldwork in societies other than one's own. However, to some extent this is an illusion. In the reality of the Palestinian camps or the Shi'i southern suburbs of Beirut, I did not feel particularly powerful; it seemed to me that most of the women I met were fully capable of asserting their own priorities and were certainly not prepared to discuss anything about which they did not feel comfortable. Sayigh describes the relationship between the researcher and the research community as intersubjectivity (1996: 145), a concept, she suggests, 'that calls into question all stages of research...It focuses critical attention...on the theory and politics of the representation of "other" cultures, and on the meaning and consequences of research for the researched' (145–46). In many cases, the researched are classified as disadvantaged in some respect. However, as Harding argues, 'the oppressed have the capacity to see more clearly. They may be socially disadvantaged, but they are *epistemologically privileged* [emphasis in original]; they are better placed to produce "maximally objective" knowledge' (1991).

Language and Interpretation

In both practical and symbolic ways, language presents a problem in a study of this kind. I am talking, on the one hand, about the language used to contextualize the research findings and, on the other, about the words spoken by the women. By choosing to delve into their lives, I was setting these women apart and cocooning them in a shroud of impenetrable jargonized language. The act of engaging them in conversation took the form of questionnaires and focused conversations in which one party had a specific agenda whilst the other may have had no clear purpose and not even much enthusiasm to participate in the process. For example, some of the Palestinian refugee women I met were reluctant to talk about violent incidents in the past as these tended to re-kindle painful memories. At the same time many of the women, in both communities, had their own very clear agendas which they were keen to share with foreign visitors. Palestinian women frequently made a point of stressing the injustice of their situation. They expressed frustration at the inability of Palestinian exile communities to affect the peace process or improve their own lives and they noted the unwillingness of the international community to intervene. Many Lebanese Shi'i women focused on their pride in and gratitude towards the Islamic resistance movement which had saved the country from foreign occupation; many referred to the centrality of Islam in their lives.

One should listen carefully to the language that women use, noting whether it is the same sort of language that men use or whether there is a verbal female way of coping with the effects of violence on social and family life. For example, during an interview with a 54-year old widow living in a Beirut refugee camp, I heard about some of her experiences during the civil war. She has six children, she told me, and has lived in the camp all her life. Her husband was killed by a bomb during one of the camp sieges of the mid-1980s and her home was demolished four times during the war. A bomb landed next to one of her sons, causing a problem with his sight. The fourth siege which lasted for six months was very hard, she said, when they were so hungry they had to eat dogs and cats and grass. The woman's narrative was anecdotal, somewhat disjointed and at times even humorous. Throughout our conversation several of her male relatives who were sitting in the room with us interrupted the story to correct her recollections of exactly what happened and when.[1] A number of studies have revealed that women's narratives are more likely to be characterized by 'understatements, avoidance of the first person point of

---

1　Interview, Bourj el-Barajne camp, Beirut, 26 February 2003.

view, rare mention of personal accomplishments and disguised statements of personal power' (Etter-Lewis 1991: 48).

The women being interviewed will not always wish to reveal the reality of their situation. They may be suspicious of the researcher's motives or concerned about the purposes for which their disclosures will be used; or they may have an entirely different objective in mind. For example, during a series of interviews with Shi'i women in Beirut in September 2002, I heard how these women had been subjected to acts of cruelty by the enemy and had managed, with the support of Islam and the Islamic resistance, to remain resilient; rather than admitting vulnerability or defeat, most of the women narrated their experiences in terms of strength and defiance.[2] By trying to find out about the lived experiences of a small sample of Palestinian and Lebanese women, I risked subjecting them to an ordeal which may have been unpleasant or unwelcome, and – worse – may have contributed negatively to future interactions with women from different cultures. But there were other considerations such as the desire on the part of some of the women I met to tell the world what has happened to them. For example, I had an opportunity in 2003 to hear the story of a woman in southern Lebanon who had been the victim of sexual violence at the hands of enemy soldiers; this is a very taboo topic and almost no other women were prepared to divulge personal information of this kind. In this instance, the woman felt she had been badly treated not only by the men who raped her but by her own community which continued to regard her in a negative light and by the international community which had little interest in uncovering the question of rape during the Lebanese civil war and Israeli occupation.

During my fieldwork in Lebanon, I discovered that although a relatively large number of women agreed to take part in the project, many of them had a preconceived notion of what they might be prepared to say to me. Certain topics, such as painful personal information, were taboo, while others, for instance pride in the liberation struggle or the hopelessness of return, were clearly and repeatedly stated. Patterns of language emerged. While men tended to slip easily into the language of politics and the grand narrative of struggle, women were content to focus on smaller aspects of life, for example the well-being of their children and the difficulties of everyday life. For example, many Palestinian women living in camps in Beirut and the south, talked about the period during the mid-1980s when the Lebanese militia Amal besieged their camps for as long as six months at a time. Most tended to recount anecdotes relating to the loss of homes and loved ones, their own fear and the difficulties of day to day survival. Yet, taken together, these narratives provide a compelling account of the violence and uncertainty of that time.

In terms of this research, there were two considerations with regard to interpretation: the first was the interpreting – literally the translation – of words from the language of the narrator into the language of the researcher; while the

---

2 Interviews with women at the Hizbullah Women's Organization, Beirut, 19 September 2002.

second related to the responsibility of the researcher to interpret as accurately and faithfully as possible the narrative she is hearing. I agree with Passerini when she says that interpretation 'should aim at identifying the patterns in the contradictions between the content of the stereotypes, on the one hand, and the information which emerges through in-depth interviews and participant observation, on the other' (1989: 194). In addition, as she says, the 'guiding principle could be that all autobiographical memory is true; it is up to the interpreter to discover in which sense, where, for which purpose' (1989: 197). The dilemma for me was to transform a significant quantity of raw data into a theoretical account which was both coherent and also respectful of the participants.

Insider/outsider Dilemma: The Participant Observer

As a non-Muslim non-Arab researcher, choosing to examine the lives of Palestinian and Lebanese women I was venturing into unfamiliar spaces. Although I may have visited Lebanon many times, I was still a relative stranger and, therefore, my relationship with Palestinian and Lebanese space was as an outsider seeking to uncover signposts along the way from the insiders, the women who are at the heart of this research. But they too are often not completely at home. Many of the women I interviewed had been uprooted and, even though they have the benefit of shared language and culture, they may be experiencing alienation, anxiety and physical discomfort. Female spaces, as Pettman notes, 'are largely enclosed within men's power and a male-dominated public sphere' (1996: 182). There are advantages and disadvantages to being an outsider. Whilst outsider status, as Perks and Thomson note, 'is believed to accord objectivity and detachment, an "insider" perspective has the benefits of special insight otherwise obscure to outsiders' (1998: 102).

Feminist researchers suggest practical ways to tackle the dilemma of how to conduct the practicalities of the relationship between researcher and researched. They recommend unstructured or semi-structured interviewing. Open-ended interview research, as Reinharz notes, 'produces non-standardized information that allows researchers to make full use of differences among people' (1992: 18–19). One of the objectives of feminist interviewing techniques is to build a more sympathetic relationship between the researcher and the individuals who are sharing their stories. It is receptive to unexpected patterns, and stresses the importance of listening and respect. There is also the question of underlying motives, both the researcher's and the participants', and the desire of those taking part to make sense of an isolated or disjointed narrative; in other words, to place the small story into a larger historical picture. But such considerations illustrate the uncomfortable position occupied by the researcher as she tries, on the one hand, to achieve a degree of detachment and, on the other, to advance an agenda she believes might bring benefit to her subjects.

If one adopts a feminist interviewing technique, it allows a degree of creativity, not in the sense of making things up but rather of broadening the field to include subjects that were previously perhaps felt to be irrelevant. This approach works well in the Palestinian camps where conversations frequently take place in family homes and often include a woman's relatives and neighbours; in this case, the event becomes a communal endeavour in which a group of people attempts to convey a story of the camp or a story of exile. In the midst of the larger narrative, it is usually possible to extract more personal recollections, although it is inadvisable to ask questions that may be regarded as intrusive. There is sometimes a conflict, too, between facts and opinions.

Oral History: The Formalization of Memory

Everything, as Al-Ali says, 'in one way or another, can be linked back to "identity"' (2000: 39–40), and one of the key questions in this study relates to self-perception or the internalization of identity. Both Palestinian and Lebanese women possess several levels of identity: they are Muslim (Sunni or Shi'i), Arab, Palestinian or Lebanese, and reside in the Middle East. Beyond the broad parameters of these labels lie individual attributes, through which identity is also expressed, in terms of status, family circumstances, age and class. Although the specific contexts in which these women exist are far from identical, they contain important similarities. Both are intensely patriarchal, they are embattled, and they regard Islamic traditions and practices as central to their lives. Both groups also perceive themselves as being the weaker party in their respective conflicts and both have suffered problems of image. For Palestinian women in Lebanon, the specific circumstances in which they live are the Palestinian national entity, the Islamic *umma*, the Arab nation, the Israeli occupation of their land and their status as refugees. For Lebanese Shi'i women, their day to day reality is expressed in terms of the Lebanese state, the Arab nation, the Shi'i branch of Islam to which they belong, and – until May 2000 – the Israeli occupation of part of their land, which has left painful scars. I wanted to discover how these various identities are expressed and interact with each other.

This raised the question of which method would be capable of yielding the most productive results. The oral history technique, through which individuals are invited to speak about their lives without excessive restriction, is popular with many feminist researchers. Sayigh argues that oral history is a valuable tool, with the 'potential for revealing social struggles contained within the history of nation-states or national liberation movements' (1994: 4–5). My decision to use a semi-structured oral history technique as a method of gathering information was based on several considerations. First, I agree with Sangster that 'traditional sources have often neglected the lives of women, and that oral history offered a means of integrating women into historical scholarship' (1998: 87). Second, oral history is an appropriate method 'to recover neglected or silenced accounts of past experience, and as a way of challenging dominant histories' (Perks and Thomson 1998: 183), which is an important consideration when dealing with women who may have been displaced and traumatized. Third, since my research is qualitative and relies on interviews and conversations with a relatively small sample of individuals, I felt that oral history was likely to be the most effective way of gleaning a relatively broad picture of an individual woman's experiences of conflict. Finally, autobiographical revelation gives the individual woman a degree of control over, and a stake in, the procedure.

Some feminist scholars 'believe that injustices can be righted when "people tell their stories"' (Reinharz 1992: 136). Nonetheless, the decision to use oral history as a method of gathering information raises a number of methodological questions. First of all, we need to ask 'how gender, race and class, as structural and ideological relations, have shaped the construction of historical memory' (Sangster 1998: 88). Second, one must bear in mind that political ideology also shapes the construction of memory (Sangster 1998: 89). In recalling the various violent conflicts in Lebanon, the narrator will inevitably be influenced by the painful realities of her everyday life and may well seek to emphasize the political rather than the personal elements of her story. It is useful, in this respect, to insert questions as a way of guiding the woman into the desired terrain. Third, 'we must…acknowledge our *own* influence on the shape of the interview' (Sangster 1998: 92). Any interviewing process, as Fleischmann notes, 'involves multiple roles and several layers of perception. Each person, interviewer and narrator makes choices in terms of communication, understanding and presentation resulting in the production of different kinds of information' (1996: 361). My status as an outsider, a westerner and a researcher was bound to affect the woman's mode of response and the information she chose to divulge. During the course of my research, I encountered a relatively broad range of interactive situations, from the very formal and structured to the ad hoc and casual, and these also affected the shape of the interview.

Conducting the Research

The first step in the research process was to conduct discussions with a number of women's organizations working with Palestinian and Shi'i women in Lebanon and to identify key areas of concern. Second with their assistance, questionnaires were prepared for the following categories: individual women, the representatives of organizations that deal with women's rights, academics, and political and religious leaders. The set of questions for individuals was designed to establish the woman's background and her experiences of violent conflict. In the case of organizations, the questions sought to ascertain the extent of violence in the society by asking what are the organization's principal objectives, how it pursues its objectives, which segment of the population it addresses and why, and the sort of assistance or support it offers. With academics, I was trying to ascertain their own understanding of violence against women in Palestinian and Lebanese society, as well as their knowledge of other relevant research in this area. My questions to religious and political leaders, who were almost all men, focused on their perceptions of appropriate roles for women, both in political and Islamic terms, as well as the reality of women's participation in conflict. By having relatively in-depth conversations with as wide a range as possible of community members, from influential men who feel that their views and actions have an effect on the way people lead their lives to women who regard themselves as entirely lacking in power or influence, I was able to form an impression of the condition of the society.

The next step was to locate individual women who were willing to contribute personal accounts about their experiences of violent conflict. Guidelines for the interview process were relatively broad. I was seeking to find out, first, how Lebanese Shi'i and Palestinian women define violence; second, what they consider to be the differences between violence which comes from the enemy and violence that comes from within their own society; third, whether they believe that Islam provides any sort of protection against violence; fourth, what measures they envisage to protect themselves against violence in the post-conflict phase; and, finally, what have been their personal experiences of violence and their own coping mechanisms. As Fleischmann observes 'through the interviewing process and in providing their own versions of the past, women become producers of history rather than just passive objects of study' (1996: 366).

During the course of several visits to Lebanon I conducted interviews with women in the two communities. I was keen to access as broad a cross-section of women as possible. I interviewed women who participated in the resistance, women who work in political groups, women who have suffered economically as a result of social practices that discriminate against women, female ex-prisoners, women who have been the victims of domestic violence, women who describe themselves as non-political, former fighters, mothers whose children and wives whose husbands have been killed by the enemy, and women who have been deserted by their husbands. I started with a series of factual questions in order to establish each woman's background, including details of family, education, paid work and interests. Next, we discussed her experiences of the conflict situation in which she lives and the ways in which she has participated in it or been harmed or victimized by it, as well as her attitude towards the national struggle, and the roles of Islam and violence in her society. The interviews created snapshots of individual women's experiences of violence and conflict, how they perceive such violence and how they are resisting or contributing to it. My objective was to work with women on the basis of victimization and empowerment; in other words, I wanted not only to talk to women who consider themselves articulate or have already had dealings with foreign researchers but also to those who may feel they have nothing to say or those whose voices are not usually heard. For the project to be effective, it had to be able to offer space to the marginalized.

In the Palestinian case, I met women living in refugee camps all over Lebanon and also some who do not reside in camps. Although I interviewed women affiliated to the Palestine Liberation Organization (PLO), the Popular Front for the Liberation of Palestine (PFLP) and the Democratic Front for the Liberation of Palestine (DFLP), many of the camp women and other women I met claimed no political affiliation. Over a period of six years, I made a total of seven research visits to Lebanon and interviewed a wide variety of individuals in the Palestinian community: over 70 women and some men involved in political activities; the representatives of governmental and non-governmental organizations; academics; women of different socio-economic status and a wide range of ages (the youngest was 15-and-a-half and the oldest over 80 years old, from different educational backgrounds – some were illiterate while others had advanced university degrees, with differing relationships to political and social activism); women who work for non-governmental organizations; women without paid work; medical personnel; ex-prisoners; students; United Nations Relief and Works Agency (UNRWA) employees; teachers; members of the General Union of Palestinian Women and other political groupings; and women who have been injured, either physically or psychologically, as a result of armed conflict. In some cases information was unearthed during visits to UNRWA and non-governmental organization (NGO) projects in the camps: literacy projects and skills training programmes, where I had the opportunity to talk to groups of women and girls; such visits provided useful larger contexts for the one-to-one interviews.

In the refugee camps, without exception, I was received as a welcome visitor and offered generous hospitality, in the form of hot and cold drinks, snacks, fruit and sometimes meals, in even the poorest homes. My questions were designed to find out about the woman's experiences of conflict: the exile from Palestine in 1948, the Lebanese civil war, the Israeli invasion of 1982 and the Amal camp sieges of the mid-1980s, her relationship with Islam and also her reflections on daily life, including her own situation, her family circumstances, her involvement in the community and her hopes for the future. Women spoke about their memories of the past, their particular experiences and their hopes for the future. Usually they set their own struggles within the larger context of the Palestinian national movement. As the years go by, there are fewer and fewer refugees who remember Palestine; I spoke to less than ten women who had been part of the 1948 exodus. Most of the women I interviewed were aged between 20 and 50.

There is an uncomfortable gap between what Palestinian camp women want and need and the imposition by an outside researcher of an arbitrary agenda. Many of these women will no longer speak to foreign researchers, concluding that it is a waste of time, hopeless or irrelevant. The ones who do agree to speak do so for a variety of reasons: out of curiosity, as a favour to friends, in order to raise larger issues such as the Palestinian national struggle or their own sense of frustration at their current situation, or to air certain feelings that would not normally be able to be spoken about. Almost everyone was keen to tell the story of Palestine. I observed a conflict between the larger narrative and women's own often-difficult circumstances. Their conclusions tended to be a mixture of the defiant, a determination to return to their land, and the hopeless because they did not believe they ever would return to their land.

In the Lebanese Shi'i community, over a six-year period, I interviewed over 80 women and some men. I met women in Beirut, in towns and villages in the south of the country, and in the Bekaa Valley. As in the Palestinian case study, the questions were designed to focus respondents' attention on the issue of violence, broadly defined, but also to encourage them to speak more generally about their experiences during the conflict. I interviewed female members of political factions, widows of martyrs, former political prisoners, women who were involved in non-sectarian activities during the civil war, women who wrote fiction during the war as a way of dealing with the trauma and women victims of domestic violence. I interviewed the Secretary-General and Deputy Secretary-General of Hizbullah, the wife of the leader of Amal, several Hizbullah members of the Lebanese Parliament, psychologists, academics and doctors. I examined women's experiences of conflict in terms of Shi'i religious and revolutionary symbolism, but also from the perspectives of the issues that concern this research: identity, nationalism, violence and women's rights. By focusing on women associated with Amal and Hizbullah and setting their narratives against the views of a group of Shi'i women without strong political or religious affiliation, I was able to draw specific conclusions about women's experiences of and attitudes towards the Lebanese civil war and the Israeli invasion and occupation of parts of Lebanon. Most of the interviews with women took between one and two hours: a few lasted less than one hour and the longest lasted for almost four hours. They usually took place in the woman's home, although some were conducted in community centres or NGO offices. Although I was able to talk to several of the women more than once, the majority of interviews were on the basis of a single meeting. In almost all cases, I spoke to one woman at a time. However, there were a few meetings with groups of women.

For both case studies, I also extracted relevant information from representatives of organizations which deal with human rights and women's rights, for example by educating women about their rights and assisting them to assert such rights. This led to a consideration of agency by revealing some of the strategies individual women or women as a group have adopted to cope with their circumstances. Some of these organizations are secular, while others define themselves through religion. They propose somewhat different responses to the pressures which modern Muslim women in Lebanon are experiencing. By listening to what the women themselves said, specifically in terms of how they remember the past, I gained an understanding of the history and mechanics of each conflict and, by constructing a narrative framework out of conversations and questionnaires, I was able to draw specific conclusions as to women's ability to participate meaningfully in embattled environments.

Conclusion: Women are not only Victims

Although 'participating in a research project is unlikely, in the vast majority of cases, to transform the conditions of women's lives' (Kelly, Burton and Regan 1998: 37), a key element in this project was a desire to influence the debate. Thus I sought to establish whether the majority of women in the two case studies experience various forms of violence as disadvantageous or as a factor of exclusion, or whether their attitudes towards violence, in whatever form it takes, are more ambivalent. One way of doing this was by re-defining violence and the other was to find out how the various forms of violence have affected women's ability to play a meaningful role in processes of post-conflict reconstruction. By interviewing a wide range of Palestinian refugee and Lebanese Shi'i women I was testing assumptions, on the one hand, about violence against women and, on the other, in relation to Islam as a source of protection and empowerment for women, contextualized within international notions of human rights and entitlements.

The research methodology used for this study had advantages and limitations. It was effective in the sense that by adopting a relatively flexible form of enquiry, through questionnaires and directed conversations, I was able to glean information about each woman's background, her experiences of violence and conflict and her opinions, reflections and aspirations. This method revealed both individual stories and also a larger communal narrative. Harding's argument about the epistemological privilege of the oppressed is highly relevant to my two case studies. The women who took part regarded themselves as subjects and possessors of knowledge; most of them presented themselves as active participants in their own society. As feminist researchers suggest, the lives and voices of ordinary women have been neglected by conventional scholarship and my project provided a means of correcting this imbalance.

The methodology also had limitations. First, the sample was relatively small; however, while the results should be treated with some caution, certain patterns emerged, such as ways of dealing with adversity and chronic insecurity and of making sense of chaotic circumstances. Second, the methodology raised questions of truth and accuracy. In their oral accounts, Palestinian and Lebanese women were choosing to divulge certain information and to withhold other aspects of their lives. Their choices reflect concerns with the larger communal narratives and are revealing in the sense that they represent perceptions of truth which in itself is a valuable indicator. Individual women were influenced by factors such as political affiliation, strength of religious feelings and loyalty to their community. Overall, I believe, the research methodology used was appropriate for dealing with non-quantifiable situations, such as conflict, that are characterized by grey areas.

While the women's oral accounts were often distressing, they strengthened my conviction that the information could significantly enrich both my own life experience and our knowledge and appreciation of the precarious situation of Muslim women in situations of conflict and other threats of violence to which women all over the world are exposed. In essence, this study was an analysis of Lebanese and Palestinian women as disadvantaged by violence in times of conflict, but it had other aims: to reveal out how the various forms of violence to which these two groups of women have been subjected overlap and influence each other; and also to discover how some of these women – as agents – are identifying positive ways in which they can contribute to and influence the processes of change taking place in their communities.

Bibliography

Al-Ali, N. (2000), *Secularism, Gender and the State in the Middle East: The Egyptian Women's Movement* (Cambridge: Cambridge University Press).

Bahar, S. (2000), 'Human Rights are Women's Rights: Amnesty International and the Family', in Bonnie G. Smith (ed.), *Global Feminisms Since 1945* (London and New York: Routledge).

Barry, K. (1979), *Female Sexual Slavery* (Englewood Cliffs, New Jersey: Prentice-Hall).

Brownmiller, S. (1975), *Against Our Will: Men, Women and Rape* (New York: Bantam Books).

Dobash, R.E. and Dobash, R.P. (eds) (1998), *Rethinking Violence Against Women* (London: Sage Publications – Sage Series on Violence Against Women).

El-Bushra, J. (2000), 'Transforming Conflict: Some Thoughts on a Gendered Understanding of Conflict Processes', in S. Jacobs, R. Jacobson and J. Marchbank (eds), *States of Conflict: Gender, Violence and Resistance* (London and New York: Zed Books).

Etter-Lewis, G. (1991), 'Black Women's Life Stories: Reclaiming Self in Narrative Texts', in S. Berger Gluck and D. Patai (eds), *Women's Words: The Feminist Practice of Oral History* (London: Routledge).

Fleischmann, E.L. (1996), 'Crossing the Boundaries in History: Exploring Oral History in Researching Palestinian Women in the Mandate Period', *Women's History Review* 5(3).

Harding, S. (1991), *Whose Science? Whose Knowledge? Thinking from Women's Lives* (Milton Keynes: Open University Press).

Kelly, L., Burton, S. and Regan, L. (1994), 'Researching Women's Lives or Studying Women's Oppression? Reflections on What Constitutes Feminist Research', in M. Maynard and J. Purvis (eds), *Researching Women's Lives from a Feminist Perspective* (London: Taylor & Francis).

Moser, C.O.N. (2001), 'The Gendered Continuum of Violence and Conflict', in C.O.N. Moser and F.C. Clark (eds.), *Victims, Perpetrators or Actors? Gender, Armed Conflict and Political Violence* (London and New York: Zed Books).

Passerini, L. (1989), 'Women's Personal Narratives: Myths, Experiences and Emotions', in Personal Narratives Group (eds), *Interpreting Women's Lives: Feminist Theory and Personal Narratives* (Bloomington and Indianapolis: Indiana University Press).

Perks, R. and Thomson, A. (eds) (1998), *The Oral History Reader* (London and New York: Routledge).

Pettman, J.J. (1996), *Worlding Women: A Feminist International Politics* (London and New York: Routledge).

Reinharz, S. (1992), *Feminist Methods in Social Research* (New York and Oxford: Oxford University Press).

Sangster, J. (1998), 'Telling Our Stories: Feminist Debates and the Use of Oral History', in R. Perks and A .Thomson (eds), *The Oral History Reader* (London and New York: Routledge).

Sayigh, R. (1994), *Too Many Enemies: The Palestinian Experience in Lebanon* (London and New Jersey: Zed Books).

United Nations (2002), *Women, Peace and Security: Study Submitted to the Secretary-General Pursuant to Security Council Resolution 1325 (2000)*, New York.

Chapter 15

Participatory Research in Programme Evaluation: The Mid-term Evaluation of the National Solidarity Programme in Afghanistan

David Connolly

Introduction

Mid-term evaluations can espouse participatory values in their attempts to investigate, correct and bolster the components of a programme as it enters its final phase. By design, evaluations at this learning juncture herald notable advances for the programme stakeholders in terms of technical knowledge, awareness, inclusion, and decision-making, among other people-oriented objectives. Such virtues may be fashionable but it is difficult to discern their actual development during and after an assessment. This observation reveals more than mere dissonance between theory and practice since the failure to meet participants' expectations, once they have been raised by a mid-term evaluation, could jeopardize the programme that it had set out to strengthen. This outcome and the attendant tensions can prove momentous in all contexts but the inherent fragility of the post-war society suggests higher stakes and greater risks for evaluators and participants. Towards furthering our understanding of the complex relationship between participatory research and mid-term programme evaluations and in taking an in-depth look at the post-war arena, this chapter examines the mid-term assessment of the National Solidarity Programme (NSP) in Afghanistan, which took place from October 2005 to May 2006.

The NSP case study is important for four main reasons. First, as the government of Afghanistan's flagship national development programme, the following analysis yields unique insight into an official process of programme review and policy making, and with broader relevance to the crafting of the Afghan state. Second, the NSP is inherently participatory itself as an initiative for governance and economic recovery that is premised on the interplay between international and local institutional partnerships in a system of collaborative governance. At its core is the operational concept of community-driven development, which crystallizes a recent and influential approach in internationally-supported responses to the aftermath of war. Considering the NSP's multi-stakeholder ethos and its particular emphasis on enabling communities to take responsibility for organizing how best to meet their socio-economic and political needs, it was essential for the mid-term evaluation to adopt participatory research methods. Stemming from this and as the third reason, the NSP case study is important because the programme and the evaluation developed a shared interest in stakeholder participation and empowerment. The evaluation was merely one part of a larger programme cycle of participation, from community-driven assessment to project execution. In this sense, the programme and the evaluation became interconnected and self-reflective since they were dependent upon the willingness and ability of stakeholders to play a central role in delivery and research, respectively.

Last, the NSP mid-term evaluation has been selected because it explores the merits and limitations of participatory research methods in a post-war context. Afghanistan defies generalizations but field research can be influenced by common characteristics that include large-scale and protracted destruction, chronic socio-economic and political needs, persistent outbreaks of violent conflict and instability, and a model of recovery that is driven overtly by programmes and international intervention.

Not forgetting the crucial roles played by Afghans, programmes and international support in general have been hindered by two antithetical trends from the bottom-up: over-dependency and opposition. Both trends involve weaknesses in participation but in different ways and are rooted in a tradition of centralized decision-making under Soviet occupation. Therefore, it is hoped that the following discussion contributes to the more profound task of better understanding insider–outsider relationships in Afghanistan and other similar war-torn societies.

In drawing upon the author's direct experience and leading role in the NSP mid-term evaluation, this chapter argues that the participatory research methods were effective overall. This assertion is based on the ability of the methods to resolve the inevitable tensions within three central domains: meeting the aim and objectives of the evaluation; gathering valid evidence; and managing the expectations of programme stakeholders as research participants. Nevertheless, the analysis below also questions the long-term direct benefits for participants and thereby critiques part of the rationale of such formative assessments in post-war societies.

Beginning with an overview of the operational context of Afghanistan and the NSP mid-evaluation, this chapter then identifies the participatory nature of the research. The second section demonstrates how the methods played a crucial role in meeting the aim and objectives of the evaluation, and the third section examines the gathering of valid evidence despite notable constraints in the field. Expectations were well managed overall but the fourth section illustrates important differences between two core groups of participants: community leaders and household heads, and representatives of governmental and non-governmental agencies. The final section explores the impact of the assessment and its participatory methods by considering the obstacles to developing the capacities of participants through their engagement in the evaluation process. In concluding with specific relevance to Afghanistan and other similar war-torn contexts, participatory research methods are proven to be an expedient means for a mid-term evaluation but the case study demonstrates the need for more strategic methodological interventions in order to enable durable benefits for both participants and programme.[1]

The NSP Mid-term Evaluation

It is important to begin by outlining the background to the NSP mid-term evaluation and the constraints for the field research from the context of Afghanistan in 2005. In identifying the participatory nature of the evaluation, the three main tools consisted of community power surveys, household surveys and semi-structured interviews. Participatory characteristics included the multi-levelled nature of the field research, the regular consultations with stakeholders, and the use of mobile research teams to collect the data at the sub-national level.

Background to the Evaluation

The mid-term evaluation of the NSP was commissioned by the Ministry of Rural Rehabilitation and Development (MRRD) on behalf of the government of the Islamic Republic of Afghanistan. The MRRD implements the NSP but it is a national programme and thus an inter-ministerial or whole-government initiative for the recovery of governance and economic development. Since 2003 the programme has encouraged vulnerable rural communities to design and take charge of small-scale projects that address their social, political and economic needs. This concept of community-driven development is based on active and proactive participation at the grassroots level among and between community groups and other stakeholders.[2] The NSP has undoubtedly strengthened state–citizen relations. For many communities, the NSP is the first time that the state has played a role in the provision of basic services.[3] Design and delivery also has been international in composition, demanding top-down collaboration among a consortium of international donors that is coordinated by the World Bank, managed by the international development agency, *Deutsche Gesellschaft für Technische Zusammenarbeit*/International Services (GTZ/IS), and facilitated in many districts across all the provinces by 22 international and

1   The author is grateful to Dr Margaret Chard for comments on an earlier draft.

2   Communities are required to elect Community Development Councils (CDCs) in order to join the NSP. CDCs have built upon customary governance norms but have also directly challenged traditional community institutions by introducing liberal-democratic processes of decision-making, for example, the insistence on a separate women's CDC or mixed CDC in each community, in addition to upward and downward formal accountability mechanisms.

3   For instance, 88 per cent of householders surveyed by the evaluation felt that their lives had improved since the end of the war in 2001 (Barakat, Chard, Connolly, Evans, and Jones 2006: 79).

Table 15.1   Participating provinces and districts in the NSP mid-term evaluation

Province	Primary research locations (full survey, including household survey)	Secondary research locations (partial surveys of varying levels with no household survey)
Badghis	Ab Kamari	–
Balkh	Dawlatabad Charbolak	Dehdadi Nahrishahv
Bamyan	Shibar	–
Herat	–	Robat Sangi Yaka Dokan
Kabul	Estalef Kalakan	Shakadara
Kundoz	Khad Abad Chadara	–
Laghman	–	Alingar Alishang
Nangarhar	Sorkhrod Chaparhar Moohamdara Achin	–
Paktia	–	Ahmad Abad
Paktika	–	Sarawza Sharan
Takhar	–	Versage

Source: Barakat et al. 2006: 136.

national non-governmental organizations (NGOs) and the United Nations Human Settlements Programme (UN-HABITAT).

Through various forms of vertical and horizontal partnerships and the integration of governance processes and institutions, the NSP has been innovative and problem-solving by tacking at least two perennial obstacles to post-war recovery: a lack of local ownership; and weak coordination among donors and implementing agencies. Consequently, and based on the need to deliver a tangible peace dividend and a stable legitimate executive, by 2005 the NSP had gathered significant attention and optimism among Afghans and international agencies. There were teething problems but it illustrated a genuine attempt for participatory governance and that recovery on a national scale was conceivable and with some commendable results.

The Post-war Reconstruction and Development Unit (PRDU) at the University of York, UK, was awarded the eight month contract, and the evaluation commenced in October 2005.[4] The evaluation team was divided into national and sub-national components. The former consisted of a team leader and three specialists in public institutions, community development, and infrastructure. During this research at the Kabul-level, five Regional Assessment Teams (RATs), composed of Afghan and international researchers, followed the programme down from the provincial governor to household heads across 11 provinces. Table 15.1 illustrates the provinces and districts that were reached by the evaluation during October and November 2005.[5]

The agreed aims and objectives of the evaluation were to examine the achievements and drawbacks of the NSP 18 months into its implementation and to make recommendations for Phase 2. Key issues were the programme rationale; programme management and enhancement; operational delivery and facilitation – efficiency, effectiveness, and early impact; the role of Community Development Councils (CDCs) in programme management and delivery at the community level; and the long-term strategy for the NSP.

The author was involved throughout the mid-term evaluation and led the RAT for Balkh province. The reflections within this chapter are based primarily on the first-hand use of the participatory methods in Balkh. The author also draws upon his close knowledge of the research in the other ten sampled provinces based on debriefings with the RAT leaders and through playing a key role in the comparative analysis of all the provincial research findings.

Field Research Environment

The field research had to cope with significant constraints. First, the collection of the data was kinetic, with part of the inquiry dedicated to investigating the NSP as it unfolded as well as the retrospective study of Phase 1 of the programme (2003–5). As the PRDU's final report acknowledges 'millions of dollars are being disbursed as we evaluate, and policy adjustments are being made; a new version of the Operational Manual has now been completed; and planned pledges have been made for Phase 2'. (Barakat et al. 2006: viii). This could be considered a typical constraint for all recovery and development interventions but it was heightened in the case of the NSP evaluation because of the pressure for the programme to demonstrate achievements and gain vital support inside and outside the government. For example, the temporal scope of the evaluation

---

4   The PRDU was in a strong position to conduct the evaluation as it had more than ten years experience in designing and managing relevant research and training in Afghanistan among many other post-war states.

5   Research participants in each province included the provincial governor, senior representatives of the MRRD at provincial and district levels, international NGOs and UN-HABITAT that worked within the program as Facilitating Partners (FPs), and GTZ/IS as the Oversight Consultant (OC). Overall, leaders from a total of 18 CDCs and six non-participating matched communities were reached in addition to 162 household heads (see footnote 7).

was extended from July 2005 to the end of March 2006 in order 'to include commentary on some notable developments in programme management and enhancement' (Barakat et al. 2006: viii).

Unlike this latter challenge of identifying, tracing and processing complex and fast-moving information flows, the second constraint involved certain restriction in access. Whole provinces (for example, Kandahar and Helmand) could not be visited due to the threat of violence for programme and evaluation staff while certain areas of provinces were off-limits (for example, in Paktia and Nangarhar). In adding to this instability, time and resources were naturally finite which set limits for the evaluation and with direct implications, as examined below, for the participatory component.

The indelible legacy of war – large-scale and protracted destruction with chronic socio-economic and political needs – created a third constraint in the form of limited capacities among research participants. Afghans were playing key roles in their own recovery but community leaders and household heads were limited in their engagement with the surveys (see below). It was assumed that this stemmed from the debilitation of capabilities after decades of war and the ongoing instability combined with a lack of trust among Afghans, and more specifically, with international-led assessments. Time was another factor, with community leaders and household heads understandably busy addressing the more urgent demands of meeting immediate and long-term needs.

Participatory Nature of the Research

The mid-term evaluation was participatory in nature based on three main data collection tools and three main research characteristics.[6] Two types of surveys were employed as the data collection tools to gain insight into the perspectives of community leaders and household heads. Participants came mainly from NSP communities but as noted above, community leaders and household heads that were not participating in the NSP were interviewed for comparative inquiry.[7]

The community power survey aimed to assess the ability of CDCs to participate and lead in community governance and economic development as set out by the NSP. This involved 'assessing their capacity to function independently as a democratic leadership of their communities and their ability to select, plan and manage development projects' (Barakat et al. 2006: 69). The final PRDU report notes that key indicators included 'legitimacy and acceptance; participation;

---

6   The data collection tools and characteristics were repeated by each RAT to ensure consistency. The primary research was participatory but the evaluation overall also incorporated a scientific approach and a deductive/inductive approach. For more see Barakat et al (2006: 121–122).

7   These are referred to as non-participating matched communities as they were not in the NSP but were similar in profile to the sample of NSP communities based on criteria established by the evaluation. The non-participating matched communities were included to strengthen the evaluation's understanding of the programme's impact.

transparency and communication with the whole community; project management skills; record keeping; relations with government and outside bodies; and their relationship with the FPs [Facilitating Partners]' (Barakat et al. 2006: 139).

The household survey, which was the 'principal tool for assessing the impact of the NSP in respect of its goal and objectives', was designed to verify if there had been 'progress in developing community governance and project management capacity as a means of empowering communities to improve their lives'. Areas of interest included the impact of the war and the post-war period which formed the NSP baseline, the experience of establishing the CDCs and the programme, their involvement in local governance and development, and their perceptions of recovery in Afghanistan and future outlook (Barakat et al. 2006: 139–140).

The third participatory tool involved the semi-structured interview. It was essential for the interview to be flexible and reflexive since it was seeking qualitative data and in a mainly exploratory manner. In accommodating the programme's many stakeholders, the semi-structured interview had to reach a diverse range of respondents, including governmental, intergovernmental and non-governmental organizations, private consultancy firms and individual experts.

The mid-term evaluation also possessed three key participatory characteristics. In order to trace the programme, and based on the PRDU's experience in identifying and comparing the range of perspectives in post-war societies, the evaluation operated and focused down through six main levels: international, national, provincial, district, community, and household. Second, the evaluation team recognized the need to consult with the range of programme stakeholders on a regular basis in order to convey and share vital information and to validate the design of the field research. Several consultative meetings occurred in Kabul in addition to numerous briefings and debriefings among participants at the provincial and community levels before, during and upon completion of the data gathering. All survey and interview questions were refined during workshops with the RAT members and after piloting among communities living on the outskirts of the capital.

As the last participatory characteristic, the evaluation deliberately integrated Afghan and international researchers during the design of the research, field preparation, and in gathering the data in the provinces through mobile and rapid assessments. The RATs in principle encouraged the forging of insider and outsider perspectives and it was intended that this would increase the chances of more balanced and objective research.

The above outline has demonstrated the significance of the NSP mid-term evaluation and the key constraints from the operational environment of Afghanistan. The field research consisted of several participatory facets, which stemmed from shared notions of 'best practice theory' in internationally-supported interventions and their evaluations (Barakat et al. 2006: viii). It is important therefore now to examine the actual relevance and practical value of these shared notions and standards.

Meeting the Evaluation Aim and Objectives

The central aim of the NSP evaluation was to 'examine the achievements and drawbacks of the Programme two years into its implementation' and to report on its efficiency and effectiveness of implementation in addition to 'its potential impact, rationale and longer-term contribution to governance and development in Afghanistan'. Recommendations were then provided to advise on 'the approach and institutional arrangements to improve the delivery and impact of the Programme; and the long-term strategy for the integration of relevant programme functions into the institutional profile of the MRRD'. To these ends, the evaluation considered both physical outcomes and the evidence of 'qualitative sustainable impacts' in relation to local governance and poverty reduction (Barakat et al. 2006: viii).

The final mid-term evaluation report was accepted and some of the recommendations have been implemented. These outcomes can be explained in various ways but this chapter argues that the participatory tools and characteristics of the research played a salient role. In particular, based on the constraints outlined above, the participatory nature of the research enabled a sufficiently in-depth and verifiable investigation while meeting the more quantitative requirement of the client and stakeholders in Kabul to visit enough provinces, communities and stakeholders overall. In sum, the participatory methods allowed the team to tackle the universal evaluation challenge of achieving a balance between claims to representativeness and depth of knowledge.

Upon reflection, given the far-reaching war legacy and the limits of time and resources, it was crucial for the evaluators to instil trust and enable cooperation with gatekeepers and research participants. The official nature of the evaluation meant that stakeholders probably felt obliged to take part but this alone does not explain how the RATs managed to gather both in-depth and critical perspectives. Towards a more thorough understanding of this achievement, it is asserted that the methods helped develop and maintain trust and cooperation.

The flexible and reflexive nature of the semi-structured interview and the community power and household surveys allowed a rapid and negotiated access to sensitive data (Connolly 2006: 169). For instance, the design of the community power survey reduced the need to write down responses and this built trust between researcher and community leaders (Connolly 2006: 167). Similarly, it was critical for each RAT to select three different types of communities: those with a well-established CDC, project approved and at the stage of implementation; one with a recently established CDC and at the stage of drawing up a project plan; and one non-participating matched community (Connolly 2006: 168). The demonstrated ability to pre-select communities in this way, without official records, undoubtedly rested on building an excellent rapport between researcher and gatekeeper. The commitment of participants to regular consultations, the combination of Afghan and international researchers, the ability of the evaluation to include perspectives from the programme's six main levels of stakeholders, and broader reflections among the RAT leaders and feedback from the consultation workshops and meetings in Kabul and in the provinces also support this main claim.

Last, participatory methods helped in meeting the aim and objectives because they allowed the assessment to remain adaptable without sacrificing consistency. Resilience was crucial considering the volatility and unpredictability of the research context. Accordingly, the experiences of the RATs were not uniform and each one, as the PRDU final report states:

> ...had to find the most practical way to implement the research strategy within the particular constraints of time and access that they faced. Some teams were delayed by transport problems or had to wait for key informants to be available, while others were able to visit additional sites or collect secondary data in addition to the core research framework based on the common research questions (Barakat et al. 2006: 135).

For example, security hindered the research in Balkh but did not interfere with the core principles of selection (Connolly 2006: 169). The RAT for Bamyan notes that the participatory approach helped to resolve the major constraint of time both overall and with specific reference to the *Eid ul-Fitr* holiday that occurred during the research (Chard 2006: 203).

International evaluations, like the international programmes that they assess, have a reputation for subjectivity, bias and weak understanding of the local context. Against this trend, this section has argued that the NSP mid-term evaluation was able to meet its aim and objectives in part because the participatory methods utilized were selected and tailored in order to address and respect the constraints of the context. Accordingly, sound preparation allowed the right approach to be chosen, which in turn enabled a credible and legitimate entry point for the research.

Gathering Valid Evidence

The evidence that formed the basis of the PRDU's conclusions and recommendations can be considered valid despite the contextual constraints. The participatory characteristic of regular consultation, through briefings and debriefings, allowed the data to be cross-checked and preliminary findings could be tested in the field. After data collection, triangulation also occurred through the processes of analyses. These various forms of triangulation were essential but not unproblematic. Last, it is argued that validity was grounded in the evaluation's broad inclusion of programme stakeholders while also acknowledging important weaknesses in this area.

The challenges to gathering reliable and accurate data in post-war environments are well-documented. The NSP was also multi-stakeholder and multi-levelled so the team anticipated disparate and complex information flows. Regular briefings and debriefings among participants, and stakeholders more broadly, thus proved useful in clarifying trends and identifying exceptions and irregularities in the data.[8] The RATs were encouraged to adopt a focusing strategy to gaining and maintaining access in the provinces (Barakat et al. 2006: 138). Meeting with the provincial governor was crucial as the primary source of permission at the sub-national level, as a courtesy, and as a source of valuable information. In Balkh province, the research team met with the governor before, during and after the research. Similarly, communities were briefed before the survey commenced and the leaders were presented with a preliminary picture of the data collected but without prejudicing the findings of the evaluation and confidentiality (Connolly 2006: 166–167).

The use of consultations and the focusing strategy mitigated the risk that respondents would 'colour their answers based on a perceived association between the research and the operations of the FP' (Connolly 2006: 167).[9] They also helped guide the non-random sampling of household heads since random sampling was not possible due to inexact sample frames. Instead, household heads were selected based on profiles – typical or non-typical – that were provisionally identified by the FP, the CDC/community leadership, and then obviously corroborated with the household head at the outset of the survey (Barakat et al. 2006: 77).

More systematic triangulation after the data had been collected occurred via the stages of analyses. These procedures occurred in two main ways: within the provinces and by each RAT leader, followed by a series of inter-provincial comparative analyses. Accordingly, the analyses aimed to create both province-wide and actor-specific inquiries, that is, for the MRRD, the Oversight Consultant (OC), and the FPs. The triangulation of the data in these ways was obviously crucial in producing a verifiable body of findings.

It is important to emphasize that the semi-structured, qualitative and exploratory nature of the data proved particularly challenging and time-consuming based on the limits of time and manpower. This was especially true for the sets of cross-provincial analyses and there ought to have been a balance between efficiency, depth of detail and comprehensiveness in considering the qualitative nature of the data and the grand scale of the findings. The evaluation client is naturally eager to see the results of the analysis but this stage of the

---

8   This included making basic tasks easier, for example, ensuring the correct representatives at the community were surveyed.

9   The NGOs acted as FPs and worked closely with the communities. The RATs relied upon the FPs to gain access to the communities in terms of building trust and logistics. At the same time, each RAT had to ensure a clear separation between the FP and the evaluation. This was created mainly by making sure the FP was not present during the interviews and surveys and by making the aim and objectives of the research transparent to community leaders and household heads. FPs in turn had to be reassured to avoid any suspicion or misunderstanding.

process can be the most demanding. Allowing twice as long as planned is not an unrealistic estimate.

Last, the evaluation prioritized inclusiveness and made several achievements in this respect. The ability to reach each level and type of NSP stakeholder and beneficiary became a cornerstone of the participatory research and helped support claims to validity. The formative assessment also managed to look beyond the programme by gaining insight from visits to communities that were not participating in the NSP although similar in profile to the sample of participating NSP communities. The mid-term evaluation report notes that the latter were used in the absence of baseline data in order to corroborate 'the retrospective accounts of the CDC of governance before the NSP, and in order to distinguish between general post-war trends and changes directly induced by the Programme' (Barakat et al. 2006: 69).

Nevertheless, the evaluation could have been more inclusive in two main ways which demonstrate relative weaknesses in participation. On the one hand, the collective perspectives of some important vulnerable groups and subgroups, for example, the nomadic *Kuchis* group, the disabled, and farmers' associations were not, unlike widows, systematically targeted. Interestingly, these specialized needs ought to have been addressed by the NSP so in this sense the evaluation mirrored the limitations of the programme by working mainly with its beneficiary and target groups. In other words, the evaluation mainly followed the programme funding because this was its assigned remit.

Inevitably, as explained above, exclusion also occurred in relation to the under-representation of women's perspectives in the evaluation. Women's perspectives were included but there was a gender imbalance overall. Of the CDC members surveyed, 73 were men but only 13 were women. Thirty-three men and seven women were interviewed individually in communities without a CDC (Barakat et al. 2006: 138).[10] Among household heads, it was not possible to interview men and women householders in equal numbers 'due to cultural factors' both among communities but also because not every RAT had a woman researcher.[11] This created a dilemma for the research. The sample of women was considered acceptable in relation to the general level of women's engagement in the programme, as validated during the consultation workshops. However, the team recognized the marginalization of women and therefore had to try to steer between reinforcing the culture of exclusion through the research and making more effort to include the perspectives of women. This was exemplified

---

10 Of the 18 CDC communities interviewed, three were mixed, four were separate and in the other communities men-only CDCs were surveyed (Barakat et al. 2006: 70).

11 Of the total sample of NSP households: 73 men and 13 women household heads were interviewed individually with 30 surveyed jointly. It was possible to interview both men and women in Bamyan, Kabul and Balkh and only widows in Badghis and Kundoz (Barakat et al. 2006: 77–78). In the other provinces it was either unacceptable or restricted even for the RATs with Afghan women researchers.

in Balkh province where women CDC members were found to be excluded from the programme yet made significant contributions to the assessment (Barakat et al. 2006: 71).

The NSP mid-term evaluation was based on verifiable evidence. To this end, the participatory aspects of consultation and inclusiveness proved valuable as best practice principles. Nevertheless, these ingredients also placed the research under considerable strain. Triangulation was possible though highly complex and time-consuming given the number of perspectives and different levels reached. Furthermore, the examples of exclusion demonstrate that the evaluation focused on the immediate confines of the programme. This meant that certain relevant voices and needs were underrepresented and even overlooked and this is significant considering the need to be critical and corrective at the mid-way juncture. Greater resources, more reliable access, and an alternative to the focusing strategy to gaining and maintaining access would have addressed these issues.

Managing Expectations

The mid-term evaluation was effective overall in managing the expectations of programme stakeholders as participants. This assertion is based on the author's direct observations during the data gathering processes in Balkh province, his consultations with programme stakeholders, debriefings with the other RAT leaders, and the broad acceptance of the report overall. The evaluation qualified the maxim that 'knowledge empowers' based on two main types of expectations among those that engaged in the research: community leaders and household heads; and representatives of governmental and non-governmental agencies.

Communities and Households

Community leaders and household heads commonly came to the research with the assumption that their comments and specific proposals for change would directly result in immediate reforms in programme design and delivery. This belief was most sparked by the official status of the evaluation and the strong commitment of participants to improving individual and collective needs. Since it has been argued above that the participatory research methods helped instil trust and cooperation then it is wise to assume that this approach played a role in raising such expectations. That is, the participatory nature of the research sent a very clear message that local perspectives mattered.

The mid-term evaluation inevitably impacted on the NSP but the communities' views of the relationship between the two was unrealistic. In particular, not all suggestions made by community leaders could lead to change. Reform was unlikely to be immediate or perhaps even discernible in some cases at the local level. Instead, changes to the NSP, and with relevance to the broader policy process in Afghanistan and other post-war societies, is more likely to be incremental. Accordingly, the research had to manage the expectations of participants at the community and household levels. The immediate research goal was to generate interest among participants by demonstrating the importance of the surveys and the mid-term evaluation overall. At the same time, the research had to achieve a medium to long-term goal which was to instil a more realistic understanding of how the findings might effect change.

In managing the expectations at the community level, the participatory methods were useful because they enabled the researcher to clarify and better inform respondents. The space for such discussion occurred at the individual and collective levels during the surveys and during debriefings. Notwithstanding inevitable exceptions, it was found that the participatory methods struggled but ultimately worked in tempering the distorted understanding of how the communities' responses could affect the programme during its final phase.

The failure to meet raised expectations is damaging for all evaluations but the risks are greater in the post-war environment. In Afghanistan, local frustrations with the rate of recovery and the quality of the peace dividend were obvious. Accordingly, it was essential that the mid-term evaluation did not exacerbate this phenomenon. Although follow ups with participants would be required ultimately to gauge the fulfilment of expectations, the participatory nature of the research and the interactions with respondents before, during and immediately after the research together indicate that the approach mitigated the main risks.

Governmental and Non-governmental Agencies

Participants from governmental and non-governmental agencies at the provincial level were more conservative in their understanding of programme change compared to community leaders and household heads. Agency representatives generally assumed that their input in the evaluation would not result in direct and significant reform of the programme.

In explaining this assumption, it is important to acknowledge that this type of respondent held a very different stake and perspective based on their technical knowledge, expertise and professional experience of the NSP and other recovery initiatives. More critically, agency representatives tended to be more conservative based on two observed attitudes during the semi-structured interviews: the perception that reform was undesirable; or an agnostic appreciation of external evaluations and policy change in general. For the former, change would have threatened vested interests and power positions that the NSP had provided and maintained. This exemplifies the degree of fragility and vulnerability within the context or conversely it could have been an indicator of weak accountability and compliance. In explaining the second conservative attitude – distrust of the ability of evaluations to create change – it was not difficult to find cynical attitudes to international intervention and the role of government in Afghanistan as a consequence of the country's tradition of subjugation through outside interference. In particular, some of the respondents and RATs confirmed the perception among humanitarian and development professionals that external evaluations were merely procedural, for internal and upward accountability purposes and thus limited in their ability to deliver substantive reform

In appreciating the aforementioned expectations within governmental and non-governmental respondents, it is essential to consider some of the ways in which the participatory methods could have played a contributing role. On the one hand, the focusing strategy to gain and maintain access was judged to be essential given the security and political dynamics within the provinces and the constraints of time and manpower. However, this strategy undoubtedly reinforced formal and informal power relations within and between institutions in the NSP because it was top-down and mirrored existing positions. Furthermore, the presentation of participatory methods on the surface would not have distinguished the mid-term evaluation from the myriad other evaluations. The choice of participatory methods would have been considered in vogue by seasoned respondents and the methods were selected, as noted above, to reflect best practice theory.

Alternatively though, it was found, in the case of Balkh at least, that the participatory methods allowed the author to challenge preconceived expectations among agency staff. As observed during the community and household surveys, the participatory nature of the semi-structured interview granted sufficient space to clarify the aim and objectives of the evaluation, the reasons for the design of the evaluation and to check the respondent's answers as they unfolded. It also ought to be acknowledged that the NSP had opponents but it was characterized more by support from governmental and non-governmental representatives. This dynamic obviously demanded attention but overall proved advantageous in the management of expectations.

The review of these two groups has revealed the versatility of participatory research methods in managing differing expectations. The design of the two surveys and the semi-structured interview were useful tools in this respect and given the contextual constraints. Nevertheless, this section has pinpointed the limits of these methods where there is a severe imbalance in power between communities and other programme stakeholders. It has also demonstrated how a participatory approach could have reinforced expectations and where the focusing strategy in particular risked cementing existing divisions.

Impact

Participatory approaches ought to have some long-term impact on the capacities of participants through their engagement in the process of a mid-term evaluation. This final section identifies how this potential is grounded in the rationale of participatory research. It is not possible here to verify if the NSP mid-term evaluation developed the capacities of participants but the analysis questions the likelihood of this outcome based on the size of the obstacles.

Potential for Capacity Development

Participatory methods imply that capacity development is an intended by-product. The inherent qualitative nature of the process, the prioritization of stakeholders and the reciprocal transfer of information between researcher and participant all point to the possibility of long-term substantive impact. A mid-term evaluation and the post-war context both further this assertion based on need to improve the programme at the half-way juncture and the widespread appreciation that war devastates individual and institutional capacities and thereby demands a holistic and concerted response. In a mid-term participatory evaluation, benefits for participants could centre on: technical knowledge, awareness, inclusion, decision-making, and communication, among other people-oriented goals. Such outcomes would indicate sound participatory research ethics, be of value to the programme under evaluation and more practically, represent a reasonable justification for respondents who have taken the time and interest to participate. The nature of the impact would obviously vary according to the existing level of capabilities, the specific interests and motivations of participants, and their relationship to the programme.

The NSP mid-term evaluation did not explicitly promise the development of participants' capacities but, as argued above, the potential for such outcomes is implied by the adoption of the participatory approach. In particular, the community and household surveys and the semi-structured interview were designed to be driven by the experiences and viewpoints of the respondents. The evaluation was sensitive to the community-driven development component of the programme and defined capacity at this level in relation to individual and institutional interactions (Barakat et al. 2006: 76). It was also intended that the surveys would connect directly with the communities' experience of using Participatory/Rapid Rural Appraisal (P/RRA) techniques to identify and address needs in the programme.[12] The participatory evaluation was self-consciously only one part of a much larger programme cycle involving participatory needs assessment, planning and project execution. The importance of using the mid-term juncture to learn and develop was realized throughout the research and the final report. In sum, programme and evaluation became interlinked by participation and both developed a shared interest in capacity development.

---

12   In relation to Nangarhar province, Jones (2006: 274) notes the communities use of focus groups to identify problems and rank priorities for project proposals.

Weak Stakeholder Capacities

During the field research in Afghanistan and upon completion of the final report, it was clear that the development of stakeholder capacities faced significant obstacles, which is typical of post-war societies. Capabilities and needs varied across types and location of stakeholders but the contextual constraints detailed above help explain the common fundamental deficits in this respect.[13] For example, the evaluation found that CDCs overall could 'function but with difficulty due to their own lack of management and leadership skills, lack of women's participation and/ or external political and economic constraints' (Barakat et al. 2006: 76). All levels were affected, as an Afghan government minister states '[w]e have become too reliant on foreigners as we lack knowledge about reconstruction programming. We are also very vulnerable to the World Bank and the IMF [International Monetary Fund] as we don't have the ability to argue with them on their own terms'. A senior civil servant confides '[a]fter 23 years of war we no longer possess the expertise to do our jobs properly' (Barakat et al. 2006, 126). High staff turnover was another recurring constraint stemming from the fluid nature of the post-war environment (Barakat et al. 2006: 34).

The ability to learn new skills and to participate in the NSP was notably weak across the provinces visited. For example, the transfer of skills overall between FPs and CDCs was judged to be limited (Barakat et al. 2006: 128). Only 'fifty per cent of the CDCs surveyed demonstrated an understanding of and a commitment to the democratic governance model involving participation and accountability to the whole community, as introduced by the NSP'. (Barakat et al. 2006: 72). RAT leaders in Badghis and Takhar provinces revealed the high level of illiteracy and other gaps in education in understanding why participation in the programme was so low at community and provincial levels (Omer 2006: 147 and 149; Wardak 2006b: 316). In Nangarhar, cultural constraints and intimidation from warlords and other powerful individuals were cited as the main obstacles to some communities' use of PRA techniques within the programme (Jones 2006: 274).[14]

The NSP mid-term evaluation had numerous deliberate and unintended impacts and it was beyond the scope of this chapter to provide a formal assessment. Therefore, the analysis above is consciously selective though insightful nonetheless. In considering the specific weaknesses among stakeholders, and with respect to the inevitable variations, the value that the mid-term evaluation added to the capabilities of participants appears to be negligible. Despite its strong participatory techniques and characteristics, it is difficult to believe that the evaluation process would have brought long-term benefits in terms of technical knowledge,

---

13   For example, communities in the provinces of Kabul and Kundoz were facing basic shelter problems while communities in Nangarhar were addressing more developmental needs. For more on these variations, see Barakat et al. (2006: 78–79).

14   See Barakat et al. (2006: 82–85) for a statistical breakdown of the weaknesses in program participation and capacity overall at the community level.

programme awareness, inclusion, decision-making, and communication, or any other such people-oriented goals. This finding is particularly interesting because it demonstrates that the evaluation followed the NSP's mistake of assuming an unrealistic level of individual and organizational capacity. Towards creating durable benefits for stakeholders that engage in participatory mid-term evaluations, it also instructs that researchers need to develop more strategic participatory methods in Afghanistan and other similar contexts.

Conclusions

A mid-term evaluation provides unique opportunities for a programme to reach greater maturity in design and implementation. A participatory approach attempts to position stakeholders at the centre of this process of reflection and reform. Simple and logical perhaps in theory but this chapter has demonstrated that the relationship between a participatory approach and a mid-term evaluation is much more complex and less certain in practice, with specific reference to Afghanistan and other similar fragile environments.

Using the case study of the NSP mid-term evaluation, the author has argued that participatory research methods were effective overall based on the ability of the methods to meet the aim and objectives of the evaluation, gather valid evidence, and manage the expectations of programme stakeholders as research participants. Nevertheless, the case study demonstrated how the participatory methods exhibited important weaknesses and struggled in resolving the tensions within each of these three central domains. In sum, it is found that participatory research methods can be an expedient means for a mid-term evaluation in war-torn contexts but the case study demonstrates the need for more strategic methodological interventions in order to enable durable benefits for both participants and programme. The author also provides the following five main conclusions by drawing upon his first-hand experience of leading the field research in Balkh province in tandem with close knowledge of the data collection process in the other ten provinces sampled by the evaluation. These conclusions are intended to provide insight into the use of participatory mid-term programme evaluations, and more broadly, the processes of statecraft and the complex dynamics of insider–outsider relationships in Afghanistan.

First, the research environment created formidable constraints. The programme was investigated both retrospectively and as it was implemented while access to data was restricted. The participatory nature of the approach was constricted by the impact of the war legacy on participants' capacities to engage and the evaluation's finite timeframe and resources.

Second, the use of the participatory approach allowed the evaluation team to meet the aim and objectives of the assessment. The methods forged a balance between meeting the competing demands for representativeness and scope versus those for detail and depth of knowledge. The methods also provided the researchers with the tools to develop trust and cooperation among participants and allowed sufficient flexibility without sacrificing consistency in investigation.

As the third conclusion, the NSP case study demonstrated how the participatory methods gathered valid evidence. The emphasis on consultation throughout and the inclusion of all six levels of the programme were important strengths in this respect. Nevertheless, the analysis revealed two instances of exclusion and at the same time acknowledged that the number of information flows included by the research and the need to cross-check these sources had pushed the resources of the evaluation team to their limits.

Fourth, this chapter has concluded that the participatory methods were able to manage the differing expectations of two sets of core participants. In particular, it was found that the surveys allowed the researchers to temper the overly ambitious understanding of reform that was held by community leaders and household heads. The flexible nature of the semi-structured interview then challenged the more conservative governmental and non-governmental staff to be more open in their perspectives on change. Despite this versatility, it was also recognized that the participatory approach, through the top-down nature of its focusing strategy for access, risked reinforcing existing disempowering divisions between communities and other stakeholders.

The fifth concluding point is perhaps the most critical since it questions the long-term direct benefits for participants and thereby critiques some of the rationale of such formative assessments in post-war societies. In the case study, the evaluation made the same mistake as the NSP by inaccurately estimating the capabilities of participants to engage in the research. Capacity development was central to the evaluation and the programme yet impact by both was weak. Therefore, it is found that the participatory approach at best reinforced an emerging culture of participation in governance recovery and economic development.

These five conclusions are relevant primarily to the context of Afghanistan so it is important to propose two broader lessons for formative studies in other post-war societies. First, based on the dynamics of these contexts and the attendant risks, it is constructive for programmes and their evaluations to interconnect but the research methodology of the evaluation ought to be aware of and seek to avoid perpetuating flaws in the programme's implementation. Finally, as researchers, it is essential to look beyond the obvious appeal of using the focusing strategy in participatory approaches to multi-level programmes, and to determine instead how bottom-up access strategies can be incorporated with respect to the constraints of the post-war context.

Bibliography

Barakat, S.B. et al. (2006), *Final Report of the NSP Mid-term Evaluation* (York: University of York).

Brown, R. (2006), 'Paktia Province: Provincial Field Research Findings', in Barakat, S.B., Chard, M., Connolly, D., Evans, M. and Jones, R., *Final Report of the NSP Mid-term Evaluation* (York: University of York), pp. 301–305.

Chard, M. (2006), 'Bamyan Province: Provincial Field Research Findings', in Barakat, S.B., Chard, M., Connolly, D., Evans, M. and Jones, R., *Final Report of the NSP Mid-term Evaluation* (York: University of York), pp. 203–216.

Connolly, D. (2006), 'Balkh Province: Provincial Field Research Findings', in Barakat, S.B., Chard, M., Connolly, D., Evans, M. and Jones, R., *Final Report of the NSP Mid-term Evaluation* (York: University of York), pp. 163–201.

Jones, R. (2006), 'Nangarhar Province: Provincial Field Research Findings, with Feedback and Analysis from Communities in Laghman Province', in Barakat, S.B., Chard, M., Connolly, D., Evans, M. and Jones, R., *Final Report of the NSP Mid-term Evaluation* (York: University of York), pp. 265–300.

Omer, W. (2006), 'Badghis Province: Provincial Field Research Findings', in Barakat, S.B., Chard, M., Connolly, D., Evans, M. and Jones, R., *Final Report of the NSP Mid-term Evaluation* (York: University of York), pp. 143–162.

Wardak, M. (2006), 'Kundoz Province: Provincial Field Research Findings', in Barakat, S.B., Chard, M., Connolly, D., Evans, M. and Jones, R., *Final Report of the NSP Mid-term Evaluation* (York: University of York), pp. 245–264.

— (2006b), 'Takhar Province: Provincial Field Research Findings', in Barakat, S.B., Chard, M., Connolly, D., Evans, M. and Jones, R., *Final Report of the NSP Mid-term Evaluation* (York: University of York), pp. 301–305.

Chapter 16

Participatory Research Methods in Post-conflict Reconstruction Study Visits

Alpaslan Özerdem

Introduction

The use of participatory research methods has become a common practice for most researchers involved in areas affected by natural disasters and armed conflicts. It would now be quite unthinkable for most researchers in our disciplines not to consider the application of some participatory rural appraisal (PRA) techniques in addition to more conventional research methods such as interviews, observations and surveys. This has been largely in parallel to an increasing number of postgraduate courses in those areas over the last 10 years and subsequently that most research method courses in a wide range of academic programmes from anthropology, politics and forced migration to post-conflict reconstruction, development and peace studies would now incorporate some elements of such participatory methods in their syllabuses. However, the question is how effectively such methods can be taught in the environment of a classroom; and especially, how ethical it would be for students to use such methods single-handedly during their MA or PhD field research, if they would have no opportunity of conducting a supervised field work. Even if they are provided with such a field study opportunity before starting to use them on their own, how possible it would be for them to gain adequate experience in a limited period of time, considering that due to time and financial constraints, such visits are usually short in duration. The ethical concerns here are particularly critical because of the very nature of such participatory methods and how they can have a number of negative consequences on societal relationships in a conflict or disaster-affected society if they are not applied properly. Therefore, this chapter will explore the issue of teaching participatory research techniques as part of conventional postgraduate research method courses and the way such techniques can be used in study visits individually or as a group by MA and PhD students. Starting its investigation from a set of practical and ethical concerns in using such techniques by students under or without supervision in disaster and conflict affected areas, the chapter questions how such methodologies can be taught, tested and practised in an ethical, effective and efficient way in the preparation of future researchers.

Teaching Participatory Research Methods in the Classroom

Differently from those participatory assessment and evaluation training courses run by various organizations working in disaster and conflict affected areas, when it comes to teaching such techniques in a classroom environment in higher education, there tend to be two major challenges. First of all, those research method courses that incorporate PRA techniques in their timetable would need to cover them in a limited period of time and in addition to other more conventional research methods. Second, working in a classroom there would be no real opportunities of experiencing the application of such techniques, and therefore, when postgraduate students would apply any of these methods as part of their field research it would often be the first time that they would actually be implementing them.

In a typical research methods course in politics or most other social sciences, there would already be an extensive list of primary qualitative and quantitative techniques to cover and in most instances they would need to be taught over two academic terms. In other words, in the design of such a module the facilitator would have no more than 8–10 lecture and seminar sessions in each term. Unless they can be provided in specifically designed PRA modules, which may be possible in certain disciplines such as development studies, those techniques would be covered only over a very limited period of time – often no more than a couple of weeks. As students of such modules would often complain, research method courses already tend to be very intensive with their content, not leaving enough time to cover each method adequately. Therefore, the reality with the limited time available in such modules means that the inclusion of participatory research methods tends to be a careful balancing act. Nevertheless, as for many students the use of such techniques would be an essential part of their research strategy or can be effectively used for triangulation purposes, it would be much better to incorporate them rather than exclude, as a result of such time constraints. Therefore, facing the challenge of teaching participatory methods as part of conventional research method courses, the first objective needs to be to underline the advantages and disadvantages of such techniques in relation to other qualitative methods like interviews and observation.

First of all, students need to understand the main ethos of participatory methods in order to make an informed judgment on their possible applications in the field. For example, it is critical to emphasize that field research with PRA techniques should be considered as a semi-structured process of learning from disaster/conflict affected women and men directly. It takes place in those people's own settings and aims at removing the often unbalanced power relationship between the researchers and researched as much as possible via its goal of drawing on ordinary people's physical, social, economic and technical knowledge. The improvization of the research process through a constant cross-checking would need to be an integral part of a participatory research process, and it is essential that students appreciate this fundamental issue from the very beginning.

Second, the application of such methods would mean a particular emphasis on diversity in that society in terms of its ethno-religious, gender and age groups; socio-cultural and economic characteristics of its households; and its other contradictions, differences and anomalies that students of these methods need to understand and subsequently, address the possible negative consequences of their research on societal relationships. This issue is particularly important, as it raises a number of ethical questions. As investigated in other chapters of this book, the ethical concerns with the use of participatory methods is possibly one of the most significant challenges for researchers. Without repeating what has already been said in previous chapters, what needs to be emphasized here is that students' awareness on this concern is imperative. In their choice of various participatory research methods they need to consider specific characteristics of their target groups and what possible foreseen and unforeseen implications that may emerge as a result of using such methods. For experienced researchers and those practitioners using such techniques, not opening old wounds of armed conflict is always an important criterion in their selection of methods, but can such a sensitive approach be really passed to new researchers successfully in a short period of time?

Third, as another fundamental principle, the teaching of participatory methods in classroom needs to put a particular emphasis on why students need to deal with communities with respect, showing humility in their interaction with those people who are not only poor and/or marginalized but also affected by a natural disaster or armed conflict. Therefore, they would need to understand the importance of showing patience in the undertaking of participatory methods and be genuinely interested in what the respondent knows, says and does. However, one of the main challenges that students are likely to face is to find the right balance between humility and adequate leadership for efficient facilitation of their research process. For example, if they start to be influenced with each direction and emphasis that they receive from different target groups on their topic because of their humility, this would be rather unproductive for their research time in the field. It is only normal that in highly politicized environments like those areas affected by disasters and conflicts there would likely to be different interest groups that would have a particular view of events that took place, and it is even possible that they may want to distort the truth in a particular way. In such cases, the need for triangulation and humility towards the society needs to be balanced well by the researcher. Although this may seem to be a contradiction to the first rule of participatory methods, which is the research being semi-structured and flexible for changes according to input from communities, the issue being advised here is not to lecture communities or lead them in order to complete the research process quickly. On the contrary, students need to learn how to seek out those groups which are poorer, marginalized and less likely to articulate their needs, concerns and priorities. This would be necessary not only for a sound level of humility but also critical for offsetting possible biases, therefore, it needs to form an essential aspect of the teaching of participatory method in classroom.

Finally, students need to consider PRA techniques as an approach to designing and planning their research process rather than solely as research methods. Such a distinction would help them consider the issues of participation much more effectively, in other words, leading them to question their role as researchers in relation to those communities researched. The power relationship between themselves and disaster-affected communities can be more effectively established by seeing PRA an outlook which would incorporate the issues of flexibility, openness, humility and facilitation, as discussed earlier. However, these issues would be realized efficiently only if the process is planned as a team work exercise rather than an individual process that is favoured by more conventional methods. As a fundamental principle of participatory methods, the teaching of such techniques needs to emphasize the importance of team work in their application. It is often the case that postgraduate students need to consider their research from an individualist perspective, as their research is geared towards an academic dissertation in which they need to demonstrate that it is their own work. This would prove to be an important challenge for students in the utilization of such techniques, as often they would be working on their own in the field and trying to apply participatory methods without the support of a team. Therefore, it is essential to teach how students can undertake such methods without a team, and what that would mean to the effectiveness of those methods. Students need to have an awareness of the possible biases that such a condition can result in their research findings.

The teaching of participatory methods in the classroom can also make the process as interactive as possible in order to train students adequately. To start with, it is important to show why such techniques are important and when they become particularly effective. In order to achieve this objective, I design a number of interview scenarios in which students would be divided into groups to conduct interviews with a mayor in a war affected town, a displaced family in a refugee camp and a large group of villagers. Some students are chosen to act in these scenarios, while others are placed in interview groups and provided with some basic information which they are asked to use to prepare their interview questions as a group. Those who are acting are also given some overall characteristics of their individual characters but allowed to come up with their own acting as part of their own scenario development. For example, for the elite interview with a mayor, the student is asked to pose a number of difficulties to the interviewers by being patronizing, deceptive, self-centred and sexist, while in the displaced family scenario the students are given the roles of an angry father, traumatized mother and disillusioned daughters, living in the difficult conditions of a refugee camp under the watchful eyes of a camp manager who has difficulties with accountability.

In the first interview scenario with the mayor, the students tend to tackle with the typical difficulties of elite interviews and although they may have some challenges with the mayor's certain attitudes that are caricatured and exaggerated, they tend to facilitate some sort of order with their questions and are often able to ask their questions and realize that by taking a number of precautions and going to those interviews prepared for such challenges, interviews as a method can be used effectively. As long as they can coordinate their questions and make sure that the process is facilitated by one of them as the group leader, they are able to conduct such an interview. In the second interview scenario, the challenge for the interviewer group is more difficult as rather than dealing with an individual interviewee they have a family and camp manager to consider. Students realize that interview as the sole method of information gathering becomes quite ineffective in such a scenario, because without building adequate trust and rapport with the refugee family they tend to struggle with getting any answers for their questions. As the scenario includes a number of people, the conversation of the interview obviously moves from one direction to another very quickly, often with different perceptions and issues emerging from the members of the interviewee family. It becomes clear that conventional research methods prove to be limited in their effectiveness in this scenario. However, as the interview target group is a family unit, the interviewing students tend to leave the scenario with a feeling that by adapting their interview technique in a more innovative way, it can still be used in such a scenario. Nevertheless, this example presents some strong signs of how difficult it is to get meaningful responses through an interview as a research method in such a scenario.

Having conducted and held discussions over those two scenarios, the class then starts to work on the third scenario. The group of students who are tasked to visit a village to conduct an initial probe for a more extensive future study are not aware that in the community to be visited there are huge societal differences and anomalies represented by such groups as the poor, former combatants and women. Equipped only with the technique of interview to seek answers for their questions, the interviewers' visit often turns into a total nightmare from the beginning to the end. They are not able to get the message across about their visit as the community is not prepared to listen and has different interests from those outsiders. No matter how prepared the interviewer students go to such a meeting, year after year they tend to stop the exercise half way through with the acceptance that it is not working. They are not able to facilitate the process and ask those questions prepared in advance. A feedback session following this scenario is facilitated for the class to identify what went right and wrong, as is the case with the previous two scenarios, and it is essential for the class to realize that they need other techniques than interview; as such a technique does not seem to work in certain circumstances. Enabling such a realization in the classroom teaching is essential as students themselves start to search for other methods rather than PRA techniques are presented them simply as other research methods. By doing this, it tends to be much easier to explain why participatory methods require an outlook approach and the reasons for them to be interactive and flexible, and conducted with humility.

If taking students to a supervised field study is not possible then it would be necessary to create similar scenarios for some of PRA techniques that there would be a chance to try them out before attempting their application in the field. Even the research methods course incorporates a field study visit to a disaster or war affected area, which would give an opportunity to test these methods in the field, in my teaching of these methods I still incorporate some hands-on sessions for various PRA methods. For example, the introduction of timelines and sketch-maps are first of all presented as possible ways of building bridges with communities as ice-breakers. When I explain these techniques by using flipcharts and coloured pens, I can always sense a certain level of scepticism among my students for the use of such techniques as proper and serious methods for academic field research. I am often told that such techniques remind of them what they are taught at primary school or educational children's programmes on television. Such a response should not be taken as a discouraging indicator of the interest of the students for such techniques, for this is only normal as their previous exposure to research methods at undergraduate level often tends to explain the research as a planned process with the use of conventional qualitative and quantitative techniques. Therefore, when they are told that they could learn so much about a particular community's history, socio-political structures and tensions in societal relationships by simply conducting a timeline exercise, they find this too good to be true. After all, all one does is indicate some dates on a line for time and engage participants into a conversation, and therefore, how could that possibly be considered a serious research technique? Meanwhile, the value of asking a community to come up with a map of their village or neighbourhood does not always seem to be appreciated fully in the first explanation. There are always many questions about how such a technique could possibly build trust between the researcher and community, or how such a sketch-map could be used to draw meaningful information for a research topic.

Having presented a couple of PRA techniques like this, I also prepare a couple of scenarios for students to use other more complicated techniques such as wealth ranking or social diagramming. Divided into groups, students are given the necessary information on how those techniques can be applied in different environments, and they are tasked to give an interactive presentation to train their fellow students on the use of their PRA technique. After working in their group for a couple of hours, it is amazing to see how innovative methods students can actually come up with in the teaching of such methods to their peers. For example, one year the group working on ranking technique used internet dating agency selection methods as an example to explain how wealth ranking can be applied in the most effective way. Another year, students brought the ranking exercise into the context of their student needs at the university, and involved their fellow students on a subject that really mattered for them. The objective with the involvement of students in the training process is particularly significant with showing how participatory methods need to be an outlook, and obviously making the learning process as interactive as possible is closely aligned with the main goal of such techniques. Also, their involvement in the explanation of such techniques to their fellow students is a good opportunity for them to practise their facilitation and training skills which are essential in participatory research processes.

Teaching Participatory Research Methods in the Field

Most postgraduate courses are unfortunately not able to combine their research methods modules with a field study visit, but those which incorporate such a component in their course structures are able to provide a great opportunity to their students to test and learn from mistakes under supervision. The MA course in Post-war Recovery Studies at the Post-war Reconstruction and Development Unit (PRDU), University of York, UK, conducts a 10-day group field study visit in a war-affected country in December of each academic year. The visit takes place after the first two taught modules which also incorporate an intensive research methods component, including participatory research methods. The class is divided into three or four groups of 8–10 students each, and each group is tasked with a particular relief, reconstruction or peacebuilding issue depending on the particular focus of that visit. For example, during a study visit in Jordan the students focused on the livelihoods, health and education challenges faced by Iraqi refugees there, while another year in Northern Ireland, the students were asked to concentrate on a number of peacebuilding issues such as identity transformation, cultural heritage and housing. On the other hand, when we conducted our study visit in Lebanon, the focus was the relief and rehabilitation needs of populations in the aftermath of the 2006 summer war with Israel. As for the preparation for the visit, divided into groups students start to work on their specific focus in early November, which would give them time to establish some primary group work dynamics among themselves and understand the context that they will operate in during the study visit as much as possible. Holding regular meetings, this preparatory process ensures that the students embark on their visit with a thorough understanding of socio-political, economic and cultural characteristics of the field study country.

Such field study visits usually start with a one or two day orientation workshop in which a number of representatives from national authorities and the international community present briefings on their activities. Hence, students can further build their contextualization by meeting a wide range of actors and understanding how they attempt to tackle those relief and reconstruction issues that they would be exploring during their visit. As well as meeting some key stakeholders, the PRDU, through their local partner organizations and academic institutions, also sets up a number of introductory meetings for all study groups. However, this would be as much planning assistance as students would expect, because afterwards it would be up to them to follow up the links from their orientation workshop and organize further meetings and start to apply their research strategy through a snowball approach. Although the groups would not have a supervisor with them all the time, their work is supervised by a system of briefing and debriefing meetings at the beginning and end of each day. The groups can also ask for assistance with the planning or application of a particular participatory research method at any time. During these study visits students are encouraged to apply a wide range of research methods, but the choice of techniques to utilize is left to them as this represents an integral aspect of their learning process. The objective here is to facilitate a conducive environment in which they start to use participatory methods as an outlook and make their decisions accordingly. If it seemed they were about to make a mistake, they could be assisted to adjust their strategy with the application of different techniques, but it is also important to let some mistakes be made. Learning from first-hand experiences will likely be the most effective method and no matter how many times good practice guidelines for participatory methods are repeated in the class, at the end it is important for students to find their own way with them.

With the use of participatory methods in field study visits there are two main concerns that need to be addressed carefully. First of all, such visits would need to be undertaken in a limited period of time. Ideally, it would be great to be able to spend at least three to four weeks in the field so that students can have plenty of time to plan and use such techniques. However, considering that those visits often need to be integrated in a tight academic timetable and require a substantial budget for travel, accommodation and subsistence expenses, met by students, it is necessary to limit their durations. With that reality in mind, students need to utilize their in-group resources in the most effective way possible. On each given day in the field, dividing themselves into further sub-groups can mean that each team can accumulate considerable amount of information over a few days. However, this does not mean that students need to work with too much haste, which can easily create a number of biases or prevent certain biases from being addressed effectively. Also, they are not always able to work with the same community during their study visits; therefore, there would be difficulties with the application of different PRA techniques to build up a cohesive picture. Although, this may be a problem for group study visits for MA students, PhD researchers could be more flexible in their planning and implementation, as they are able to make these decisions themselves according to the specific needs of their research, which is not the case for MA field study visits as they are to a large extent planned for students. PhD research can also utilize a much longer period of time and work with the same community, if necessary, so that participatory methods can be truly effective for gathering insightful information from ordinary women and men of that community. Bearing in mind time limitations in MA study visits, it might be advisable to encourage students to go for more straightforward techniques such as timelines and sketch-mapping initially in order to test their facilitation abilities and understand the difficulties of using participatory methods.

It is interesting to note that students tend to be highly apprehensive about using PRA techniques. On one hand, they seem to identify their value but on the other hand, they are not quite sure whether such techniques would actually work for them in enabling the gathering of insightful information. It would be good for students to go through their plans for participatory methods with their supervisors just before their application. The debriefing session on the night before can be used to consolidate those plans and share them with supervisors, and the final points and last minute clarifications can be made during the morning briefing session of that day. Having applied them, it is always a rewarding experience to see students coming back from their field work in the evening and talking about their great experiences with various PRA techniques. The discovery of the fact that by using some of these simple techniques they can build up a good level of rapport with their interviewees seems to be a great learning point for them. From that point onwards, even interviews turn into a method that can be adjusted and moulded according to the specific characteristics of target groups. For example, a school visit turns into an experience of MA students doing drawings with school kids and in that process talking to them about their lives, education experiences and homes; or interviewing youth would no longer need to be talking to them in a formal interview environment but on a football pitch while playing football or in a youth centre through a focused discussion group facilitated by some of the PRA techniques.

On the other hand, as the second main concern with the use of participatory methods during field study visits, it is important to recognize the ethical dimension of such undertakings. It is clear that the exercise taken is for primarily learning reasons and although it is important for students to practise such research methods under supervision before starting to use them on their own, the issue of practice should be considered carefully. There are a number of ethical concerns to be borne in mind. First of all, such study visits work with communities that have gone through a traumatizing experience such as an armed conflict or natural disaster. For example, interviewing a refugee family could easily open wounds of having lost their relatives and friends before or during displacement, experienced unbearable fear and torture during conflict, horrendous difficulties of forced displacement in their day-to-day lives, missed educational and economic opportunities, or having been disillusioned with their future and humanity in general. Second, certain groups among disaster and conflict affected communities might have particular vulnerabilities such as child soldiers, orphans, war veterans and those who experienced rape. Third, having experienced all these losses, difficulties and animosities in their lives, how ethical would it be to ask them to take part in a learning exercise which at the end, is very unlikely to have any direct contributions to their lives? When such methods used as part of needs and capacities assessment undertaken by relief and reconstruction agencies to plan their programmes, there is an obvious objective for them to involve in such PRA methods, but when a group of MA students or PhD researcher asking them to invest their time and answer questions that can mean revisiting painful experiences, there is not such a justification. Finally, there is always the risk of the whole field research experience turning into some sort of disaster tourism. If disaster-affected communities start to feel that their privacy is not respected, they are treated as objects of a learning exercise and belittled with the whole experience due to the one-sided power relationship between themselves and students, then naturally, there would no longer be any justification for the continuation of such a visit.

What can be done to address such ethical concerns? To start with, it is important to note that such concerns would not be the case for only student field study visits. However, the main objective of learning brings a different dimension to these concerns, as some may argue that this would be like conducting medical tests on human beings before conducting laboratory trials. However, it is possible to address some of these concerns to a large extent. First of all, students need to be absolutely clear about the objectives and motivations of their time in the field. Once they know why they are there and what they are supposed to do, then the next issue to consider is the need for them to be honest and open about their research intentions with their interviewees and communities involved in PRA methods. It should be should be explained to them at the beginning that they have the option of not taking part or withdrawing from the research process. Secondly, connecting the learning experience with a research task makes the whole experience much more targeted and specific so that when communities involved in the process see the value of research process for students' learning then they would often be happy to take part in them. Third, the facilitators of such visits can set guidelines in terms of which would be acceptable groups to involve in the process, and which groups the students should avoid unless they take part as observers during outreach visits of the organizations working with such vulnerable people, if this is possible and acceptable for both those organizations and beneficiaries. Dealing with trauma and certain groups would obviously require particular knowledge and skills, and unless such expertise is available among students, then such groups should be excluded from the process. Finally, the way students approach and interact with these communities and ask their questions, as well as the way they are dressed, sit and talk would all play a role in whether communities' experience of the process is demeaning or rewarding one.

Over the years I have been to such disaster and conflict affected environments both as a researcher and supervisor numerous times, and I think that as long as a researcher, whether a student or senior academic, approaches such communities with respect and humility, most of these ethical concerns can be addressed easily. By adopting PRA as an outlook rather than a set of research methods can also be quite useful for this purpose, as it would require the establishment of a much more finely tuned balance of power between researchers and researched. Given that this point is explained clearly at the beginning, in most cases, even not gaining anything in return is not an issue for disaster-affected communities. On the contrary, having a researcher being interested in their experiences because of who they are, rather than as a potential beneficiary group or for reporting in the media, has a certain empowering impact that should not be neglected. Asked sensitively and in a considered manner, disaster-affected people would usually be willing to share their experiences no matter how difficult that may be for them. It is only a matter of self-reflection of students on their position vis-à-vis communities and being able to exhibit constructive empathy when they plan and implement their research methods that could deal with these ethical concerns effectively.

Finally, the testing of different PRA techniques in a field study visit would show that some of them would not be possible to apply unless there is a certain period of interaction and they can only be used after establishing a substantial understanding of the community. Therefore, they may not be suitable for short study visits but one of the main advantages with some postgraduate courses like the MA in Post-war Recovery Studies is that they may incorporate a work placement component during which students would have more opportunities to use such research techniques. For example, the students of MA in Post-war Recovery Studies undertake their internships over a period of eight to ten weeks, mainly in conflict-affected countries. While they carry out their work placements with renowned international organizations and national and local authorities, they also have an opportunity to gather data and information for their dissertations. It is for this purpose that they can consider the use of participatory research techniques if their dissertation topic would lend itself towards such methods. Having undertaken the group field study visit under supervision means that they could have much more confidence with the use of PRA techniques on their own. They could still get feedback from their academic supervisors in York and work supervisors in the field, on the use of such methods, but overall, they need to act as independent researchers and take the whole responsibility of research planning and implementation. Experience in York shows that the transformation of students with the knowledge and ability of using participatory methods from November to the time they undertake their internships from March to June is often quite amazing and demonstrates that by giving the necessary opportunities it is possible to train students in such methods in a fairly short span of time.

Conclusion

The inclusion of participatory research methods such as PRA techniques is now frequent for postgraduate courses in disaster, conflict and peace studies. However, the challenge of whether such techniques can lend themselves to effective teaching as part of conventional research method courses in a limited duration without much opportunity of practice is what this chapter sought to address. Differently from training courses organized for practitioners that would have a strong practical element, or adopting a learning-on-the-job approach taken by some organizations, teaching such methods to postgraduate students needs to tackle a number of obstacles. First of all, it is imperative to ensure students understand why such participatory methods are needed, and when and how they can be particularly effective for academic research. The framing of PRA research methods as an outlook in order to define and establish the main contours of the research is essential for students so that they can distinguish their use from the application of more conventional research methods. From the way the community is contacted and initial interaction was established, to the selection of translators and equipment/materials to be used in those methods would all need to be considered carefully. It is all about equipping students with the necessary skills to make informed decisions on the politics of conducting their research, and to establish sound and equal power relationships between themselves and those communities they would be working with in their research. Second, in relation to these power relationships the need for humility needs to be judged carefully. It is absolutely critical that students accept and internalize the importance of humility, because the consideration of PRA as an outlook would demand the placing of the women and men of the community, no matter how marginalized, vulnerable and inarticulate they are, at the centre of their research process. However, this should not mean that they would not need to facilitate the process through an effective coordination perspective. Lecturing communities should definitely be avoided but being impressionable would also not be helpful for their research either. Finally, in ensuring students take an outlook approach to participatory methods and adopt a well balanced humility towards the community, the need for flexibility to change, adapt and improve research plans is also something students should be taught carefully.

If the teaching of participatory research methods cannot benefit from the opportunity of practising in the field under supervision, then the process would be strengthened by the incorporation of some group work based around set scenarios or hands-on exercises. Although the preparation of the tasks, getting students working on them, presentations by students and ensuring that they are followed by extensive discussions and feedback would all be quite time consuming, they can be highly effective to show what such methods can actually manage in a very effective way. The direct participation of students through a trainers-of-trainers approach can provide a number of opportunities in the inclusion of such classroom practices. In order to make the subject more accessible and interesting, the input of students is often quite critical and such peer-teaching proves to be a good methodology for effective learning.

If conducting a group field study visit as part of research methodology course is possible, then obviously this would be an ideal scenario for students. Engaging in such a visit under supervision in a disaster or war affected country would provide students with a number of opportunities to practise participatory research methods. Nevertheless, such a study visit would need to consider certain logistical and ethical issues in their planning as they are not free from difficulties. As those visits would also have a limited time in the field, the structure of the visit needs to enable students to use their resources and capacities effectively. Although some planning to initiate the process is essential, it is also important to leave students with a certain level of independence to decide on what research methods to incorporate and how to use them in their overall research strategy. Rather than trying to have a mistake-free process, students need to be allowed to make mistakes but as long as they are made in a supervised environment, they would primarily remain in the realm of planning. In order to ensure this, there need to be clear guidelines on who cannot be incorporated in the process as a target group, what techniques cannot be used or how certain methods need to be adopted to make them possible as part of such a learning process. Even a limited period of time in the field would be highly beneficial to give students the opportunity of trying out different methods and test themselves with their uses.

Overall, it cannot be emphasized enough why such field study visits are so essential to strengthen students' skills and capacities with participatory research methods. Having conducted their study visit, the students of MA in Post-war Recovery Studies write a field study report on their specific research focus. Although visits are undertaken in a small group, essays are written individually and this also gives an extra challenging dimension to the task of such a field work. As their essays would be examined according to their own merits, students would need to establish effective teamwork dynamics so that they do not only carry out the study as a group, but also share all findings among all members of their group effectively. As their field study report would include a section of the field research methodology, they would have the opportunity to reflect on how their fieldwork went and how it could have been undertaken in an improved way. After the field study component, MA in Post-war Recovery Studies students would also have the chance of applying a wide range of research methods during their work placements which are often closely linked with students' dissertation topics. It is only through a step-by-step approach that students can be equipped with a set of research methods skills that can be applied in different contexts both as a practitioner and researcher.

Chapter 17

Conclusion to Part II

Alpaslan Özerdem and Richard Bowd

Introduction

The previous seven chapters in Part II attempted to seek insights into the application of participatory research methodologies in environments affected by armed conflicts. Each one of them represented a number of characteristics and merits through the ways that they enabled a deeper exploration of the three main groups of challenges faced by researchers: a respondent element, a researcher element and an effectiveness element, as explained in Chapter 9. Therefore, it is important to remember those qualities before deriving the main conclusions for this section.

First of all, using a combination of ethnographic methods, life histories, elite interviews, and such participatory rural appraisal (PRA) techniques as landscape mapping, institutional diagramming; social network mapping and social capital indicators, Bowd's application of participatory research methods took place in a largely unexplored theoretical context: that of the promotion of enhanced social capital in a post-genocidal conflict environment and its implications for reconciliation. The chapter explored how such methods contributed to the understanding of social capital and reconciliation in war-torn areas.

Second, although similarly focused on the reintegration of former combatants in an African country, the chapter by Asiedu presented the use of door knocking technique as a trust building approach, while Podder investigated the use of such participatory methods and their particular ethical challenges in child soldier focused research programmes. In post-conflict environments where the lack of trust poses a major concern, Asiedu demonstrated that the door knocking approach, as a complimentary measure to participatory research methods, can strengthen research validity by easing the process of gaining the trust and confidence of communities before and during the research process. On the other hand, Podder tried to deal with the challenge of trust through affiliation with a well respected international organization amongst the research's target group, and tackled the question of how such methods can be used effectively in environments where the distinction between civilian and combatant is highly ambiguous.

Third, although both undertook academic-centred research, Holt and Robins highlight the way such participatory methods can also be used for the empowerment of war-affected communities. Blended with the critical feminist theory, rather than imposing them from outside, in Holt's use of participatory research methods the participants, their needs and their priorities were involved in the process from an early stage. Meanwhile, Robins saw the application of participatory research methods as an opportunity for advocacy work by enabling a co-dependence between the research agenda and the desire of research target group who is formed by the victims of human rights abuses and disappearances for the dissemination of their needs.

Fourth, Connolly's chapter took the application of participatory research methods to the context of a mid-term evaluation. Through the application of such participatory methods as the community power and household surveys and semi-structured interviews, the complex relationship between participatory research and program evaluations was investigated. Finally, Özerdem explored the effectiveness and ethical aspects of teaching such participatory methods as part of conventional postgraduate research method courses in the class and their testing in the field for the preparation of future researchers.

Respondent-Related Challenges

All case studies in this section showed that access, both physical and emotional, is one of the main challenges in the application of participatory research methods. Differently from development and disaster environments, the magnitude of this problem is particularly the case in conflict environments as research is often undertaken in divided societies. Therefore having access to research target groups would likely overcome not only such inaccessibility problems as bad road conditions and other forms of poor infrastructure, but also negotiating with those who would have the power to control such an access to war-affected populations. In the case of Bowd's research with former combatants in Rwanda, he had to work closely with such gatekeepers as national authorities and local actors for reintegration. Meanwhile, Podder affiliated herself with an international organization and initiated her research in Liberia by focussing on the program beneficiaries of this organization as an entry point in order to enable a snowball process. Similarly, the affiliation with local associations for the families of disappeared people in Nepal was the way Robins dealt with the physical access challenge. On the other hand, the application of door knocking was the way for Asiedu to identify gatekeepers for his research in Sierra Leone and, as well as assuring his physical access to research target groups, he also managed to gain emotional access so that his respondents were less likely to hold back information as a result of lack of trust. Podder's affiliation with an international organization meant that emotional access was also much easier, as the programme staff had already established constructive relationships with her research target group; therefore, it was much easier to be accepted as an outsider and conduct her interviews for life histories.

Once access was gained the next highly critical challenge in the research processes was that of informed consent; due to the invasive nature of participatory research methods. The chapters in Part II identified the importance of gaining an informed consent of those war-affected people who take part in the process as. To deal with this issue, Bowd asked each respondent 'if they understood what the research was about and what was to be asked of them and were informed they were free to withdraw at any time', as this is particularly important for such cases in which research methods would remind participators of their traumatic experiences of conflict and losses. To lessen the potential of re-traumatization, Robins conducted his interviews in either a family or small peer group 'where support is available to those telling their stories and will continue to be available in the family or community once the interview is complete'. On the other hand, Robins pointed out that respondents were grateful that 'an outsider was taking an interest in their issues, and that this was the first time anyone had consulted them on their opinion of their needs and the action they sought'. Furthermore, the issues of trauma and vulnerability are also particularly pertinent in research on child soldiers, and Podder had to take a number of precautions to ensure that her research first of all did no harm emotionally, and those adult combatants and child soldiers involved in the research process were clearly explained the purpose and scope of the research. By directing her in-depth interviews towards open ended story-telling, she allowed a free and participatory research process and ensured an 'extremely honest, approachable and frank' interaction with her respondents. In Connolly's case, the respondents of evaluation 'probably felt obliged to take part' due to the official undertaking of the process, which in return may have affected their critical perspectives of the project.

Holt's research with refugee women in Lebanon identified a number of other interesting respondent-related challenges. First of all, she tackled the issue of language used by both the researcher and the researched. She was concerned that she was perhaps cocooning refugee women 'in a shroud of impenetrable jargonized language', while for many of the women who took part in her research '[c]ertain topics, such as painful personal information, were taboo, while others, for instance pride in the liberation struggle or the hopelessness of return, were clearly and repeatedly stated'. Moreover, women who took part 'had no clear purpose and not even much enthusiasm to participate in the process'. On the other hand, for Robins, the advocacy approach meant that families interviewed could easily see that 'the research could potentially offer them indirect benefit', making their participation more purposeful and willing. This is particularly important as, highlighted by Holt; respondents are often 'suspicious of the researcher's motives or concerned about the purposes for which their disclosures will be used'. It is in relation to this challenge that all case studies highlighted the importance of assuring respondents with anonymity. For Bowd's research with former combatants this was critical to attain a good number of informants, gain their trust and, more importantly, protect them 'from any danger the information they provide may place them in'. As pointed out by Robins, confidentiality and the anonymous transmission of statements are all consent related issues underlying the importance of why it should be considered carefully in research planning and application.

Researcher-Related Challenges

Who the researcher is seems to be as critical as those challenges related to respondents. For example, being a female researcher meant a number of challenges for Podder in Liberia, which ranged from dealing with blatant emotional overtures from male expatriates to restrictions in her freedom of movement in certain areas and times. Meanwhile, being a male researcher restricted Asiedu from gaining access to female respondents due to cultural and religious practices in local communities and Bowd had to deal with being a white man and its cultural connotations in Rwanda. Asiedu utilized his door knocking approach to identify female fixers to assist him in involving female respondents in his research process, while Podder made sure that her research assistant accompanied her in most interviews. Therefore, it is clear that gender relations between the researcher and the researched play a significant role in the establishment of trust and rapport with communities in participatory research.

Another common denominator in all cases was the challenge of being an outsider and the way this affected research in different ways. For example, being affiliated to a western university and international organization Podder 'was viewed as one of privilege' creating a power barrier between the researcher and her respondents. Holt experienced this as being a non-Muslim non-Arab researcher, and although she had visited her case study country a number of times before her research, she 'was still a relative stranger'. To deal with it she 'began by acknowledging traditional power relations and the imbalances caused thereby between the researcher and the "objects" of her research and then made a conscious effort to hand over as much of that power as possible to the participants'. Such issues are particularly important as they inform the level of interaction that the researcher can ensure in the application of participatory methods. Being too close to communities could affect researchers' objectivity in their way of thinking and not being close enough on the other hand, could easily have huge detrimental impacts on the successful implementation of participatory methods. As part of his door knocking approach, Asiedu participated in various social functions to overcome the challenge of being an outsider as much as possible, while Bowd used the development of a geographical map of the area to build up a rapport with community members and gave 'an understanding of, and confidence in, what they were doing which was crucial to gaining rich data in the subsequent PRA techniques'. Getting too close to communities was a particular risk in Robins' research due to its advocacy element, as the associations for disappeared people 'determined the goals of the research process and the methodology' and, as was pointed out clearly, this would 'only work where the research agenda seeks articulation or addressing of issues that the community prioritizes'.

The collection of sensitive information and exposure to war traumatized people and their problems could also have a negative impact on the researcher. Conducting a research on child soldiers in Liberia where communities experienced gruesome war tactics or in Nepal where people's loved ones disappeared due to human rights abuses meant that Podder and Robins had to deal with traumatized adults and children, and researching in such an environment could easily take its toll on the researcher's emotional well-being. Similarly, the women's oral accounts in Lebanon were distressing for Holt, but at the same time, they also enriched her 'own life experience and our knowledge and appreciation of the precarious situation of Muslim women in situations of conflict'. Overall, all contributors in this section have made some reference to the difficulties of emotional composure and being able to deal with the stress of conducting research in a demanding environment due to its taxing psycho-social, physical and security conditions. However, it is interesting to note that although they all had different ways of dealing with stress and trauma, they did not necessarily have built-in mechanisms in their research processes. This aspect did not seem to be recognized as a critical issue, though it could have easily had serious health ramifications on themselves.

Effectiveness-Related Challenges

As explained in Chapter 9, effectiveness-related challenges are based on the reaction between respondent and researcher elements. For example, emotional access, sensitivity and insider–outsider relationship that would all have clear impacts on effectiveness are actually constructed from a combination of challenges reviewed in the previous two sections. Therefore, the focus here will be on another three fundamental issues: application of participatory methods, managing expectations and research ethics.

It is interesting to note that all contributors had different reasons and their own trademarks in the application of participatory research methods. For example, almost all of them used semi-structured oral history techniques for different reasons. For Holt, it was 'the most effective way of gleaning a relatively broad picture of an individual woman's experiences of conflict' as it gave 'the individual woman a degree of control over, and a stake in, the procedure'. Similarly, Bowd wanted to understand how a former combatant's 'perceptions of conflict and their role in it feeds into their personality, and how he or she subjectively constructs his own identity'. On the other hand, for Podder, the 'free flowing process of sharing ex-combatant experiences greatly enabled the respondents to feel they had legitimate grievances which made them fighters', and which 'made many of the younger respondents and women, reflect on their current situation more objectively'. However, she interspersed them 'with some structured questions on age, affiliation, status and mobility during the different phases of the conflict' so that the method would 'keep a tab on timelines and experiences prior to and post-demobilization'.

Both Holt and Podder also used participant observation as one of their main research techniques, while it was more like a supportive method for other contributors, and as pointed out by Podder, the 'observation of behaviour, mannerisms, communication and body language in intra-group and inter-group interactions revealed important insights'. However, while she and Holt did not use any particular PRA techniques, Bowd and Asiedu introduced them in all stages of their research. For Bowd, the process of PRA and the time spent with community itself was particularly significant as it 'served as an introduction period to the community' and provided 'vital data concerning the physical and social constitution of the community and community dynamics'. For him also, such techniques as landscape mapping, institutional diagramming and analysis and social network mapping were means of enabling 'further triangulation and comparison through offering an additional perspective from the same respondents'. Connolly, as part of his mid-term evaluation, employed the community power and household surveys in a participatory way, and in addition to semi-structured interviews, they formed the main means of information gathering in his research. Furthermore, 'the design of the community power survey reduced the need to write down responses and this built trust between researcher and community leaders'. He also held many 'briefings and debriefings among participants, and stakeholders more broadly, thus proved useful in clarifying trends and identifying exceptions and irregularities in the data'. Such examples are frequent throughout the text but the main lesson emerging is that there is a great level of variation in the interpretation and flexibility in the application of participatory research methods. The researchers in this section used them in such a way that they fit into their overall research aim and objectives, and all of them agreed that the main attraction of these methods remains with the fact that they could create their own hybrid methods or, like the case with Bowd's social capital indicators technique, they can even be invented during the research process.

Managing expectations emerged as a critical issue in the application of participatory methods in an evaluation context, which brings an additional dimension to the insider–outsider debate and power structures between the researcher and the researched. Connolly's evaluation stakeholders 'came to the research with the assumption that their comments and specific proposals for change would directly result in immediate reforms in program design and delivery'. As explained, this was largely due to 'the official status of the evaluation and the strong commitment of participants to improving individual and collective needs'. In a situation like this Connolly had to address a number of possible biases that may affect the way community leaders and household heads shared their experiences. Similar concerns with respondents' raised expectations were also the case with more academic-centric research undertakings. As pointed out by Asiedu, Bowd, Holt and Podder, they had to make a specific effort to explain that there would be no direct, tangible return as a result of their research to their war-affected communities as for example, this might be the case after a needs assessment conducted by an NGO. On the other hand, Robins' research experience on disappeared people represented a distinctive example for managing expectations, as to a large extent those expectations formed the main thrust of his academic research. As explained, such a:

participatory engagement with family associations permitted a level of access and acceptance by the research subjects that would not have otherwise permitted the ethnographic approach that was sought…This engagement was predicated on the victims' own agenda and resulted in an advocacy approach that concretised the mutuality of interests of the researcher and the researched.

Finally, as is the case with the challenge of managing expectations, the contributors in this section also identified a number of other ethical concerns and considerations and as pointed out by Robins in his research:

the individuals and families concerned were poor, of low formal educational attainment, often women and very often from socially marginalised ethnic or caste groups. They are also people who have survived the traumatising effect of conflict, live in an environment that may still be highly divided and are being questioned about the issue of a disappeared relative that is potentially traumatising.

In other words, ethical concerns were largely due to the legacy of conflict on the well being of individuals and societal relationships. However, the relationship between the respondent and the researcher from an outsider–insider perspective was also a significant factor in the emergence of ethical dilemmas, some of which were presented in the previous sections.

Meanwhile some of those ethical concerns were quite issue-centric, as was the case with Podder's research on child soldiers, that is, data collection through adult care givers, or children's understanding, interpretation and coping mechanisms being different from that of adults. Asiedu's door knocking approach itself also raised some ethical concerns, as it involved gift giving which might be considered as a way of enticing respondents 'to reflect the views of the researcher and compromise the research findings'. In line with variations in ethical concerns, the case studies also recorded different ways of approaching them. For example, although he noted its possible ramifications as research biases, Asiedu continued with his door knocking methodology for its greater benefits for identifying appropriate gatekeepers, dealing with translation inaccuracies, more effective snowballing benefits and enabling construct validity. Meanwhile, although the discussions in PRA techniques applied by Bowd were at times 'somewhat heated' and this could have been considered as exacerbating war-damaged societal relationships and the researcher would have been expected to 'ensure everyone had their say', he wanted to observe the situation as 'the way in which people communicate and interact provides an indication of social capital and reconciliation'.

Overall, the key lesson from all of the case study chapters in this section can be summarized as the importance of flexibility and considered approach in all aspects of participatory research methods. It is clear that the process is full of challenges which are not only obstacles to prevent the research from being conducted but often they are very much the integral aspects of that very research undertaking itself.

They are not only contextual matters but also what would constitute as the main characteristics of the research. For example, the researcher-related challenges seem to emerge as a result of their combinations with those related to the respondent, and what the effectiveness of the research is all about is in a way how those two actors interact with each other. It is clear that the relationship between them is influenced, managed or even controlled by a myriad of surrounding elements, but participatory research methods seem to provide a much greater level of response flexibility to such obstacles and characteristics than more conventional methods.

Chapter 18

Conclusion: A Comparative Analysis of the Use of Participatory Research Methods in Development, Post-disaster and Post-conflict Contexts

Alpaslan Özerdem and Richard Bowd

Introduction

The primary objective of this book was to understand and explore the use of participatory research methods in the three distinctively different contextual environments of development, post-disaster and post-conflict. As literature on participatory methods often concentrates on why and how such methods should be used in the development context, the main contribution of this book to knowledge therefore, is the way it incorporates post-disaster and post-conflict environments as its other areas of focus. Having investigated the challenges faced in their application in those three environments and how researchers and practitioners deal with them in different approaches, a set of conclusions on the use of such methods were already highlighted in Chapters 8 and 17. Therefore, the overall conclusions will aim at a comparative analysis for the use of participatory research methods in the three different contexts, and in order to achieve this, the chapter will use the taxonomy of participation, power and empowerment to analyse the similarities and contrasts between them. Following this analysis, the chapter will end with a set of recommendations for an improved practice in the use of such methods.

Participation, Power and Empowerment

As explained in Chapter 1, the concept of participation and how it can be turned into practice is still a highly controversial issue debated by both practitioners and researchers. The utilization of local knowledge and what that constitutes and in the way it has been highly romanticized in certain circles of practice and academia were some of the issues that have already been elaborated. Furthermore, the case study chapters demonstrate that the most critical issues to be borne in mind are those related to such considerations as whose knowledge, and how it could be assessed and incorporated in a research process, and finally whether or not it is actually an achievable objective, as the realities of their contextual challenges often force them to remain as rhetoric only.

As explained in Chapter 3, Anna Mdee made a special effort to deal with the issue of local knowledge from its identification to the incorporation into the research process by dealing with various power issues in Tanzania. In her research, participation meant partnership with 'active local community researchers' and a specific focus on the role of local researchers as 'community mediators and representatives'. There was a clear recognition of the possibility that there may be a different focus on the priorities and implementation of the research from insider and outsider perspectives. Therefore, for Mdee, the use of participatory research methods had to 'go beyond the "quick and dirty" application of PRA tools to have a deeper "community" involvement in the research from inception to final analysis'. However, Mdee's realization regarding the power relationship between the researcher and the local research team was striking, as she explained that 'given imbalances in knowledge, power and resources' it is impossible to ensure an 'absolute equality'. It seems that no matter how hard Mdee tried to overcome such a power relationship between herself and the local researchers, they continued to consider her as the boss. More importantly, in terms of whose knowledge that really matters to have a comprehensive understanding of the situation, as Mdee rightly points out that it 'is not helpful necessarily to see the poor as "experts" on their own poverty', as there could be a wide range of socio-economic and political factors that would prevent them from possessing such knowledge. However, what is highly crucial to consider is that the real value of participatory research methods is the fact that it 'is more concerned with a philosophy of respect and humility, a way of accessing specific local knowledge and of beginning a long-term interaction of reflection and action that necessarily must extend beyond the boundaries of a particular community'. In other words, approaching community as the sole source of knowledge can be misleading but this does not mean that community should be disregarded. Subsequently, the only way to benefit from whatever knowledge they have would be through respect and humility.

In another development context, Richard Jones' research in Rwanda was 'to define poverty from the prospective of different communities primarily in terms of perceptions of wealth'. Participatory research methods were utilized in the development of poverty baselines for the preparation for the 2001 Rwandan Poverty Reduction Strategy Paper (PRSP). However, as explained in Chapter 4, Jones experienced a number of challenges for the participatory characteristics of his assessment strategy. First of all, the perception of his identity as *mzungu* meant that participants were often exaggerating the difficulties of their circumstances 'due to expectations from outsiders' and as part of group dynamics that key informants attempted to influence the findings of his research from their own set of interests. Similarly, in the context of a drought recovery and famine mitigation intervention in Zimbabwe, John Burns and Andy Catley in Chapter 5 had to deal with the issue of participation for such questions as 'how a participatory approach can be used to measure the real impact of a project using indicators of impact defined by project participants' and 'how participatory tools can be used to produce representative results on project impact in the absence of any meaningful baseline data'. In Jones' work with the development of baseline data, participants were not willing to be explicit with their wealth status in front of others 'presumably not wishing to arouse jealously' and also many of them 'had the perception that their problems could be immediately resolved due to the large amount of money that white people inevitably have'. Meanwhile, as Burns and Catley's research was for an impact assessment, the participants' expectations for the continuation of the project were once again an important source of bias as it was likely that they may have responded to certain questions with a particular objective in mind. In other words, these examples of conducting participatory research in development contexts show that the approach is certainly not a bias-free undertaking. It is true that the likeliness of various generic biases such as elite, professional, geographic, seasonal or socio-cultural biases can be reduced by the utilization of more participatory methods, but such an approach also has its own possible shortcomings. As will be recommended in the second part of this chapter, the key with overcoming successfully such possible biases lies with the design and implementation of triangulation methods effectively.

In the post-disaster context too, such participatory methods seem to have encountered similar challenges. The research undertaken by Bimal Kanti Paul and Sohini Dutt in the aftermath of the Cyclone Sidr in Bangladesh had to deal with the challenge that some villagers expected post-disaster assistance as a return for their participation in surveys and group meetings. As explained in Chapter 6, they 'were confident that talking with a member of the research team would guarantee them receiving American relief aid'. However, the issue for the main focus of discussions here should not necessarily be on such expectations from disaster-affected people, as after all, considering the urgency of their basic needs and reconstruction assistance, it is only expected that they continue to make such judgments even though the contrary was explained by the research team. In other words, such a reality is hard to change and it is very much to do with human psychology and the way human beings cope with adversaries in their lives. Hoping is often an important aspect of coping with the challenges of such disaster-affected environments. Such expectations for example, do not seem to be the case when the research is not part of a humanitarian disaster context, as was the case with Rohit Jigyasu's research which explored 'the potential role of local knowledge, resources and strengths of rural communities in India and Nepal for formulating long term planning and mitigation measures to reduce their disaster vulnerability, especially to earthquakes'. In order to achieve such an objective, participatory research methods provided the only real opportunity to understand and assess local community perspective on disaster mitigation and preparedness issues. Stated differently, to overcome the existing power structures that may have prevented to gather information in order to build a truthful and reliable picture of the reality with disaster vulnerability, Jigyasu utilized participatory methods as effective tools to enter in those communities and act as a voice for them. What seems to be the most critical factor in the structuring of power relationships between the researcher and the researched therefore, is whether or not there are conditions and reasons that the researched could expect something in return as part of their participation. In addition to the insider–outsider type of power structures based on the discrepancies of resources and capacities between those both sides, the research undertaken as part of development programmes and in post-disaster environments would also need to deal with the challenge of expectations and its influence on the use of participatory methods.

In addition to dealing with the challenge of expectations and its impacts, it is important to recognize that the interaction between the researcher and the researched through participatory research methods would form its main contours by the nature of participation in that relationship. Jigyasu, in Chapter 7, outlines two main scenarios. In the first one, participation takes place in the process of empirical data gathering but the researched would be detached from the entire research process. In order to achieve such a higher level of participation, Jigyasu suggests that 'the researcher needs to earn the trust of the community or other stakeholders' and they 'should also have enough time at their disposal'. These conditions are not always easy to achieve in a development context, but particularly difficult in post-disaster environments as a result of the urgency of problems faced by populations. In order to deal with the challenge of limited time that the participants could invest in the research process, which was coupled with the needs of the research for a substantial caseload, Burns and Catley decided to interview up to nine participants at a time. They had to make such a trade off between the quality and quantity factors, as they were aware that this decision could have resulted in peer biases. However, it was necessary due to timeframe limitations. Similarly Kanti and Dutt experienced the problem of adequate time that could realistically be expected from their research participants to invest in the research process. As a matter of fact, even the researchers themselves often do not have sufficient time to undertake participatory research methods due to a set of financial constraints and other work commitments. Although, they try to address this issue through the involvement of local researchers, as Mdee points out a short intensive PRA exercise would fail to recognize many complicated social-cultural nuances in that community. She stated her concerns as:

> One of my difficulties with PRA is that, despite claims to the contrary, it is often very difficult to see how PRA tools used in short periods of time can capture fully the different voices of the community – considering in particular the dominant discourses and potentially biases of such voices.

Furthermore, apart from Mdee's research in Tanzania the time for proper participation for both the researcher and the researched was a critical issue in all of the case studies of the first section, which is also the reality for most research undertakings. On the other hand, the challenge of participation can be even more difficult in environments affected by armed conflicts, as gaining community's trust would be even more difficult with deep socio-political divisions created or exacerbated by wars.

All of the case studies in the second section highlighted the importance of trust building with communities in order to undertake participatory research methods. Richard Bowd in Chapter 10 detailed his approach in the context of PRA techniques such as landscape mapping in order to introduce himself to the community and allow participants to have adequate time for building trust, while Sukanya Podder tried to overcome this challenge by affiliating herself with a trustworthy international organization. On the other, Victor Asiedu's door knocking approach was purely for this very objective of trust building. Working in the context of Sierra Leone where communities experienced terrible war tactics by different belligerent groups, for him to enter a community and start asking questions about the community and former combatant relationships needed a mechanism that would be appropriate to local customs and expectations, and also achievable in a limited period of time. He explained in Chapter 11 that:

> in many traditional African communities, visitors are customarily required to present tokens to their hosts because it is assumed that they have come from cities with all the fancy items. Apart from that, tokens are offered to show an appreciation or to return a favour, and in this regard, for the time spent with respondents.

He continued by stating that having offered his gifts and had:

> a short deliberation with their elders, the chiefs used their authority to grant me permission and asked their subjects to give me the necessary assistance for the research. The door knocking at the chiefs' palaces was very necessary in the sense that in certain places I visited, people wanted to know whether I have been officially introduced to the chief as a form of assurance that my mission was not covert, but of importance to the communities.

Overall, it may be hard to claim that gaining trust of communities is less of a problem in the development and post-disaster contexts, but the issue with post-conflict environment is that the community is likely to feel much more vulnerable to external actors as its normal coping mechanisms and social protection mechanisms are likely to have been badly damaged as a result of the armed conflict. Consequently, a certain level of suspicion towards the motives of researchers is almost inevitably, to be expected in the application of participatory methods in such environments. Furthermore, it is necessary to recognize that research trying to understand the root causes of the conflict and existing socio-political and economic divisions can easily negate the very tenuous peacebuilding prospects between individuals, institutions and communities. For example, for Bowd to consider the divisions between groups in Rwanda, specifically Hutu and Tutsi, which were necessary to understand social capital mechanisms and reconciliation in relation to the reintegration of former combatants, it was necessary to focus on the impacts of the genocide. However, in the post-genocide Rwanda context it was very difficult to find anybody who would be prepared to talk about such ethnic differences, and secondly, asking such questions could easily make communities suspicious about the motives of the research. More importantly, there is also a very significant ethical question to consider in terms of exacerbating post-conflict relationships by focusing on such differences. Therefore, in such a context as Bowd dealt with in Rwanda, or Podder and Asiedu's research contexts in West Africa, the issue of trust building becomes the most significant issue for the successful application of participatory research methods.

For power relationships it is also important to bear in mind certain differences between the three contexts of this book. As explained in Chapter 1, power relationships in any community are very fluid and such binaries as urban and rural or elite and masses would be highly constraining to explain the realities of socio-economic and political structures. In parallel to this, knowledge also is a highly dynamic instrument, and what is evaluated as knowledge is often no more than the reaction between the researcher and the researched. In other words, although it may be a very cynical view, the fact is that local knowledge can easily be packaged in different ways, for example, by the variations in different outsider agendas. Therefore, it is imperative to be aware of the factors that shape such a power relationship in the design and application of participatory research methods. In order to soften the contours of power discrepancies between herself and communities, Mdee opted for a wide range of techniques such as life history interviewing and diagramming for interpretive biography; local interpretation through diary keeping, observation and analysis for auto-ethnography; and other methods consisting of in-depth interviewing and participant observation, process documentation, institutional mapping and a review of institutional records and documents. It was hoped that by applying different methods, sometimes in conventional and other times in a more modified way, there would be a greater level of equilibrium between the researcher and local researchers, and the research team in general and communities. Nevertheless, her research experienced major 'tensions relating to power, resources and capacity in the interaction', as for example, there was a risk of having 'over expectations about local researchers' as they may not be able to use certain tools as effectively as expected, such as diary keeping in Mdee's research, or the transferability of concepts are highly difficult even though the researcher may have visited the research context for a number of times and be fully aware of its characteristics. On the other hand, Simon Robins' research experience in Nepal highlights an interesting issue in regard to power structures and how they can be used for the benefit of both the researcher and the researched.

As elaborated in Chapter 13, Robins undertook his research in cooperation with the local associations of families of the disappeared people. In this research too, the expectations were high, and so much so that the entire process was planned and implemented with the participation of those associations and the research process was utilized as a tool of advocacy. The expectations of participants involved in the process, and their ramifications in the creation of power relationships, were handled in a way that the entire process was a win-win scenario for both sides. Therefore, for the researcher to expect participants to invest their time in the process, and for participants to expect the researcher to investigate the issue thoroughly went hand in hand with each other. For example, in terms of the outcomes of his research the final report allowed 'the dissemination of the results as a tool of advocacy' and hence the associations 'benefited from the expertise of the researcher whilst gaining a degree of ownership over the research results'. The very nature of the research from an advocacy perspective was critical to overcome those challenges related to the equilibrium of power relationships between the researcher and the researched. Robins unpacks this issue further by pointing out eloquently that:

> a participatory research design demands that the researcher yield some control of the research agenda, and indeed the research question, to the researched. Whilst this can be considered a violation of the positivist view of social research aims, it is a prerequisite of participatory research design and indeed of any emancipatory approach.

This is particularly significant in addressing the relationship between participation, power and empowerment issues which are the main objectives of participatory research methods.

In order to ensure a certain level of emancipation and equal power relationships between herself and refugee Palestinian women in Lebanon, Maria Holt adopted a flexible approach in her enquiry through the application of both questionnaires and directed conversations as then she 'was able to glean information about each woman's background, her experiences of violence and conflict and her opinions, reflections and aspirations'. Furthermore, through a feminist interviewing technique, as explained in Chapter 14, Holt's research led to 'a degree of creativity, not in the sense of "making things up" but rather of broadening the field to include subjects that were previously perhaps felt to be irrelevant'. In other words, with such an approach Holt was utilizing an important characteristic of the Palestinian camps 'where conversations frequently take place in family homes and often include a woman's relatives and neighbours'. This helped reduce the view of Holt as 'a non Muslim, non Arab researcher' as the experience became 'a communal endeavour in which a group of people attempts to convey a story of the camp or a story of exile', preventing the emergence of sharp power relationships between herself and her respondents.

From a mid-term participatory evaluation perspective, David Connolly presents a disaggregation of benefits for participants according to their capabilities, interests, motivations and relationship to the post-conflict reconstruction programme concerned. As the discussions in Chapter 15 elaborated, from gaining 'technical knowledge, awareness, inclusion, decision-making, and communication' to ensuring 'sound participatory research ethics', the attempts for empowerment as part of the research process represented 'a reasonable justification for respondents who have taken the time and interest to participate'. However, gaining and maintaining access through the project's own decision-making structures in order to overcome security and political dynamics of the operational environment meant that the participatory evaluation 'strategy undoubtedly reinforced formal and informal power relations within and between institutions in the NSP because it was top-down and mirrored existing positions'. Moreover, Connolly rightly points out that the power relationship can also be the reverse in which 'participatory methods would have been considered in vogue by seasoned respondents and they were selected…to reflect best practice theory'. In other words, what this reminds us of is that the power relationship between the researcher and the researched does not always incline for the advantage or superiority of the former, as the latter can also have means and capacities to manipulate the process if wanted.

Overall, the post-conflict case studies in the second section indicate an important characteristic for the divergence of power–participation relationship into the opportunities of empowerment of participants, or in most cases, the lack of it. It seems that although the researchers tried hard enough to ensure an enabling environment for a more conducive framework of power relationships between themselves and their targeted communities, they often found it quite difficult to eradicate them completely. Unless, the community and local organizations are directly involved in the planning and application with such objectives that are beneficial for them, the aim of full participation remains to be only partially satisfied. However, the blame here is not solely with the researcher, as the case studies in both sections showed that the researchers went to their targeted communities with a genuine interest in their participation. It is possible to argue that some may have been more successful in this quest than others, but the issue can be judged properly only when the other component of the equation, the researched, is brought into consideration. The researcher can do only so much in the creation of an enabling participatory research context, but the main characteristics of that very environment are completely outside the researcher's control and it is in relation to this very fact that to assume the possibility of a full participation of communities is only an expectation but unfortunately, not the reality. It is clear that there are many challenges in the identification of whose voice should be heard and what that means for the politics of the researcher and the researched relationship, but more importantly, there is not any convincing evidence that a full participation of local communities in research can actually be achieved. This participation takes place for various reasons at different levels according to the characteristics of the relationship between the researcher and the researched. However, it is important to point out that what is understood from participation is a highly contested and varying concept, and claims for its realization and success needs to be considered carefully. With this in mind, therefore, it is now necessary to conclude on the relationship between participatory research methods and such conventional research principles as truthfulness, reliability and validity, and in order to achieve this, the next section will focus on the triangulation of participatory research.

Participatory Research Methods and Triangulation

As the preceding analysis on the participation–power relationship indicated that some of those challenges with participation would be impossible to overcome completely, and ironically, while this may be the main weakness of them, the main strength of their application emerges in the context of triangulation. Conventional social research methods in terms of interviews, observation and surveys would have some use in the contexts of development, post-disaster and post-conflict, but often in a modified way. All case studies in this book indicated that each use certainly has its time and place, and the researchers used them extensively with certain target groups such as the use of semi-structured interviews with the representatives of national authorities, international organizations or other elite groups. In most cases, they were adapted to the realities of the research environment and particularly to the special characteristics of environments affected by disasters and armed conflicts. However, one important issue that has emerged in all case studies was the flexibility and effectiveness of participatory methods for the purposes of triangulation, and particularly for the triangulation of findings from more conventional methods.

Burns and Catley in their participatory impact assessment task carried out the triangulation in a number of ways but most importantly, they took the advantage of using a multiple selection of techniques. For example, the results from different methods such as focus group discussions, household interviews, and key informant interviews were compared with each other, as well as comparing the results from different scoring exercises for the identification of common patterns and trends between them. Similarly, Bowd used the institutional diagramming, social network mapping and social indicators technique to triangulate the findings from those methods themselves but also more conventional methods like interviews and life histories. For example, the social capital indicators technique facilitated the triangulation of 'of proxies and proxy variables for social capital' by discussing them 'with community members who identify particular community events, formal and informal networks and associations, among others, that contribute to social capital in the community'. Through this technique not only the findings from institutional diagramming and social network mapping were triangulated but also it was 'particularly useful in deciphering ways in which social capital formulation occurs within the context of a developing country'. Connolly also stated that it was the 'participatory characteristic of regular consultation, through briefings and debriefings' that 'allowed the data to be cross-checked and preliminary findings could be tested in the field'.

Overall, these examples indicate that through the employment of a wide range of participatory methods, the researcher is able to create more opportunities for triangulation, and ironically, such a need becomes a major necessity for the very nature of those methods, as 'narratives and self-reports always carry the possibility of bias, concealment, or exaggeration' and furthermore, Podder's 'close interaction with trainers and beneficiaries in the IOM programme, together with elite interviews with programme managers and government officials provided a valuable triangulation tool, enhancing validity by including policy perspectives to balance former combatant and insider views'. Nevertheless, as pointed out by Burns and Catley, the advantages of participatory methods easily outweigh their weaknesses, and ironically, 'the limitations of these methods are what give them the flexibility and advantage over more conventional approaches'. The participatory impact assessment used in their research provided 'a balance between practicability, participation, and scientific rigor, and an over emphasis on one of these comes at the expense of one or more of the others'. In other words, it is critical to emphasize that especially in the application of participatory research methods by practitioners the balance between such considerations as participation, practicality and scientific rigor needs to be maintained carefully. Nevertheless, the case studies indicated unanimously that PRA techniques for example, could be effectively used for triangulation purposes, and by increasing the number of tools that can be applied to collect data is an effective insurance policy for the reliability and validity of findings.

Recommendations

In the final part of this book, the discussions will be directed towards the development of some general conclusions for an improved application of participatory research methods. Rather than presenting a detailed set of recommendations, the objective will be to collate the main findings under the headings of flexibility and multi-disciplinarity, diversity and interpretation, trust and confidence building, and finally the ethics of participatory research methods, which all can serve as the main principles for an improved practice.

Flexibility and Multi-disciplinarity

The experience with the application of participatory research methods presented in this chapter shows that the main strength of such methods is in fact all to do with their flexibility. There are no fixed menus and approaches for the utilization of those methods, and flexibility can exist to such a degree that the research strategy and new research methods can be created and developed in an inductive way. All case studies point out the importance of pre-field research preparations, but at the same time, they also indicate the reality of the need to be prepared for the unexpected. No matter how much pre-field research preparations had been placed in the process, the fluidity of research environments is always a critical issue to be borne in mind. This is particularly the case with environments affected by disasters and armed conflicts. Therefore, a research process that is clearly structured with pre-defined research methods would likely have a limited use in real world research. All case studies in this book indicated that the researcher needs to have an open mind about the research strategy and methods employed in their research. Without that data collection is likely to be significantly affected at the first obstacle or even collapse completely. Therefore, participatory research methods and their application should be considered as a set of possibilities, and although there could be some plans made for the use of certain techniques, the researcher would need to be well prepared to make last minute changes in order to adopt the realities of that very context and time.

It is also important to note that unexpectedness should not only be considered from a negative perspective, as the dynamics of that particular environment can also provide various opportunities as well as challenges. For example, an interview with a gatekeeper could easily open up so many different opportunities for the research to take shape in different ways that unless there is a high level of flexibility with the adaptation of the research strategy and its methods quickly, they cannot be used effectively. The snowball effect for sampling for example, is truly efficient if and when the researcher can come up with the most appropriate data gathering technique for each new respondent type.

For a greater level of flexibility one of the main tools that can be used should be the multi-disciplinary approach to the research task in hand. In a conventional sense, this would be forming research teams by people from different academic and professional backgrounds, so that the likeliness of biases based on the researcher's own identity and professional experience can be reduced to a minimum. Although, this could be achieved in research undertakings as part of major research projects, and well-funded impact assessments and evaluations, the reality for many researchers is that they often have to undertake their research on their own. Even the employment of adequate number of local researchers is often a major challenge for most researchers, and especially for those students working on their MA or PhD theses. Nevertheless, even within such circumstances, the adoption of multi-disciplinarity in the conceptualization stage, that is, being able to structure the strategy and use of research methods from different academic perspectives, would be an important assurance for a coherent and insightful set of findings.

Specifically, supported by an innovative and inclusive thinking on the strategy and techniques of their research, researchers can undertake their work in a more reflexive way. This is particularly important for participatory research methods, and their main strength is the way they could actually be adapted to the characteristics of different environments. There are no specific rules for the use of PRA techniques and as the case studies in this book demonstrate, participatory research can come in all different formats and combinations.

Diversity and Interpretation

In highly dynamic environments such as the contexts of development, post-disaster and post-conflict the research process is likely to encounter, work with and focus on a wide range of actors from donors, international NGOs and national authorities to local NGOs, grassroots organizations and communities in general. Furthermore, even within communities there would likely be a high level of heterogeneity consisting of different socio-economic and political groups with varying interests and agendas. In parallel to such diversity, researchers often opt for methods that would allow the categorization of such differences in approaches and opinions so that the strategy would emerge in certain themes and patterns. To a large extent this is something an effective research process would and should try to achieve, however over-categorization can easily remove the benefits of having such diverse perspectives. As Jigyasu points out 'by assuming the role of a journalist, collecting, checking and cross-checking information from various sources, not to establish the truth but to understand diverse perspectives of various government, non-government and individual stakeholders', it is possible to maintain a good level of flexibility. More importantly, the application of various participatory research methods in different ways could provide just the right level of sensitive response in the gathering of such diverse information. This is one of the most significant advantages of participation, or at least theoretically, it provides additional opportunities to tune the strategy in the most sensitive way so that such diversities are captured effectively.

On the other hand, for the protection of diversity and ensuring its reflection in research findings, the interpretation of information is as significant as the actual data collection process itself. As pointed out in the preceding sections, for a full participation it is essential to ensure that participants are not only the source of information but also decision makers of how to gather that information. Holt argued that both the translation 'of words from the language of the narrator' and 'the responsibility of the researcher to interpret as accurately and faithfully possible the narrative she is hearing' would play a very significant role for the entire context of participation, power and empowerment relationships. It is clear that without such a sensitive approach voices can perhaps be heard, but they would not be turned into knowledge. Data analysis is as significant as the actual data collection process itself, as without appropriate checks and balances, the findings from the research can easily be manipulated for the benefit of a particular perspective or approach. Nevertheless, it is also a fact that interpretation is an essential undertaking to constructing something meaningful from a large body of raw data and information, and one way or another it would be inherently open to a certain level of biases. However, as a bare essentiality the process should be flexible enough to reflect on the diversity of perspectives obtained in the field research, as without this the whole purpose of utilizing participatory research methods would become redundant.

Trust and Confidence Building

The importance of trust-building with respondents for the successful application of participatory methods has been covered by most case studies in this book and some of them have even proposed particular approaches to achieve this goal. However, the question is how such a quest can actually be achieved and what factors seem to play a significant role in this process. In order to explore this issue, the following three elements of time, resources and skills will be the focus of recommendations here. First of all, it is clear that time, and the way it is highly limited for the application of participatory research methods, was highlighted as a major concern by almost all case studies. Although, the rhetoric of such an approach advocates for the researcher to have plenty of time to get to know communities before initiating the process and allow sufficient time for reflection and learning from communities, the reality is that they are often undertaken in a hurry. Time constraints with both the researcher and the researched are significant factors, as on one hand, the researcher could dedicate a limited time for research for financial considerations and other commitments, and on the other hand, if the researched does not see a direct benefit from the process it would be difficult to ensure their involvement in an extended period of time. It is this very issue that poses a number of questions for the technical limitations of the participatory research approach, because if proper participation cannot be achieved due to time constraints, then it would be hard to expect its expected gains and consequently, that would leave the whole practice as a façade without much substance. However, if for example, PRA techniques are considered more like ice breakers, methods of introduction to communities or additional means of triangulation, and then perhaps the shortcomings created by the time constraints would be less of a critical issue for the research.

Secondly, the availability of necessary resources such as adequate number of research team members with appropriate backgrounds and capacities would be critical for the application of participatory methods as the primary means of research. The use of PRA methods would require the work of a team rather than a sole researcher. In order to facilitate various techniques while taking notes and making appropriate observations at the same time would be impossible to achieve for a single researcher. Such techniques are particularly useful when there is adequate number of researchers with specific roles to undertake in each method, and the facilitation of team members would be as important as the successful incorporation of respondents in the process. Also as pointed out earlier, it is essential to cover appropriate professional backgrounds with a good gender balance so that the team would be sufficiently equipped to interact with participants.

In addition to the appropriateness of team members' professional backgrounds for the research task, it is also important for them to have a set of well developed conflict management and negotiation skills. Participatory methods are prone to conflicts and disagreements as part of the very nature of group dynamics and the way individuals interact with each other in a group environment. However, such skills are particularly necessary when the research environment is badly affected by the impacts of an armed conflict. Even in a development context such concerns as the share of natural resources and land disputes can be the potential causes of disagreements, and as participatory methods place their focus on differences rather than similarities, and they aim to empower communities as part of their participation in the process, which is predominantly a political approach, the researcher would often need to deal with heated arguments, disagreements and sometimes major disputes. In such an environment unless the researcher is equipped with appropriate conflict management skills the problem can easily intensify, exacerbating damaged societal relationships further. This is an important issue that will be addressed further in the next section, but before moving to the challenges related to ethical concerns, it is important to recognize the way confidence building plays such a significant role in the creation of trust between the researcher and the researched.

The issues of time, resources and skills are clearly important, but some of those are hard to remedy for a number of reasons such as financial constraints, and it is often the reality that the researcher undertakes participatory research methods in less than ideal conditions. However, when it comes to trust building some measures can be highly effective and would not necessary require the investment of large resources, and the most important of those measures is clearly the assurance of confidentiality. The promise of anonymity and obviously, keeping that promise is possibly the bare minimum of ensuring confidentiality but it is not necessarily enough to build a good level of trust. In order to gain a high level of trust, as pointed out by Asiedu, the process 'requires a period of familiarization through playing of games, going out, eating and sometimes drinking together', which is not often possible for researchers for various reasons explained earlier. Therefore, to support the bare minimum requirement of confidentiality, the researcher's transparency and honesty about the research process and its objectives, and the way this is explained to respondents would likely to play a critical role in trust building. An honest approach to communities with respect and humility, and giving them the opportunity to withdraw their consent at any phase of the process in order to protect their privacy would be the first step for the initiation of an environment of trust.

Ethics of Participatory Research Methods

Conducting research in the real world would certainly need to consider a number of ethical issues. From the researcher and researched interaction perspective, those ethical concerns could be identified as those which might have an impact on the physical and psychological well being of respondents as well as such considerations as those related to their dignity, privacy and respect. Those ethical concerns would need to be made part of the planning and application of any social research being undertaken in all types of environments. For example, they would vary from the particular vulnerabilities of refugee women and child soldiers due to their experiences of armed conflict to the trauma experienced by the impact of a natural disaster. However, the main ethical concern that will be investigated here is to do with the very participatory characteristic of participatory research methods and its impact on divided societies. As pointed out earlier, those societies affected by protracted armed conflicts are likely to have deep societal scars as the way civil wars tend to dissolve the glue of cohesion between different ethno-religious groups.

As a result of the manipulation of differences and the 'us and them' dichotomy used by nationalist politicians and warlords of such environments, the signing of a peace agreement signifies only the beginning of a negative peace period. The transformation into positive peace is often a hazardous and painful process for war-affected populations during which the trust and confidence between different groups are likely to be highly sensitive and weak at most times. It is such a context that participatory research methods often take place, and therefore, it is essential to consider their harmful consequences on communities.

One of the main challenges with the use of PRA techniques for example, is that the community is often led to face its war experiences and divisions created in its recent history. Questions can lead people to remember their trauma and losses and unless managed properly some of those techniques could easily open up old wounds and be highly damaging for peacebuilding efforts. The way PRA techniques are primarily centred on the difference in a community carries a certain level of risk, but the problem emerges for two main reasons. First, due to limitations of time, resources and skills as explained earlier, the application of such techniques may not consider such nuances and sensitivities in a society properly and consequently, the process itself can easily do harm on societal relationships. However, the second issue is even more significant as in most cases, participatory research strategies have little to offer to mend strained relationships as a result of their impacts. Wounds are often left open for communities to deal with by their own means. Without means and resources for counselling or community work, there are serious ethical issues in the way communities are made part of such research processes without being supported without any means of assistance once that process is over. Therefore, it is essential to consider such consequences at the planning stage and take necessary mitigation measures for both the application and post-implementation periods.

Index